THE PEOPLE OF THE SIERRA

Alcalá de la Sierra

THE PEOPLE
OF THE SIERRA

Second Edition

JULIAN A. PITT-RIVERS

THE UNIVERSITY OF CHICAGO PRESS

CHICAGO & LONDON

First Published in Great Britain by Weidenfeld & Nicolson Ltd., 1954
Protected under the International Copyright Convention

ISBN: 0-226-67009-0 (clothbound); 0-226-67010-4 (paperbound)
Library of Congress Catalog Card Number: 70-153710

THE UNIVERSITY OF CHICAGO PRESS, CHICAGO 60637
The University of Chicago Press, Ltd., London

For

JULIO CARO BAROJA

in admiration and gratitude

Contents

List of Illustrations

Preface to the Second Edition

THIS BOOK is republished in its original form with only minor corrections and without the many expansions and reorientations I was tempted to make. In patching up a book published fifteen years earlier, especially a first book, one risks losing more than one gains, for it can no longer then claim the reader's indulgence in the same way and the very improvements may in a sense detract from its unity. So let it remain frankly what it was, the work of an apprentice. I had studied anthropology for less than two years when I was first allowed to start research in the field, and though I returned to the university for a couple of months a year during the next three I spent in Andalusia, my reading was guided by the problems I had encountered there, and I still had only the frailest general education in my subject. This ignorance may not have been a bad thing under the circumstances, for too wide a range of theory is perplexing to the beginner, if not actually stultifying. Nevertheless, I would like to underline that the book was intended as a theoretical work, not simply as an ethnographical account, and if it is not stuffed with the usual copious discussion full of detailed references this is due to the publisher who consented to put it in print only on condition I cut most of the "erudition" out. I was, of course, scandalized by this request and went to consult my teacher, Professor Evans-Pritchard, who reassured me that such scholarly trappings are mainly either mystifying or redundant: the reader who is not already acquainted with the theories invoked is not much enlightened by the references to them, and he who is should be able to see their relevance for himself. Evans-Pritchard quoted his own study of the magical thought of the Azande as a case in point[1]: the book is a critique of Lévy-Bruhl's

[1] E. E. Evans-Pritchard, *Witchcraft, Oracles and Magic among the Azande* (Oxford, 1937).

theories of how natives think; yet Lévy-Bruhl is mentioned only in a single footnote.

I have seldom regretted taking his advice, but there are nonetheless some matters on which I would like to comment either because the conditions of the period in Spain forced me to an extreme discretion which has sometimes led to misunderstanding or because looking back at the book from the standpoint of the present I can see some interest in placing it in its historical context within the discipline.

On the first point I was much concerned to avoid causing reproach to the members of the local community who had given me their confidence and, in the case -of the leaders, had sometimes gone so far beyond the call of duty in providing me with information that it might have been felt they had betrayed the secrets of their office or profession. Since they were unique in their roles, it was impossible to disguise their identity without disguising that of the pueblo, and I therefore gave it, and the communities immediately surrounding it, false names. However, since my intention was to deceive only the potential troublemaker, not the scholar, I left the ancient Latin names unaltered: Lacidula and Accinipa are true places even if they are no longer so called. Moreover I felt sure that anyone seriously interested in identifying the community would have little difficulty (even were he ignorant of the ancient history) in discovering, by simply taking his map and measuring the distances to places mentioned, that Alcalá de la Sierra is really Grazalema, from which it becomes obvious from the description what are the real names of the surrounding towns. Anyone who went to the area could check the conjecture from the photographs and the description. Moreover, I have always readily given the true name of the place to anybody who bothered to ask me.

I was overcautious perhaps, for the book was no sooner out than I received a furious letter from my friend, John Marks, *Times* correspondent in Madrid at the time, saying: "I know every pueblo in Andalusia and where the hell is Alcalá de la Sierra?" At least my excessive precautions enabled me to feel free in my relationship with my friends in the town to whom I sent a couple of copies of the book

(though they none of them knew any English). I was grat-
ified on my return there a few years later to be greeted
by the remark: "It appears, Don Julián, that you have
written a novel about us". I was delighted to confirm this
slightly inexact appraisal. The information in the book is
in fact true, except for changes in the names and nicknames and the deliberate printing of the map on page 143
back to front. When I wrote that there are no individual
personalities in this book I trusted that the conventional
lie that disculps the author of a *roman à clef* would be recognised for what it was. I was relieved, when the book was
reviewed, that no critic headed his article "Corruption in
Fascist Spain", for it would have been awkward for me to
deny that, for those who wish to give it such emphasis,
this is what the book is about (though I put it very differ-
ently myself). Apart from a few scholarly journals, the
Spanish press ignored it, and no one deemed me to have
abused the national hospitality or added to the *leyenda negra*.

The question of concealment poses a problem which
other disciplines do not face—at least in the same way.
For a town-planning sociologist to conceal the identity of
the town he was replanning would defeat his purpose. A
biographer would hardly think of concealing the identity
of the person he was portraying (though writers of personal memoirs are frequently published posthumously or
at least after the death of their victims to avoid the con-
sequences of their indiscretions). On the other hand a
psychoanalyst who published the identity of his case histories
might subsequently have difficulty in persuading anyone
to lie down on his couch. The anthropologist's position is
somewhere between these extremes. If it were possible for
him to conceal the individual persons without concealing
the community, there would be no problem for him, but
he cannot black out their features as the physical anthropologist can when he photographs his subjects in the nude.
It is characteristic of small rural communities that the
people within them *are* unique and in fact part of the
reason for studying them is this: one can here grasp the
individual in his entirety, the total man. Once the town
is identified then everyone knows who is meant. It is natural enough, therefore, that those who hold the good name

of their profession in esteem should avoid acting in such a way as to bring opprobrium upon it. Moreover, there tends to be formed a professional etiquette in this regard, lest the act of concealment imply that the study is injurious. The authors of an excellent monograph on an American small town whose identity they had carefully concealed are reported, nevertheless, to have seen their names posted the following year under the last float in the pageant which represented two apes shoveling dung.

The loss involved in concealment is variable. From the point of view of the theoretical interest it is small: it increases according to the amount of concern attaching to the ethnography of the area. Since at the time I wrote there were no other ethnographical studies of Andalusia in English (and since my intention was primarily theoretical), I did not feel that much was lost by concealing the location of the place. Now that this is no longer the case I am glad to be able to give its correct name.

The need for discretion also influenced the presentation, for I judged it premature to publish my materials on religion and Anarchism at that time and decided to reserve them for a later book, which I still intend to write. It is not possible to discuss the plebeian religion of Andalusia, other than as folklore, without treating the agrarian Anarchists who, in their iconoclasticism, their temperance, and their respect for education and the sanctity of words recall the Puritan revolutionaries of the English seventeenth century. The distinction between politics and religion, as we conceive of it in our own society, has no anthropological validity. Anarchism therefore, as an anticlerical faith, a schism in the structure of belief, belongs to this other volume. Here it is dealt with only insofar as it throws light upon the history of the social structure. (I believe it throws a great deal.) It is highly significant that the Sierra de Cádiz was the cradle of agrarian Anarchism,[1] and Grazalema

---

[1] In contrast to the mountainous region of the province of Cordoba, which remained conservative and Catholic. The development of the movement therefore took a different course in the two areas, and the greatest tragedy for those interested in the subject is that Diaz del Moral never went on to add to his magnificent study of Anarchism in Cordoba the volume he promised on the province of Cádiz.

important in its annals, and this fact was one of those which attracted me to the area in the first place, since I was already attempting to formulate in anthropological terms the problem of the relation of the community to the nation. The Anarchists' rejection of all authority other than that which derived from within the local community clearly represented an extreme position with regard to it.

A further effect of my concern to be discreet, the only one I regret, was that I could not give the figures on which my conclusions regarding the economy and family structure were based, since this information was not public at the time. It would have been evident that I could only have gathered it from documents I was not entitled to have seen. I can only ask the reader to believe that when I make an observation regarding landholding or relative frequencies of types of marriage, I based it on what purported to be the official records, checked by what I knew to be the case from the samples provided by my field-work.

It would be quite wrong, however, to suppose that my "ideological neutrality" was adopted out of discretion. On the contrary, it was fundamental to my theoretical and methodological standpoint.

My training in anthropology, such as it had been, was mainly concerned with Africa, especially east Africa. I went therefore into the field armed with the models of lineage systems and age groups, but devoid of any which turned out to be relevant to the social structure of Andalusia. I spent a week in the French Basque country on the way there, inspecting for an alternative site should I find it impossible to work in Andalusia, and perhaps such intellectual baggage as I had would have been more useful to me there, but Andalusia, as I eventually came to discover, has indeed very little in common with Africa for all that that continent has been proclaimed to begin at the Pyrenees. Consequently, by the time I had hit upon the important conclusion that there is no lineal principle to be found in the dynasties of nicknames and that the ages were not "grouped", I was left with no alternative but to think things out for myself.

Rather naturally I groped for a higher level of abstraction at which the principles I had been taught would not be wasted. Lineage systems, in Evans-Pritchard's analysis, are after all no more than the principle of social solidarity organised into a hierarchy of binary oppositions, and so forth. It was understandable then that the work which became my bible while I was in the field should have been the *Sociology of Georg Simmel*.[1] His kind of totally abstract sociology, which depends upon form and quantitative relations, provided me with a mode of transition from what I thought was anthropology to what I saw with my eyes. In addition, the sensitivity of Simmel to the modes of human feeling and values gave me the clues to an attack on my problems from an intuitive standpoint. Finally, his ideas about conflict and above all secrecy furnished me with the means of passing from the structure of a primitive society in which custom is universally recognised and consensus easily established to that of a complex society in which "understandings" are confined by social barriers and the most important knowledge is not "common". On the other hand, the writer who may be called to mind at various points in this book, Tönnies, is one I read for the first time only after the draft of my thesis was finished, though I am fully prepared to recognise my debt to him through MacIver, whom I had read with care and admiration.

In short, the whole book can be read as no more than an explication through an ethnographic example of Simmel's great essay on secrecy and the lie. I could not have chosen a better terrain on which to demonstrate it, for the Andalusians are the most accomplished liars I have ever encountered. I use the word *accomplished* literally, for it requires training and intelligence to distinguish rapidly when the truth is owed and when it is to be concealed, and to acquire conscious control over facial expression is an ability which takes practice from childhood.[2] Consequently, the reproach commonly levelled at them by other Spaniards

---

[1] Translated by Kurt Wolff (Glencoe, Ill., 1950).

[2] Schopenhauer used such an observation to explain, by a very teleological argument, why men have beards and women do not. Since women, unlike men, possess a natural talent for dissimulation they do not need them.

is that they are fickle, treacherous, and always acting. Such stereotypical evaluations never give more than half of the reality, and it is logical rather than paradoxical that the Andalusians should be people profoundly concerned with the truth and with the true state of the heart, a point which has escaped the tourist literature but which will, I trust, be evident to the reader of this book. When knowledge is something to give or to deny you become concerned with its exact worth; it takes a money changer to detect false coinage.

This explains also why the British, who are poor liars and poor truthtellers also, making do much of the time with a blend of half-truth and self-deception, are greeted in Andalusia with that particular mixture of indulgence and admiration—indulgence toward children who control their muscular reactions so gracelessly and admiration for those who still cherish the bold ambition to be frank. Let us face it: we are all fumblers by Andalusian standards, but they envy our innocence even while they also take advantage of it.[1] Impressions of this kind gave me my first leads to understanding the culture and social structure of Grazalema, but had I carried them no further I should have written only the travel book the publisher was hoping for and which, alas, I have laid aside for too long now to finish.

I should like to say something more about my concept of value, since this study is constructed around it. Reading

---

The rarity of beards in Andalusia might be explained by the same theory.

Simmel (p. 330) went further: "The secret in this sense, the hiding of realities by negative or positive means, is one of man's greatest achievements. In comparison with the childish stage in which every conception is expressed at once, and every undertaking is accessible to the eyes of all, the secret produces an immense enlargement of life: numerous contents of life cannot even emerge in the presence of full publicity. The secret offers, so to speak, the possibility of a second world alongside the manifest world; and the latter is decisively influenced by the former."

[1] It appears therefore rather inept to label the Andalusian rebels "primitive," as Eric Hobsbawm has done (*Primitive Rebels*), unless one is to adopt a point of view similar to that of the Victorian anthropologists who called all people primitive who did not share their ideas and assumed that they "advanced" if they came to do so. Hobsbawm was referring to their political conceptions which he believed would inevitably evolve to become similar to his own. In fact they showed no sign of doing so and the recent resurgence of anarchist ideas among student rebels elsewhere does nothing to validate such an evolutionary scheme.

about Africa, one has the impression that its people have
a remarkable capacity for stating their customs and beliefs.
Norms, it appears, are in everyone's mind and are constantly referred to as guides to conduct. The ethnographer
of Africa has never waited for an answer about the correct
thing to do. He is among a race of lawyers, it seems, ready
to argue every point and quote precedent. But the unfortunate ethnographer of Andalusia, when he is not told
simply that each man does what he wants ("lo que le da
la gana"), is likely to discover afterwards that he has been
misinformed. I found it necessary to devise some other
means of discovering the norm than asking for it in so many
words. I had to construct from observation the scales of
preference and pressure which go to building the framework of desires and sanctions within which individuals determine their conduct. I expressed the result as "values".
I was not at the time acquainted with the work that had
been done under this heading in America—especially at
Harvard—and I fear it would only have confused me had
I attempted to read it, for I came to the study of values
as a way round the difficulty of obtaining stated norms;
they are not in my usage purely ethical but in the first
place cognitive values, concepts whose ethical content is
built into them and becomes apparent only according to
context, a part of the ethnography, not, as in the work of
the late Clyde Kluckhohn and those connected with him,
a moral structure abstracted from stated norms.[1] My treatment of this theoretical problem is not spelled out here
(though all references to the word "value" are noted in
the index) and the reader concerned to pursue the point
is advised to see my paper "Honour and Social Status"[2]
which I intended as a demonstration of how the concept
of values should be handled.

This concept of values is connected, of course, with my
usage of "social structure" as the relationship between activities rather than individuals or groups. This was not what

[1] The most sophisticated demonstration of this method is John Ladd's
The Structure of a Moral Code (Cambridge, 1957).

[2] In J. G. Peristiany (ed.), *Honour and Shame: The Values of Mediterranean
Society* (London and Chicago, 1966).

I had been taught, but in a modern complex society people do not belong only to permanent groups defined by birth, kinship, or age, but are allied also by wealth, interests, accomplishments, and voluntary associations.[1] The emphasis is on the actions then rather than the actors. The social structure thus appeared to me to be composed of more than groups of persons labelled according to their status, but to be, rather, a kaleidoscope of changing relationships dependent upon context. Hence the individuals with whom I was dealing faced choices of allegiance and defined themselves by the attitudes they adopted. They were not simply members of a given tribe and tribal segment.

The inhabitants of the Andalusian pueblo are simultaneously members of both the community and the state, but the two are different not merely in terms of their size and level of organisation, but by nature. Though the state is composed of municipalities, which provide the legal structure of the communities, the individuals who compose the nation are differentiable in terms of whether they are concerned primarily with one or with the other. Hence the kind of hierarchy through which the community is integrated into the state is not something like the Nuer lineage system, which reaches the peak of authority (such as this is) in the figure of the Leopard-skin-chief, but in people five hundred miles away whose authority is infinitely more effective but only indirectly; it is distant and abstract and therefore incapable of application save through channels of command which reduce abstract principles to actual personalities. These channels of command were therefore the network through which the state was integrated, but in fact they could be seen to depend upon relationships of quite another type at every level. These were social and economic, not political. It therefore appeared to me that one must define the structure of the nation before attempting the definition of the state, which remained always a somewhat superficial imposition (and from the point of view of the Anarchists an unacceptable one).

[1] It appears from the ethnographics of the last decade that in simple societies, also, such impermanent associations play a much larger part than was formerly realised.

Such a viewpoint necessarily committed me to a concern with the wider social structure of which both region and community were part and, though it was perhaps going outside my province, to compare this to other parts of Spain, I risked a fleeting comparison between the parallel growth of a revolutionary working-class movement in the south and of separatism in the north (p. 136). The point may be used to illustrate the way in which the total structure can incorporate alternative forms which upon the surface look very different. I had already explained how the word *pueblo* can denote not only place but people, and not only community but class. Both Anarchism and Carlism were "popular" movements in the sense that they both derived their roots from the pueblo. Brenan at several points makes the analogy between them, not only in their overt characteristics, such as their taste for violence as a means of establishing agreement on certain essential values, but in their common nature as reactions of the traditional pueblo to Liberal Centralism (*The Spanish Labyrinth* pp. 147, 150, 205, 214 n.). Both creeds were somewhat unrealistic in their aims and equally unsuccessful in their results, and both demanded for the attainment of salvation a change of heart in the local community and an end to the interference of the state in its affairs. They differed in the direction in which they sought this salvation. For the Anarchists it lay in an imaginary future in which the values of the pueblo could be reaffirmed after the destruction of the state and its agencies within the pueblo (including the new land-owning class), while for the Carlists it lay in a return to an equally imaginary past where God and the Old Laws were to be placed on high once more. It was the difference between the projection of a similar ideal into either the future or the past, and into either atheism or theocracy.

The social structures of the north and the south were not the same; above all in the mode in which the communities of each were related to the nation they differed. In the south the rulers were the old absentee landlords and the new rich who had bought up the church lands and commons and remained associated essentially with the state and the national upper class. The Church, deprived of its wealth and thereby of its role of patron, became dependant upon those who had acquired its lands and it thereby forfeited the allegiance of the pueblo. In the north where the good land was divided into small holdings and the common lands were for the most part hillside pasture, which could not be exploited as an agricultural estate or a bull-farm, such a new class did not emerge. The moral leadership of the local community remained in the hands of its traditional rulers, the clergy and its rather modest upper class with whom it sided in the creed of Carlism. After the Carlists had finally been crushed, the regions which possessed a distinct cultural tradition turned to regional autonomy. Navarre stuck to Carlism and Carlist Aragon made its peace with the state and saw the emergence of Anarchism in the next generation.

Both the Carlists and the regional separatists on the one hand and the Anarchists on the other opposed the authority of the centralist state, but the former did so in favour of the region, which included the local upper class (pueblo in the sense of *a* people) and the latter did so in favour of the local community (pueblo in the sense of plebs). Hence the moral schism occurred at a different level in the social structure in the two cases and on a different axis, geographical in the first case, and in terms of class in the second—or putting it another way, vertical or horizontal—according to the nature of the local social structure.[1] The question hinged upon the nature and affiliation of the local upper class. The Federalist movement in Andalusia represents a transitional stage in this development. It centred upon the urban middle class, which made its peace with the state as soon as agrarian Anarchism raised a threat. Equally, one might argue that the rise of Anarchism is the consequence of the failure of Federalism.

In this book I have dealt only with the Andalusian scene and that horizontal schism which gave birth to Anarchism and set the conditions under which the social structure was

[1] The suggestion of a possible alternative between such a vertical and horizontal split may seem more acceptable than fifteen years ago with the conversion of labour strongholds to Welsh or Scottish nationalism, a change in the reverse direction to that which occurred in Andalusia.

subsequently to evolve. I have not attempted to describe the systems of belief save insofar as this affects the social structure. Nor have I tried to make any evaluation of the political and religious ideas of the Grazalemeños, nor still less to set myself up as a judge in their disputes. What I might feel about them does not appear to me to be capable of adding anything to my analysis. This attitude of detachment which is necessarily connected with the argument of the book had methodological roots without which I should perhaps never have been prepared to forego the joys of partisanship. I made it a matter of principle to distinguish the ethnography from the analysis.[1] Even though an ethnographical account necessarily implies a theoretical standpoint, as I wrote in the Introduction, the premises from which it should derive are hardly to be found in the ethnography of the society itself or one would be saying nothing that one's informants do not say better. Still less should the ethnographer look for them in the ideology of his own society, for the whole aim of anthropology is to attain some degree of abstraction with regard to it, a foothold outside it from which it may be possible for him to transcend the values by which he lives at home. He must therefore recognise as a preliminary step to the investigation of another culture that the ideology of his own society is no less an ideology than that which he is studying. It is part of *his* culture. For anthropology gives western civilization no special dispensation. Its premises must be drawn from the comparison of the whole corpus of *other* cultures. It was perhaps then an advantage for me to come to my task, not only unencumbered by any religious or political faith, but armed insofar as I was armed at all, with the training of an Africanist. At least in my reading I had been outside the West.

The ethnographer who does not lay aside his own culture risks the discovery that he has used the people he was studying only as a mirror to return him his own image and prove to himself the correctness of his prejudices. He must project himself into their lives, leaving his own be-

[1] The distinction is examined in my paper "Contextual Analysis and the Locus of the Model," *European Journal of Sociology*, vol. 8 (1957).

hind, or he would never grasp their viewpoint, but if he fails to regain his detachment he will never know what it is he has learned. The best field anthropologists have been those who were most successful not only in penetrating behind the natives' eyes but in reinterpreting what they saw through them. It is understandable, then, that they should sometimes have been attracted by what they saw and wished to retain their visions of Arcadia. Hence there is often a good grain of truth in the quip that, in the naked savage he has portrayed, the anthropologist has discovered no one but himself. Malinowski fought against the self he discovered in the Trobrianders by calling them "niggers" in his private diary. Other anthropologists have been less resentful of their self-discovery, and in the unlikely event of anyone detecting a resemblance between the Andalusians and me then I confess I shall not be displeased.

It is never possible to detach oneself entirely from one's natal culture—what on earth should we be if it were?—the culturally homeless anthropologist cannot exist, however he rebel against his past; such an ideal is unattainable. Yet if he does not strive for objectivity placing his moral judgment in abeyance, he will fall only into pedestrian ethnocentrism. The worth of a work of social anthropology relates largely to the degree to which it achieves a genuine detachment. The reader must be left to judge whether this book does so.

Preface to the First Edition

THIS BOOK is about a Spanish town. More precisely, it examines the social structure of a rural community in the mountains of southern Spain. To demand the reader's attention for a whole volume in order to interpret to him the habitual goings-on in so insignificant a place might be asking too much of him, but that in order to do this it has been necessary—or, might I say, through doing this it has been possible?—to say a good deal about the nature of Andalusian society, and even to sketch certain hypotheses of sociological theory. Yet this is not a discourse on the principles of social organisation. On the contrary, my concern is to set forth facts and only such general formulations as are required in order to relate them one to another. For I believe that every description of social life carries in the method and terms it employs an implied theory of society, while on the other hand theories which aim to lay down the principles of sociology, however great their potential value, remain until an observer can make use of them in a particular instance something uncertain, unassessable as an unopened seam of gold which may not, when brought to the surface, repay the cost of mining it.

Nevertheless, there is one point of theory to which I would like to draw attention before I begin, and that concerns the meaning of the term "social structure", since this is used by some writers in quite another way. They use it to mean the composition of a society in terms of percentages of persons belonging to one or another category of age, sex, monetary income or status, and so on. This is not what a social anthropologist means by social structure. For him the word "structure" implies something composed of interdependent parts, and the parts of a social structure are not individuals but activities or institutions. A society is not an agglomeration of persons but a system of social relations.

How exactly such a system "works", what is the nature of the logic governing it, is a matter upon which much doubt rests. Is a social system a system in the same sense as a legal or an economic system, as systems of grammar or physiology, or the solar system? This question is one which I prefer to leave to philosophers to whom it properly belongs. But many excellent monographs have examined different institutions among different peoples and have shown how they determine and are determined by the other institutions of their society, how, in a word, their activities and beliefs are consistent with each other. So, in this book, I have attempted to define the values attaching in Alcalá to possessions and status, to sex and the family, to political authority and the moral code of the community, to the supernatural and the natural and to show how they are related to one another and to the social structure of the whole country.

It will be seen that these values are not uniform in the sense that they are not shared equally by all members of the community, as one is led to believe is the case in simpler societies, but rather they (and the social perception upon which they depend) vary according to the position of the individual within the structure. This variation which gives rise to strife in certain contexts, leads also to logical inconsistencies which yet are not sociologically inconsistent. They devolve, rather, from the necessity to reconcile conflicting social ties within the same community and within the same individuals. The modes in which this reconciliation takes place give to the structure of this society many of its characteristics. If this book makes any contribution to sociological theory it does so through tracing the conflict of ties to the divergent demands of the local community and the central government and suggesting that, while the resolution of the problem is peculiar to this place and time, the problem itself is one which exists in all centralised states.

At a less general level this book aims to throw light upon the culture of Andalusia through defining its structural background. Such typical features as the popular bull-fight and the bandit, the witch and the cult of the gypsy, are shown as components of this social system, as possessing their structural *raison d'être*.

In a final appendix it attempts to reinterpret the social history of the sierra of Andalusia and in particular the rise of the Anarchist Movement there in the nineteenth century.

This book makes no claim, on the other hand, to contribute anything to controversies regarding Spanish politics, and any attempt to put the facts contained in it to polemical use is likely to do violence to them. In examining the values of another society I have been at great pains to avoid, myself, making any "value judgements".

Those whom I would like to thank are many. There is, first of all, the debt to be acknowledged in a first work to my teachers, Professor E. E. Evans-Pritchard, Professor Meyer Fortes and the late Dr. Franz Steiner. Secondly, to those who lent me the assistance of their advice when I first approached the problems of Spanish culture and history. Of them I would particularly like to mention Mr. Gerald Brenan, Mr. Raymond Carr of New College, Oxford, and Mr. Arthur Lehning, formerly of the Institute of Social History of Amsterdam. I am grateful to many other Spanish friends who patiently forgave my ignorance and endeavoured to help me towards an understanding of their culture. To the Hon. Mrs. Joan Rayner I am indebted for her photograph which forms the frontispiece.

Finally I take this opportunity to express my friendship and my admiration for the people of Alcalá. Save for the natural beauty of the land they live in, fate has given them few material advantages. With less wealth they are more hospitable than more fortunate people. In the face of greater disadvantages they dress more finely upon feast days. The benefits of learning have not been showered upon them yet they are often masters of the spoken word. Their manners and their feelings possess a natural refinement. Convinced at first that I must be a spy (for what else would an Englishman be doing in Alcalá?), they behaved nevertheless with the greatest kindness and courtesy.

I have been anxious to avoid indiscretions which would repay most heinously the friendship which they gave me, and have taken such steps as are necessary in order to prevent implicating either directly or indirectly any living person. Thus, for example, while all the nicknames mentioned are authentic, I have not given them to the people to whom they belong. There are no individual personalities in this book.

CHAPTER I

El Pueblo

(i) The Boundaries of the Community

LIKE MANY other Spanish place-names the name Alcalá derives from an Arabic word. It means a fortress, and it is normally possible to discover in places which bear that name the remains of Moorish fortifications. There are four towns called Alcalá in Lower Andalusia; Alcalá de Guadaira, where the bread of Seville is baked: Alcalá de los Gazules, on a knoll in the southern plain: Alcalá del Valle lies in broken country east of Olvera: while in the mountains between Ronda and Jerez stands Alcalá de la Sierra.

The name as well as the masonry of the town testify to its Moorish history, but Alcalá de la Sierra is older than the Moors who built upon the site of a Roman town named Lacidula. It appears to have come into prominence only during the later Moorish period when it was the stronghold of a Berber tribe. For some two hundred years it stood upon the frontier of the kingdom of Granada, and the Christians sacked it during the campaign which put an end to Moorish rule in Spain. Nor was that the termination of its troubles for nearly ninety years later, in 1571, it played a leading part in the rebellion of the Moriscos and was the scene of another year's embittered warfare during which it was burned down again. After this, the town was resettled and rebuilt by people from the plains to the west, and has remained ever since in a backwater of the national life, uncelebrated in Spain's history and unmarked upon its maps.

Richard Ford, that indefatigable traveller, visited it a century ago and does not appear to have been seduced by it. "Plastered like a martlet-nest upon the rocky hill," he wrote, "it can only be approached by a narrow ledge. The inhabitants, smugglers and robbers, beat back a whole division of the French who compared it to a land Gibraltar. The wild women, as they wash their parti-coloured garments in the bubbling stream, eye the traveller as if a perquisite of their worthy mates."

I cannot claim to have been aware of being regarded in that fashion, and I selected the town in the first place, among many other considerations, because I was invited into the *casino*, the club, and given a drink more promptly here than in any other place I had been. This was due, I think, not so much to the greater generosity of those of Alcalá, certainly not to their greater wealth, but to the fact that, being more cut-off than other towns, my appearance there in winter was more of an "event" than elsewhere. This first encounter was for me the prelude to an attachment which lasts still.

The mountains around Alcalá look bare and very precipitous, but they are not devoid of vegetation. Between the rocks lie grassy hollows and glades of evergreen oaks whose abundant acorns are the best fodder for pigs and whose wood makes charcoal for the towns in the plain. Below the grey crags and wooded spurs stretch valleys of not very fertile soil. The hillsides are lined by watercourses which are torrents for a few weeks and, for the rest of the year, dry pebble-beds edged by the oleander and the iris. But the bowls of the valleys are scattered with springs whose waters zigzag down the slope, charted by poplar-trees, white farmhouses and the geometric patterns of irrigation. These springs have never been known to dry up, for they are fed by underground reservoirs replenished each winter from the hollows in the high ground.

The towns of the sierra are much smaller than those of the plains and appear on the map to be situated somewhat closer together. El Jaral is only eight miles from Alcalá as the raven flies, but the road there is more like twenty miles long, for it descends into the valley, skirts round the foot of the mountain and then rises once more to El Jaral. The valley across which both towns look out is known as the *campiña*, the plain. It is not called a plain because it is flat but because its agriculture resembles that of the flat country to the west, arable land divided in large properties with few trees. That is the reality which the peasant's eye sees. The tourist's eye sees a rampageous landscape of swelling hillsides and tilted escarpments brought at last to the sky-line by a flat-topped crest upon which are strewn the broken columns which once supported the temples of Accinipa.

Not quite as far as El Jaral in the other direction lies Benalurín, where Napoleon's troops burned the church: and following the road round the mountain one comes to the town of San Martín, no farther from Alcalá than Benalurín by donkey-track, but it must be a sturdy donkey to do the journey. San Martín, back to back with Alcalá and separated from it by the mountain, faces Cádiz and the Atlantic eighty miles away. Beneath the mountain in a cleft lies Jacinas and beyond that the cork-covered and bandit-ridden foothills, and beyond these the corn lands of the Andalusian plain.

These towns are much alike at first sight. The houses, whitewashed and red-tiled all, cluster together on knoll or mountain-flank overlooking their approaches. Jacinas is an exception for its siting is based upon the reversed principle. The rocks fold round it on three sides, and its lowness affords it as much protection as height does to the others. The only town whose situation is not strategic is Guadalmesí, but it has grown into being in the last thirty years. It is the only modern town in the area.

Just outside each town, a matter of two or three hundred yards, are the cemetery in one direction and the *calvario*, the chapel, in the other. The cemetery is usually below the town, the *calvario* above. There are no detached houses. The built-up area begins and ends as abruptly as the Spanish day.

Outside the towns there are not many habitations. In the plain the big farms are homes for no one, though the fore-man lodges there with his family. Labourers are housed there while they are working, but they keep their families in the town. There are sometimes apartments for the owner where he may come with his family to spend a month during the summer. Yet areas of small-holders' farms are commonly found on irrigated land, or within one of the colonisation schemes founded within the last thirty years.[1] The straggling

---

[1] "Interior colonisation", as it is called, is not confined to the last thirty years. In the village of Algar near Jerez a colonisation scheme was founded by a

collection of mills and *huertas*, or irrigated gardens, is a feature peculiar to the sierra.

The wealth of this area appears to have been declining for a long time. The liberation of the Americas from Spanish rule damaged the commercial supremacy of the port of Cádiz, and the loss of Cuba finally destroyed it. There are few modern manufactures in the area. The development of modern means of communication, of modern industry, the improved technique of agriculture in the plain and the phylloxera have each in one way and another contributed to a general decline in prosperity among the towns of the sierra. Jacinas with its flourishing leather-factories is an exception: but Alcalá has been particularly hard hit by these developments, for it formerly exported wine and in addition it possessed a cloth industry which was the pride of the region. Its products were once advertised as far afield as South America. Ninety years ago the population was double what it is today.

Some people might see in this economic decline an explanation of the intensity of social unrest which developed in the area during the latter years of the last century. The trial which made the secret terrorist society called the Black Hand famous in the eighties concerned people from this sierra, and local tradition has it that the Black Hand was active in Alcalá itself. At the beginning of the Civil War in 1936 these towns were not lacking in revolutionary ardour.

But to return to Alcalá today. The number of inhabitants living in the town is 2,045. The number of dwellings is 604. Considering the size of the average family—five to seven children is normal and up to ten is not exceptional—it appears that there are sufficient houses for the number of families. People complain of a housing shortage, but the relatively low rents (10 per cent of a day-labourer's monthly income is normal), and the fact that few houses are lived in by more than one family would indicate that it is not very acute. Moreover, the population is still falling.

nobleman in the eighteenth century. An account of this, as well as of many other features of the area, is contained in *Viaje de España*, by Antonio Ponz (Madrid, 1787). See also *Los reyes y la colonización interior de España desde el siglo XVI al XIX*, by C. Bernaldo de Quiros (Madrid, 1929).

Houses vary in size. There are fine three-storeyed mansions in the centre of the town, built in the eighteenth century by the wealthy clothiers. But no house has any pretensions to nobility, and where arms are found over the door they are those of one of the religious orders which, before the church was dispossessed, owned property here. The seigniorial lordship of Alcalá belonged to the Dukes of Arcos together with that of three neighbouring towns, but there is no evidence that they ever kept up a residence in any of them.

More modest houses have two storeys whose top floor may be no more than an attic, while the upper town is composed mainly of single-storeyed dwellings where the greater number of poor families live. Almost all have a yard at the back, including perhaps a stall for an animal, an open veranda where the cooking is done and a trellised vine. The only modern buildings are a cloth-factory and a gaudy villa put up by a retired lawyer at the entrance to the town. In spite of its incongruity it is much admired.

The hillside which folds round Alcalá is scarred by what were once streets which housed the greater population of a former epoch. The buildings are of uncut stone, granite boulders collected from the slopes, plastered both inside and outside and whitewashed. From the houses which have fallen into disuse the doors and roofs and windows have been removed—much material was taken by the builders of Guadalmesí—and the jagged walls, washed bare, have become almost indistinguishable from the rocks behind them. The ruins now serve as pens for animals. The buildings which have been abandoned in this way lie on the outskirts so that the town appears to have shrunk in upon its kernel, leaving streets of goat- and hog-pens between the inhabited dwellings and the hill.

In this way it has retained the compact appearance typical of the Andalusian town. Nor is it strange that this should be so, for, quite apart from the fact that the outlying streets were inferior, more precipitous and the houses rougher, the life of the community centres upon the fountain, the church, the town hall and the shaded square where people walk in the evening. The distance of a house from these is something of a measure of its desirability. In

addition, people do not like to live in isolation but prefer the
crowded atmosphere of the street. The climate is warm for
half the year and much time is spent out of doors. The old
women sit in their doorways by day. The young people do
their courting there in the evening. The streets of Alcalá
may be said, in fact, to be the social centre of a community
which stretches for eight kilometres around. This is called
the *término* of Alcalá.

This territory is the rural area of the township, and a
further 1,740 people live within its bounds. Of these about
half live in a village called Peñaloja, which stands beyond
the mountain at the far end of the *término*. The remainder
may truly be regarded as country-dwellers, people living
upon isolated farms or in the mills or cottages in the valley
below the town.

One of the facts which an examination of the statistics
reveals is that the relation of houses to number of inhabitants
is very much lower in the town than in the country. In
Alcalá it is 1 : 3·4, while in the country it is 1 : 5. This is
because the families who live in the country almost all own
houses in the town. These remain vacant for the greater part
of the year, being used only to store grain which must be
concealed from the visting inspector, and to house the family
when they go to stay in the town. Nor is this an innovation
which the black market in agricultural produce has made
possible and also necessary—possible through the increased
wealth of the small-holder and necessary on account of the
inspector's visits, though this explanation would seem reasonable at first sight. On the contrary, it is an ancient tradition
that every family possess its house inside the town, and this
tradition is common to the greater part of Spain whose
empty countrysides bear witness to it.[1]

This desire to live in compact communities—for so we
must for the moment consider it—is one of the prime conditions of the social structure of central and southern Spain,
and corresponds to that strong sentiment of local patriotism
which has been observed by many writers upon Spain,

---

[1] The parts of the country where the agricultural population lives entirely
in central communities rather than in farms upon the land corresponds very
roughly to the distinction between "dry" and "wet" Spain.

and which is a recurrent theme in Spanish literature. Geographically, Alcalá is something of an exception with 25 per cent of its souls living in the country. In its sentiments, however, it is no exception. This identity of place and community is clearly revealed in the language. The word for "town", which might equally be translated as "village" since it covers any community of from a few hundred to thirty thousand inhabitants, is *el pueblo*.[1] And this word means, not only in the dictionary but also in everyday parlance, both the place and also the people who belong to that place. This conception of the pueblo as a human community expressed in a geographical idiom was well illustrated to me when people explained; "Peñaloja is a street of Alcalá." This in spite of the fact that ten kilometres and a mountain pass separate the two places. Moreover, the language reinforces this identity by a converse example. The word *población*, meaning population, is most commonly heard in the sense of a populated place, a city, town or hamlet.

Membership of the pueblo is acquired primarily by birth. Those born within the town remain "sons of the pueblo" until their dying day, no matter where they go to live. They will remain "sons of the pueblo" not only for legal purposes, as in the parish register; "Hijo de Alcalá, empadronado en X . . ." ("Son of Alcalá, numbered among the neighbours of X . . ."), but also in people's minds, for it is likely that they will never bear any nickname other than that derived from the place of their origin; "El Alcalareño" or "El de Alcalá". This does not follow if a man goes to such a distance that the name of his town is unknown, or to a big city where nicknames have not quite the same significance. A man from another province may be known by his province, or if from farther away still, by his region. Thus a man of Alcalá is: "Alcalareño", "Gaditano" ("of the province of Cádiz"), "Andaluz" ("Andalusian"). I was known in Alcalá as "el Inglés".

---

[1] I use the word "town" rather than "village" because although it is the residential unit of agricultural workers, it also has shops, a market and a municipal administration. Moreover, I do not wish to use both words and make a distinction where the language of the people themselves makes none.

Legal membership of the municipal commuity, *vecindad*, neighbourship, is acquired by the act of *empadronamiento*, inscription in the parish register as a neighbour of the pueblo. This is performed automatically after two years' continuous residence or after six months should it be solicited. Public functionaries, on the other hand, receive the legal status of neighbour upon taking up their post. This status entitles a man to vote in municipal elections, to hold municipal office and to participate in the privileges of the community such as common pastures and agricultural and social benefits. The quality of neighbour has greater effects in the sphere of law than the place of birth, yet the moral quality derived from the latter enters into the definition of the personality for legal purposes in a term which reveals its mystical importance. The word *naturaleza*, nature, means, when applied to a person, simply his place of birth.

The inhabitants of a pueblo are frequently designated by a collective nickname.[1] Those of Alcalá are called "the Lard-eaters", a reference to their fame for raising and fattening pigs. Those of Benalurín are the "Bumpkins". In this instance the people of Peñaloja are differentiated from those of Alcalá by a separate nickname.

In addition, each pueblo is distinguished by the possession of a patron saint who stands in a particular relationship to the community. The pueblo is under the protection of its patron to whom, in many cases, it was formally dedicated at its foundation. The name of the town sometimes derives from this fact. Thus, Villaluenga del Rosario, Puerto Santa Maria, San Pedro de Alcántara, San Martín. The festival of the patron is always a holiday of importance and in many cases it is combined with the *feria*, the lay festival and market. Though devotion is not accorded uniquely to the patron of the pueblo, there tend to be strong feelings regarding him and not only on the part of persons of religious zeal. In this regard Alcalá is distinguished once again from Peñaloja by separate patrons.

The sentiment of attachment to the pueblo is counter-

[1] There is an article by Gabriel Maria Vergara Martín in the *Boletín de la Real Sociedad Geografica*, Vol. XV, 1918, which gives a collection of such nicknames from different parts of Spain.

balanced, as might be expected, by a corresponding hostility towards neighbouring pueblos. Thus, for the Alcalareño, those of Jacinas are boastful and false, those of Montejaque cloddish and violent, those of Benalurín are mean, those of El Jaral drunken and always drawing their knives. There appears to be little objective basis for such accusations, but such as exists is worth noting. Jacinas is a rich town with twice the number of inhabitants now as Alcalá. It threatens on account of its greater wealth to oust Alcalá from its place as judicial centre of the region. There is far more animosity in Alcalá towards Jacinas than towards any other town. Montejaque is an entirely pastoral community, and shepherds' manners are held to be uncouth by agricultural people. Benalurín is a poor pueblo which cannot afford to pay high prices. While El Jaral is where the wine-growing country begins.[1]

This hostility finds expression in various customs. It is usual for the boys of a pueblo to object to the visits of *forasteros*—a word which I shall translate as "outsiders", since it means a person born elsewhere—for the purpose of courting one of their girls. In some places they follow the practice of ducking the visitor in the fountain when he first comes, but allowing him to come freely thereafter. In others, however, they ambush him and beat him up whenever they are able to catch him there. Two Alcalareños have had to break off their engagements on account of the rough treatment which they received in their fiancée's town. Such a custom applies only to the town itself. A girl who lives on a farm within the *término* of another pueblo may be courted with safety.

Each pueblo possesses a collection of ballads recording local history, and of sayings and rhymes in which the praises of the pueblo are sung and derogatory observations are made

---

[1] Casual conversation does not always reveal the animosity between pueblos, for the educated tend to laugh at it, while the informant may feel the solidarity of the area in face of a foreigner and give an account in which each pueblo seems more marvellous than the last. When travelling, one day, up the valley of the Rio Genal with a local man, I was amazed at the praises which he bestowed on each pueblo in turn. Coming finally to the most miserable of them all, I asked whether this was not a rotten place. "This one?" he replied, "No, indeed, a fine pueblo. A very rich pueblo. It has many acorns."

of its neighbours. So, a common expression of denigration is
to say of someone that he is:

"Mas bruto que el alcalde del Gastor."
"Rougher than the mayor of El Gastor."
or
"Como la gente de Jerez que mientras no tocan no ven."
"Like the people of Jerez who can't see without touching."

A rhyme inspired by the same spirit can usually be found
for any pueblo, and I give one which is known in Alcalá:

"En el pueblo de Zahara	"In the pueblo of Zahara
Hay dos cosas regulares	There are two things which aren't up to much
Una p'arriba y una p'abajo	One in the upper town and one in the lower
Y en medio los mula'res."	And in between are the dung-heaps."

In the folklore of its neighbours Alcalá is represented in a
similar light, but within the pueblo its name is heard only
in the most complimentary contexts. A ballad recounts how
a visiting official was outwitted and put to shame by the
noble people of that place, and a more ancient saying tells
that after the Resurrection the Saviour stopped off on his
way to Heaven at the *calvario* of Alcalá, a signal honour which
has afforded the inhabitants special protection ever since
from the damage wrought by thunderstorms. In a rhyme
the excellence of Alcalá is contrasted with the wretchedness
of its neighbours:

"El Jaral corral de cabras	"El Jaral is a pen for she-goats
Guadalmesí de cabritos	Guadalmesí for kids
Benalurín de cabrones	Benalurín is for he-goats[1]
Y Alcalá de señoritos."	And Alcalá for gentlemen."

The most proud saying of all comes from the town of
Jimena, which challenges the rest of the world in terms of
piteous contempt:

"Ay! que pena	"What a shame!
No ser de Jimena!"	Not to be from Jimena!"

[1] The reader unacquainted with the symbolism of the Mediterranean
countries is referred to the word *cabrón* in the glossary.

But, typically, the neighbouring pueblos have found a line to add:

"Y arrastrarse el culo en la arena."
"And drag your arse along in the sand."

for the people of Jimena enjoy a local reputation for being short in the leg.

The festival of the patron saint is the day upon which the hostilities between pueblos are traditionally expressed. Upon El Jaral's Saint's Day the young men are supposed to fight with those of Villa Fadrique, and it is told that upon the day of St. Martín, in the village of that name, the young men would hurl rocks down the hillside upon those of Jacinas coming to attend the occasion. Another story recounts how the latter attempted to make away with the image of St. Martín during an open-air ceremony, and how, foiled in their design, they later stole the bull from San Martín's bull-fight (an affair in which the animal is hauled through the streets by a rope attached to its horns) and dragged it half-way to Jacinas, when the boys of San Martín, rather than submit to such an affront, slew it with a dagger upon the border of their territory. A bull's head painted upon a rock commemorates the event. This kind of thing is common throughout the greater part of Spain. The traditional fighting between two towns near Seville, Mairena and El Viso, is well known, though today it takes place only between the school-children of the two towns. At the fiesta of Haro in the Rioja, not many years ago, the bull-ring was festooned with an announcement reading: "A hearty welcome is extended to all outsiders with the exception of those from Logroño."

Pueblos are commonly linked in pairs, each one, supposedly, hating its rival above all others. Thus, El Jaral—Villa Fadrique, Montejaque—Benaoján, Ubrique—Grazalema, even, on a far greater scale, Cádiz and Jerez. Today, with the rise of Jacinas, its rivalry with San Martín appears to have diminished, for the latter is poor now and economically dependent upon its more powerful neighbour, but at the same time its rise has accentuated the tension with declining Alcalá.

Yet in none of these cases does fighting take place today.

Though there is likely to be indiscriminate fighting upon Saint's Days because more wine is drunk then, it cannot be said to be anything but casual. So, it is permissible to wonder whether these enmities are anything more than a piece of folklore which people enjoy repeating, whether the fights ever took place in fact or whether, as has been suggested in the case of the ritual murder of the Shilluk kings, the myth was not always sufficient. There are reasons to believe, however, that these stories, though sometimes much exaggerated, are in essence true and that recent times have brought a weakening of the spirit of local chauvinism.

The body of custom, the folklore which was studied under the influence of Machado who founded the review *El Folklore Español* in 1883, is generally similar throughout Andalusia. In speech there is a recognised Andalusian accent which is thought to be funny by the rest of Spain (indeed it is as much a necessity for the stage comedian as is a Yorkshire accent in the English music-hall). The methods and implements employed in agriculture vary little save in accordance with the demands of the terrain. The pattern of land-tenure varies, but the same customary law, the same forms of exploitation and co-operation are found. In spite of the continual attribution of this or that characteristic to the people of one province or another, there seems to be little variation in the values underlying social behaviour throughout Andalusia.

Yet, if the spirit of custom is the same, there is a proliferation in the detail which distinguishes one town from another. There are differences of speech, both of accent and vocabulary from one pueblo to another. Benaocaz pronounces the "ll" as in Castile and not as a soft "j" like the surrounding pueblos. There are distinctive intonations in the speech of Zahara, Villa Fadrique, Montejaque and Benalurín which make it possible, it is thought, to tell where a man is from as soon as he opens his mouth. Between Alcalá and Jacinas there is little difference in intonation, but there is a difference in vocabulary and in the use of language. Differences are particularly noticeable in the customary slang and in obscene language. Women swear more and more shamelessly in Jacinas than anywhere else, so the Alcalareños say.

Courting is done in much the same way everywhere; but in one town the young couples talk through the window, in another they stand in the doorway. The modes of celebrating religious festivals vary from place to place. The essentially dramatic interpretation of religion in Andalusia clothes itself in individual customs in each pueblo. Moors and Christians, Romans and Jews, dancing acolytes and dancing devils lend picturesqueness to the local fiesta, giving a distinct character to that of each pueblo. And these distinctions are found not only in the feasts of the patron saints but in most of the important days of the calendar, and not only in the processions but in the pueblo's activities for the whole day.

Differences in material culture stress the same point. Men carry their lunch in one town in a bag of woven palm-leaf, in another in a basket, in a third in a cotton bag. In Alcalá mattresses are filled with wool, even in the houses of the poorest. In Guadalmesí, where people are less poor, many are filled with straw. Certain pueblos have established excellence in a particular craft. These observations are far from complete, nor are they significant to the study of social structure, in their detail. What is significant is that they should exist, for they are the ways whereby membership of the community is defined. They maintain the basic premiss of the Andalusian peasant's political thought, which is the moral unity of the pueblo. Thus, it is sincerely believed that the women of Benaocaz have stronger characters than their menfolk and than the women of other pueblos.[1] And even where the veracity of such an assertion might be questioned, the legitimacy of this method of generalisation is not.

[1] "En Benaocaz la hembra na' ma'
    Y en Villaluenga ni el macho ni la hembra
    Y en Grazalema huye que te quema'"

"In Benaocaz only the women (i.e. are worth anything)
    And in Villaluenga neither the men nor the women
    And in Grazalema flee lest you get burned."

This is the statement of a sociological truth, but the first line is founded upon an historical legend. It is said that when the Catholic Monarchs visited the town of Benaocaz only the women came out to greet them. There are several variations of this legend. (Cf. Pedro Perez Clotet, *La serranía de Ronda en la literatura*, an address to the Ateneo de Cádiz, 1940.) With regard to the danger of burning in Grazalema, see p. 197.

CHAPTER II

El Pueblo

(ii) The Community and the World

IF THE cultural reality has been given before the facts of
political organisation, it is only in order to stress the more
permanent of these two interrelated aspects of the community. Each in the long run acts upon the other; but since
this is the study of a community and not of the political
structure of the country, it seems proper to begin by defining
the community as it exists upon the ground and in the minds
of its members, before examining the laws which regulate its
government. The same law applies, in Murcia or Galicia, to
pueblos whose social structure is very different.

When Granada was conquered by the Christians it was
annexed to the Kingdom of Castile, which was still separate
from the Kingdom of Aragon, the two being united only by
the marriage bond of their sovereigns. Since that date the
work of centralisation stretches down—not without periods
of regression[1]—to the present day. The local rights which
derived either from an autochthonous tradition or from
charters accorded to townships during the Middle Ages have
today virtually disappeared, except for certain regional
diversities in matters of private law. The country is governed
from Madrid. Yet the regions cling firmly to their cultural
traditions. Within them, the provinces show only slight
variations, but they, not the regions, are the political segments of the structure of the state. It is also the regions not
the provinces which are divided by natural barriers and by
historical tradition. The provincial system was only intro-

---

[1] Notably through the sale by the Crown of seigniorial rights in the seventeenth century. Garcia Oviedo (*Derecho Administrativo*, 1951, p. 315) sees a
tendency against centralisation from 1877 to 1935. This is discussed later,
p. 219.

duced during the latter half of the eighteenth century, and
the present division was established in 1834. Thus, while the
country as a whole is both a cultural and political unit, the
region is today chiefly a cultural unit and the province
chiefly a political one. How membership of these groups
defines a person has already been discussed. What this
membership means to the individual varies according to his
social status and must be discussed elsewhere. For the
moment we are concerned only with the lowest level of
political segmentation, the pueblo.

All the municipalities of the province come directly under
the orders and administration of its civil governor. The
province is divided, however, into *partidos*—*partido judicial* is
the full term—for certain purposes, the chief of which is the
organisation of justice. The advisory council of the governor,
the *diputación provincial*, is made up of one mayor from each
partido elected by the others from among their number. The
Church also uses this unit in its administration, though the
dioceses do not always correspond to provincial territories.
The Civil Guard is also organised by *partidos*.

The syndicates, the government labour organisations, are
controlled directly from the provincial office which is
situated, normally, in the capital. A single syndical headquarters in the pueblo under the secretary of the syndicates
administers the affairs of all those of Alcalá.

At the level of the pueblo power centres in the hands of
the mayor, just as at provincial level it centres in the hands
of the governor. The mayor is responsible to the governor
and to no one else. All the other official bodies require the
co-operation of the Town Hall in one way or another, and
they are to a greater or lesser extent subject to the mayor's
authority.

How these various organisations function in detail must
be left till later. Let it be underlined here that, excluding
Peñaloja whose mayor is a delegate of the mayor of Alcalá
and whose presence within the *término* appears in view of its
geographical position something of an anomaly, they all
centre in the town. Nor would it be practical for them to
operate in any other way, given the geographical and ideological formation of the peublo. Power is therefore vested in

a very few hands, those of the governing body of the pueblo, the persons of influence: the officials and the resident wealthy. The officials are mostly outsiders, appointed to their office by the state (though they may be paid by the Town Hall), and are only temporarily part of the community of the pueblo. Neither the mayor, nor the priest, nor the judge, nor the secretary of the Town Hall, nor the Secretary of Justice, nor the Chief of Posts, nor three of the five schoolmasters, nor the doctor, the vet nor the chemist, nor the state tax-collector, are sons of the pueblo. Nor the head of the municipal guards, nor any of the civil guards, (It is a firm principle with the latter that no man is ever posted to his own pueblo.) While of the large landowners, the majority though sons of the pueblo live now in Malaga or Jerez, sixty-odd miles away, and come to Alcalá only for the summer months. The sentiment of solidarity with the pueblo is a thing felt far less strongly by these people, for whether sons of the pueblo or not, their ambitions and interests, both social and material, revolve within far wider horizons. "This place is dead", "Nothing ever happens here", they complain. Except perhaps for the elderly women, very few of them would not move to a larger town if they had the chance. (During the past forty years several wealthy families have sold their lands and moved elsewhere.) These people all lead lives whose interests focus to a large extent upon objects outside the pueblo.

But the lives of the working-people are contained within narrower horizons. The *término* of their town defines the extent of their relations with organised institutions. For a man's health, there is the town's doctor; for his animals its vet; if he requires to borrow money, there is its branch of the Monte de Piedad, the agricultural bank; for the rites of birth, marriage and death, there is its priest.[1] If he wishes to prosper, he must be on reasonably good terms with the authorities, for while they work together they are too powerful to be defied. On the other hand, the man who is well thought of by them need fear no outside interference. When a man is arrested on suspicion in a strange place, the first

[1] The distinction between civil and religious rites, introduced under the Republic, has been abolished.

1. The lower fountain

2. The upper fountain

thing done by the Civil Guard is to communicate with the commander of the section in the man's pueblo. His subsequent treatment will depend largely upon the character which he is given.[1] Travel, other than on foot, is expensive and to do so other than for business reasons is a luxury which few can afford. From ten to twenty men go down every year to the plain to work in the harvest, and others go from time to time on various pretexts, but their families and their interests remain in Alcalá. A special pass is required to leave Andalusia to work elsewhere. Some have never been to Jacinas, and some have never seen Ronda. To have seen the sea other than from the top of a mountain is to have travelled, and though many have been as far as Africa or the Pyrennees in military service, this experience is something apart, like a relative in America, which gives knowledge of another world but does not affect everyday life in the community.

The concentration of political power at municipal level appears so natural in Andalusia that, though it provided a basis upon which the system of *caciquismo*[2] rested, the doctrine of Anarchism, the movement which attacked that system, never questioned it. The concept of the pueblo as the unique political unit was so deeply embedded in the outlook of the peasants that it became a corner-stone in Anarchist policy. The Anarchists sought, in fact, not to break this political monopoly, but rather to become empowered with it and to eliminate the governing class which represented external influences. An example of their activity may be drawn from the neighbourhood of Alcalá. A successful rising in the town of El Gastor at the end of the last century was followed by a declaration of the Republic of El Gastor. Its men marched over to Alcalá and invited the inhabitants to follow their example and declare a republic also, entering into a defensive alliance with them. They had been in secret touch with people in Alcalá and elsewhere and hoped to secure their

---

[1] The traditional attention which the law pays to the "good name" of a person is to be found in the dispositions relating to *Buena conducta*. See Emilio Calatayud Sanjuan, *Enciclopedia Manual Jurídico-Administrativo* (1933), p. 323.

[2] A system of "political bosses" which obtained during the period between the second Carlist war and the first dictatorship. Cf. G. Brenan, *The Spanish Labyrinth* (1942), who gives an extensive bibliography of the subject.

position through a series of these alliances. According to some accounts they marched over to conquer Alcalá. While the matter was still under discussion, the forces of the Civil Guard rallied and sent a column upon the scene, whereupon the Republic of El Gastor vanished into thin air.

The insistence upon municipal independence in the policy of the movement was tempered, as time went on, by practical contingencies which required a certain measure of centralised organisation. Yet this was an adaptation to the necessity for co-ordinated action rather than a change of heart. The same spirit reigned and was to be discerned in the events of the Civil War. The rise to power of the Anarchists in the towns of the sierra in June 1936 was followed by the establishment of "communism" : Money was abolished and a central exchange bureau was set up in the pueblo which collected all produce and redistributed it in accordance with a system of rationing. Thus, though clearly the situation demanded extraordinary measures and this example cannot be treated as conclusive, the assumption of power by the Anarchists rendered the pueblo not only, theoretically, an exclusive political group but exclusive economically as well. There are some indications that this conception of the pueblo in the minds of small-town Anarchists created tension between the regional leadership and the local community. The Anarchist leaders from the large towns attempted, in the interests of organisation, to interfere with what the small-town Anarchists regarded as the autonomous rights of the pueblo which they themselves embodied, and in that they were often resisted.[1] The very word pueblo cloaked the disagreement. For, in addition to the two meanings which have been given above, the word has a third meaning: "people" in the sense of *plebs* as opposed to the rich, and although the people of Alcalá recognise this meaning, it is for them synonymous with the other meanings, for the rich do not really belong to the pueblo but to that wider world which has already been delimited as theirs. In this sense the pueblo is a potentially revolutionary force which at any time may rise

---

[1] Cf. Gamel Woolsey, *Death's Other Kingdom* (1939) for an account of a right-wing person defended by the Anarchists of his village from those of Malaga on the grounds of being "un hijo del pueblo" ("a son of the village").

to see that justice is done—as in the rebellion of Fuenteovejuna,[1] or as in a story told of Jacinas, when the priest
apparently omitted to observe the same courtesies in the
burial of a poor person as he had in the case of a wealthy
widow. The pueblo demanded the same treatment for both.
"Sinó se levanta el pueblo",[2] said the story-teller. A final
example is provided in the words of one of the leaders of the
Anarchists in Alcalá, a man named "Argolla". When the
forces of the Right had taken Alcalá they wished to avenge
the victims of the Left with a public execution, and this man
was given public trial. When he was charged with the murder
of those who had been shot there he replied that it was not
he who had condemned them but "el pueblo". He would
make no other answer to the charge.

The main market for the products of the area is found in
the large towns of Ronda, Jerez, Cádiz, Seville and Algeciras.
And it is from them that manufactured articles reach Alcalá.
It is by these centres of trade, rather than by the neighbouring pueblos of the sierra, that the economy of Alcalá is
complemented today. Entrepreneurs from them establish
trading centres in the town to buy up such commodities as
game, eggs or esparto grass. The visiting copers buy the cattle
and wool. Contractors come with lorries to buy the charcoal,
or the merchants of Ronda come with donkey-trains to
fetch it. The couriers of Alcalá bear produce as far as Jerez
on their donkeys, returning with such purchases as they are
charged with.

Yet there is a considerable volume of trade between the
towns of the locality. First of all, in controlled agricultural
produce. For the foodstuff-control organisation does not,

[1] The pueblo of Fuenteovejuna in the province of Cordoba, angered by the
tyrannical behaviour of the *comendador*, rose one night in 1476 and murdered
him. When the judges came to inquire who was responsible for his death they
could get no answer but "Fuenteovejuna". Cf. Diaz del Moral, *Historia de las
agitaciones campesinas Andaluzas* (Madrid, 1929). Lope de Vega wrote his play
Fuenteovejuna upon this incident.

[2] "Otherwise the pueblo would have risen." Diaz del Moral (*op. cit.*, p. 24)
describes the popular revolt: "La muchedumbre se hace pueblo" ("The
multitude becomes a pueblo"), and refers to the seventeenth-century expression: "La gente se levantaba en forma de pueblo" ("The people rose in the
form of a pueblo").

in fact, get its hands on more than 50 per cent of the crop. This is easy to understand. The officials who are responsible in the town for countersigning the returns of the farmers are farmers themselves. Less than what is sown is declared, and upon the declared area only about half the harvest is admitted. It is always an inexplicably bad year. In addition, the farmer is permitted to retain the grain to sow the following year and a certain amount for his subsistence in lieu of rations. Since the price paid by the government for the grain collected bears no relation to the real price, a farmer who made an honest declaration every year would soon be bankrupt. The official grain is taken away by the inspector, and other grain, inferior, so people say, is sent to the town to provide the inadequate bread-ration. This is milled by the officially authorised mill, an electrical one, situated in Alcalá. The crop which remains undeclared follows a different and less unnatural course from producer to consumer. It is ground illicitly in mills which are officially closed, and eventually it furnishes the unrationed bread which is sold openly throughout the country. There are a great many mills working unofficially in the area, powered by the waters of the sierra. Alcalá has some fourteen of them, some of them converted from old cloth-factories and fulling-mills.[1] The grain which they grind comes mostly from the plain of Guadalmesí. It is borne by donkeys which make the journey singly or in pairs, sometimes at night, for fear of the inspector. There are also two olive-mills in the valley, both of them authorised, though how much of the oil produced is declared to the inspector can only be a matter of conjecture. The miller smiles and changes the conversation when he is asked how much he mills.

One can see then that agricultural produce flows in two parallel channels: the official and the illicit. But the latter is so essential, so much more extensive and so generally accepted, that it dwarfs the former and makes it appear not so much as an attempt to keep down the cost of living of the

[1] Six of these mills were matriculated already at the time the law making them illegal was introduced, and they are paid compensation for being denied the right to mill (at the rate of 7,000 pesetas per annum). In fact they mill just as much as those who are paid no compensation for not milling. All of them pay the municipal tax upon industry.

poorer people,[1] but rather as the central government's method of levying tribute in favour of a parasitical hierachy, the food-controllers. Be this as it may, the inspectors enjoy a wide reputation for corruption, and popular feeling is high against them; the consumers on account of the inadequacy and irregularity of the rations, the producers since they would prefer to sell the whole crop at the unofficial price, and both together because it is thought to be an immoral organisation which meddles in the affairs of the town and imposes unjust fines.

Apart from illicit trading between pueblos there is a certain body of local trade, though less than formerly. A cork-factory in Benalurín supplies itself from the area. The cloth-factory in Alcalá buys most of its wool locally. There is a chair-factory in Peñaloja whose products are common throughout the area. There is also a certain trade in the produce of the irrigated gardens, for crops ripen earlier in Jacinas, while some pueblos have no irrigation. Farmers sometimes send a son with a donkey-load to get the better price in a neighbouring town. The high towns specialise in hams which cure better at their altitude. On the other hand, many local industries have succumbed to the economic changes of modern times. The cloth production of Alcalá has been much reduced. The leather industry of Jacinas uses imported leather today since local skins are less well cured. Mill-stones are no longer quarried locally but are imported from regions of harder stone. The blacksmiths of the pueblo no longer make agricultural implements. In many items local craftsmanship has given way to the manufactured product. These changes have meant not only a change in the directions of economic co-operation but also a contribution to the general impoverishment of the area, which, being country unsuitable for modern agricultural techniques, has benefited little from their improvements. The money which leaves the community in this way does not return in exchange for increased production.

---

[1] There are three rationing scales whereby the well-to-do receive fewer rations than the poor. It is argued that they can afford to buy upon the black market. This argument involves a logical contradiction between the aims of the control order and the aims of rationing, but its equity cannot be denied.

The degree to which towns are economically independent of one another can be inferred from a comparison of price-levels which vary from place to place according to supply and demand, and to the success with which traders manage to corner an article in short supply. Manufactured articles are always more expensive in Alcalá than in Ronda, and, except when local crops come on the market, agricultural produce also. The cost of transport, due partly to the nature of the country and partly to the bad conditions of the roads and the shortage of motor vehicles, is responsible for this. Motor transport is not used for local trade, and animal transport is costly: for, apart from other considerations, the quantities seldom justify the use of a two-ton lorry, which is the smallest transport vehicle employed in the area. What, in fact, has happened is that while great advances have taken place during the last century in long-range communication, local communications remain much as they were one hundred years ago. In a sense they have deterio-rated, for the scarcity of beasts following upon the war has made them more expensive, and their upkeep is relatively more expensive also. In addition, though roads have been built, they take longer and less direct courses than the tracks which, not being built for motor vehicles, use steeper gradients. And since the roads exist, the upkeep of the tracks has been allowed to fall off.

Another factor is the lack of economic uniformity at national or provincial level, which means that there are stable and general prices only for things like newspapers, patent medicines, etc., while the fiscal liberty which the Town Hall possesses favours local variations. Variations in local taxation are sometimes considerable, and accentuate the local variations in price level.

Wages also vary a great deal from one town to another. During the harvest they reach, in Jacinas and in the plain of Guadalmesí, the figure of double the agricultural wage in Alcalá. They are always appreciably higher in the plain of Jerez. Theoretically, a minimum wage is laid down for the whole province, but it is the custom for employment to be given with meals ("con la comida"). A worker can only claim the wage-rate if he is employed without meals ("a seco"). The difference between what he is paid and the the wage-rate is technically a subtraction for his food. It is recognised that the labour involved in cultivation of the lands of Alcalá and the poor return which they yield does not permit payment of the same wages as in the plain. Yet, in spite of this, men are unwilling to go there if they can find a job in their own town. "It is all very well making a lot of money," they say, " but away from home it costs twice as much to live, and you have no friends there so anyone may take advantage of you." A labourer who is an outsider appears to be at a disadvantage because he does not belong to the community. The majority of those who go away to work do so in answer to the summons of a friend already established as a permanent employee upon a farm which requires additional labour. Moreover, at certain times in the past, the provincial governor has issued an order forbidding men to seek work outside their own pueblo.[1] The Civil Guard were then entrusted with the enforcement of this order, sending home those who arrived from outside.

For the most part, the economic relations of Alcalá lie towards the north and east, not towards the other towns of its *partido*. The main road passes to the north of Alcalá. The railway station lies to the east on the Ronda–Algeciras line. Fish comes almost daily to the pueblo by one or other of these routes; a man with a donkey meets the fish lorry from Cádiz on the main road. It is also sometimes brought from the railway station. Grain for the mills comes from the northeast, and it is in that direction that the transhuman flocks go after the harvest. The wine drunk in Alcalá, other than a small quantity vinted in the town, comes from the same direction.

The main shopping and business centre is Ronda. The motor-bus runs in the morning from Jacinas to Ronda via Alcalá and returns by the same route in the evening. This means that while it is possible to go by that means for the day to Ronda, to go to Jacinas involves spending two nights there as well. Though one kilometre nearer by road, the journey to Jacinas is more arduous to animals on account of

[1] This was originally the *Ley de los términos municipales* of 1933. Similar legislation has been brought in at various times since the war.

the mountain pass. Also, Ronda is five times the size of Jacinas, and a place of much greater importance.

An examination of the parish register gives some indication of the range of human contacts.[1] Those born in other pueblos number 13·4 per cent of the population. This includes both families which have moved into Alcalá, single persons who have married into the town, and children born to Alcalarenian parents while away. In addition, it represents a time-span of the last seventy years or so. The total number of persons born elsewhere is 433. Of these, 300 were born within a radius of fifty kilometres. If we break up these 300, we find that 226 come from the north-east side of the mountains and only 74 from the south-west. Graded according to the towns from which they come, the four highest figures are: Montejaque, 60; El Gastor, 50; El Jaral, 41; and Ronda, 35. Fifth in order comes Jacinas with 22, the highest figure from the south-west and from the *partido* of Alcalá.

To sum up, then, Alcalá is tied to the other pueblos of its sierra by a common material culture, by the exchanges of goods and services between similar economies, by a certain tradition of being mountain people who consider themselves tougher and more moral than the people of the plain because, perhaps, they are poorer, and by membership of an administrative unit, the *partido judicial*. It is linked to the north and east by a very different set of ties, by complementary economies and by human contacts including kinship. The difference in the nature of these two sets of ties might be summed up as ties based upon similarity, and ties based upon reciprocity, or one might also call them corporate ties and diffuse ties.[2] At the present stage, rather than seek a pair of "portmanteau" concepts into which to fit the various but

[1] The hamlet of Peñaloja is torn between its administrative dependence upon Alcalá and its economic dependence upon the nearer and better communicated Jacinas. It is therefore excluded from the statistical data here considered.

[2] It might be possible to say, using Durkheim's terms, that Alcalá possessed "mechanical solidarity" with the mountain pueblos and "organic solidarity" with the towns of the plain. However, as will be seen, neither set of ties constitutes solidarity in itself. Where I use the word solidarity I shall use it to mean the identification of members of a group through a common allegiance *in a specific social situation*, and their differentiation thereby from non-members. I do not wish to imply any necessary attachment between members of a group. It is a sociological, not a psychological term. Groups, not individuals, possess it.

by no means complete observations which have been made, it is more useful to make one further observation, namely, that these ties are exercised in the main through two different elements of the society of Alcalá. A further examination of the parish register brings this point to light.

Of persons living in the town itself 11·7 per cent were born elsewhere, while of those living upon farms within the territory of Alcalá the percentage is 17·1 per cent. Yet the former includes the families of all the officials who are outsiders, and of the landowners who live in the large towns where their children are born these days. Together these two classes make up about one-third of the outsiders resident within the town. The following table shows the exact percentages of outsiders (*a*) among the inhabitants of the town, and (*b*) among the inhabitants of the country.

Place of residence	Total	From under 50 km.	From over 50 km.
(*a*) The town:	11·7%	6·9%	4·8%
(*b*) The country:	17·1%	14·6%	2·5%

The great majority of the officials and of the children of the landowners were born more than fifty kilometres away, and if, therefore, these be excluded, then the figures are even more emphatic; there is double the percentage of outsiders among the mills and farms than in the town. So that it appears that the path towards assimilation into the community lies through the peripheral countryside. The reasons for this are many. To begin with, those who live outside the pueblo live correspondingly nearer to another town with which trade and human contacts are easier in consequence. In the second place, they are largely persons of a certain substance—tenant and owner-farmer, miller, charcoal burner, and so on—men of independence who work for themselves and do not depend upon a daily wage. They travel about in pursuit of their business, and their contacts are more extended as a result. Millers are seen to change their place of residence more frequently than any other class, and many of them, if not born outside, have passed part of their lives working in a mill in another valley. In addition, their position today on the margin of legality alienates them from the official administration which centres in the town. Owner-farmers are sometimes outsiders and so are tenant-farmers, brought in by landowners who may have interests in other pueblos and who in at least one case prefer to employ an outsider.[1] The outsider, who comes seeking work, goes round the farms asking for a job rather than ask for it in the town. Or he may come at the invitation of the farmer. He lives upon the farm and returns home once the work is finished. If he remains therefore as permanent employee, he is likely to do so as a country-dweller.

No doubt other reasons could be found to account for the higher percentage of outsiders in the country than in the town. For example, the importance of marriage in bringing an outsider into the community and this will be discussed later. It is enough for the moment to point out that the same classes which are more free in their movements are those who are most likely to marry a girl from another pueblo.

It may appear surprising that in a place which has a high birth-rate and a declining population there should be so many outsiders. The number of sons of the pueblo living elsewhere is certainly far greater, though it is not possible to know exact numbers. Prior to the Civil War, some went to America. Many went to Jerez during the last century. Today they go in all directions—wherever it is possible to make a living. Most of all have gone to the Campo de Gibraltar in recent years, where the end of international hostilities has brought a boom in its traditional industry, contraband.

The Civil War has carried away many men and some whole families, creating gaps which outsiders have filled, dispersing people throughout the country. But for this, the problem could be seen far more clearly.

Yet how do people behave towards outsiders? The stranger, as in Ancient Greece where he was protected by Zeus, enjoys a special status. It is a duty to assist him, for the reputation of the pueblo is felt to be at stake in his eyes. The visitor of wealth or standing is treated with great

---

[1] In somewhat the same way certain of the officials prefer to get their domestic servants from another pueblo. "It is better," they say "if one's servant-girl does not have a family in the place. The household money goes further."

courtesy and hospitality. He is probably invited to a glass of wine in the *casino*, the club. People inquire what brings him and put themselves at his disposal.

This standard of hospitality is a very noble feature of the Spanish people, yet its analysis would not be complete if one were not to point out that it is also a means whereby the community defends itself against outside interference. For a guest is a person who, while he must be entertained and cherished, is dependent upon the goodwill of his hosts. He has no rights and he can make no demands. On the other hand, the good name of the pueblo is his protection. For the sake of that, the members of the community prevent one another from taking advantage of him.

The vagrant labourer who comes in search of work is in rather a different position to people who come for business or pleasure. For one thing he is potentially taking the bread out of the mouths of the sons of the pueblo. He is also a potential black-leg who will work for less than that which is being paid there.[1] In addition, those who purport to come seeking work may be in reality shameless vagabonds, ready to steal or commit any felony. For a man who wishes to escape criticism in his own pueblo must go elsewhere, where the sanction of public opinion is less effective over him. A man's behaviour is not necessarily the same once he has left home. Among those who go away to seek a living, some are prepared to beg who would be ashamed to do so in their own village. Stories circulate in the valley telling how this or that beggar from outside is really a prosperous person in his own village, to whom no one would dream of giving alms. Men who rob the crops, seldom do so within the *término* of their own pueblo. To work as a prostitute is something which a girl must go away for. To do so where she had a family would be regarded as very shocking, quite apart from what they might have power to do in order to prevent her. The power of public opinion is very great. It is expressed in one word *el quedirán*—the "what-will-they-say". It is recognised that people are virtuous for fear of what will be said—"por

---

[1] The labour from the poor villages of the mountains was used to break strikes in the plain of Jerez at an earlier period. *Vide* V. Blasco Ibanez, *La Bodega* (Valencia, 1905).

miedo del quedirán".[1] Those arrested for stealing in the
término of Alcalá are almost invariably from El Jaral, Villa
Fadrique, or El Gastor. In this way the low opinion of the
character of neighbouring pueblos is reinforced. Not that
stealing by residents of the valley is unknown, quite the contrary. Yet, when it happens, the case seldom comes before the
law. Private action is preferred, for to call in the Civil Guard
against a neighbour would be considered very "ugly". At
the same time, there is a far greater inducement to beg or rob
when away from home, in that other means of maintaining
oneself are no longer available.

When men come seeking work they are treated at first, if
they are unknown, with a coldness which contrasts with the
reception afforded to the affluent.[2] People are chary of
giving work to a man whose reputation they do not know,
for he may take advantage of the fact that his good name
matters less to him away from his own pueblo. The first
question asked of any outsider is: Where is he from? Yet if
a man has a friend there then he is alright, his friend is
responsible for him, and if someone can give him a good
name, then he may find work. The importance of friendship
and acquaintanceship is very great. One often hears men
boast: "Here everybody knows me" or "I am known in
every town from here to wherever-it-is." A good name is a
literally valuable asset.

Discussion of friendship as an institution must be put off
till later. The Andalusians are well known for the fineness
of their manners and the volatile quality of their sympathies.
Lovers of the new, they are quick to enter upon terms of
friendliness with a fresh acquaintance and people who settle
in a pueblo do not take long to be absorbed into its life. Within a couple of years they will have developed relationships of
reciprocal trust, and enter into co-operative ventures such
as share-cropping with the people of the pueblo. The senti-

---

[1] Much of the murder and church-burning during the Civil War appears
to have been committed by outsiders for, perhaps, the same reason. Cf. G.
Brenan, *The Spanish Labyrinth*, footnote on p. 189.

[2] The two contrary forms of behaviour contain a common factor: distrust.
Whether he is entertained or treated off-handedly, in either case he is obliged
to keep his moral distance. The fact that he does not belong to the community
gives him a particular standing.

ment of hostility towards those of other pueblos and the
reality of co-operation appear to exist comfortably side by
side. How is this compromise effected?

The hostility towards an enemy depends upon his remaining
in the enemy camp, and one who leaves his native town to
settle in another escapes most of the distrust which is attached
to it by those among whom he goes to live. At the same time,
there is a tendency, among those who regard themselves as
educated persons, to consider such sentiments old-fashioned
and brutish. Nevertheless, the prejudice persists for many
people in Alcalá, and though it may be hidden in the daily
give-and-take of living, it is always liable to be brought out.
When I was moving into a farm-house in the valley where
the tenants were people from Jacinas who had come to
Alcalá fourteen years earlier, I was warned by several
persons on no account to trust them, on the grounds of their
origin. One man, in particular, an intelligent craftsman,
added great feeling to his warning, saying: "My father was
a man of the world and of great wisdom, and he used to tell
me, 'Never trust a man from Jacinas, for not one has yet
been born who was not a twister!'"

In fact, however, most of those who gave their warnings
against the family in question had additional grounds for
distrusting them: present jealousy or a past quarrel. For
every person possesses a number of different guises under
which he may conduct social relations, and which one he
appears in is largely determined by the present circumstances. He is not only an outsider, he is also a member of
many other categories of age, status or occupation. Consequently the suspicious origin of a person is recalled only
when the context warrants it, when, that is to say, he has
given offence or some past offence of his is remembered.
Then his antecedents are brought up as an explanation:
"What do you expect from him, he is from Jacinas?"
Until that moment the fact of his birth-place was overlooked.
The personal tension becomes transfused into a structural
one.

The sociologist may detect here a principle with which he
is familiar in other contexts, whereby the tensions of the
internal structure are projected outside the group where they

serve, as an exterior threat, to strengthen the group's
solidarity.[1] It is always the people of the next-door town who
are the cause of the trouble, who come stealing the crops,
whose wives are unfaithful, who swear more foully, are more
often drunk, more addicted to vice and who do one down in
business. In all things they serve as a scapegoat or as a
warning.

Yet this very principle implies a degree of proximity and
co-operation. If we are to blame the people of the next
village, then they must have some share in our enterprises.
If their shortcomings are to provide a compensation for our
own, we must be concerned in their affairs. It has been
suggested earlier that the hostility between pueblos is
weaker today than formerly. It is now possible to put forward a reason for this. The pueblos of the sierra are no
longer as closely co-operative. The focus of their social
relations has shifted.

To sum up, then, the pueblo is a highly centralised community, both structurally and also emotionally. In Spanish
political jurisprudence it is the "natural" unit of society
compared with which the state is an artificial structure.[2]
In many aspects it resembles other rural communities of the
Mediterranean. All are composed of agricultural workers
living under urban conditions, with a background of dry-
farming and olive cultivation. All possess a strong sense of
local patriotism; devotion to the *patria chica* in Spain; in
Italy *campanilismo*, attachment to the local *campanile*, the
highest building in the village. A conception of community
based upon locality runs through the cultural idiom of
Southern Europe, which is demonstrated in many ways:
for example, in their legal codes the preference for the
principle of *jus soli*, in contrast to the Germanic *jus sanguinis*;
in the institution of local patron saints, in everyday conversation the importance attached to their place of birth.

In fact, the Greek word *polis* far more nearly translates
"pueblo" than any English word, for the community is not

[1] Witchcraft and sorcery in primitive societies may often be interpreted in
this light.
[2] Article 1 of the *Ley de Regimen Local* puts the point succinctly: "El Estado
Español se halla integrado por las Entidates naturales que constituyen los
Municipios, agrupados territorialmente en Provincias."

merely a geographical or political unit, but the unit of society in every context. The pueblo furnishes a completeness of human relations which makes it the prime concept of all social thought. That is why Argolla uses the word "pueblo" in a way which recalls Sophocles. During the Reconquest pueblos were founded, with special municipal charters, for the express purpose of defence against the Moors. And in the archives of later pueblos the vestiges of a concept of purpose may be detected. Upon the foundation of the town hall of La Carolina in 1835, the municipality solemnly pledged the pueblo to defend, among other more temporal things, the "misterio de la Purisima Concepción".

This moral unity of the pueblo is achieved through a lively and highly articulate public opinion. People live very close to one another under conditions which make privacy difficult. Every event is regarded as common property and is commented upon endlessly. Where good manners demand frankness it is perhaps natural to find that individuals are well skilled in intrigue. Here the subtlety of intrigue is only matched by the wealth of imagination expended in unravelling it. People's observation is sharp, and they are quick to satirise each other behind their backs. The least eccentricity is rewarded by a nickname which will be used universally throughout the town.[1] Yet a man's nickname is particular to the pueblo. If he moves to another place it will find its own nickname for him. Another pueblo will see him in a different light.

The public opinion of the pueblo is not only exclusive to other pueblos. It possesses a unity derived from physical and moral proximity, common knowledge and the acceptance of common values. That is to say, the sanction of public criticism is exercised, not, as in the open society, by a number of separate groups which largely ignore one another, but by a single group, the pueblo. It is this which gives to public opinion its strength, its sense of the completeness of human relations. It is this which, as in a primitive tribe, makes custom king.

Looking, now, at the pattern of relations between pueblos, what surprises one is not the tension which exists between

[1] See Chapter VI.

them, but the lack of techniques for co-operation. No
organised institution appears in this role which overlays the
frontiers of the *términos*. No principle of exogamy, no county
cricket league, no Kula system, provides a framework within
which the relations between pueblos can be organised—
other than that of the political structure of the state and the
social ties of the wealthy. Kinship has some small significance
in this connection, but that honorary kinship provided by the
compadrazgo (co-godparenthood) has not, as in Mexico,
evolved in order to fulfil such a function.[1] One institution
only, friendship, reinforces the economic co-operation
between pueblos, and that exists upon an individual basis,
unencumbered—one might say, undefended—by ritual of
any sort. The instability of this institution and the reasons
for it are dealt with in Chapter V.

In fact, the exterior relations of the pueblo are conducted
by different classes of people in different ways. The influential,
professional and wealthy people link it to the structure of the
state through political and social contacts. These together
are designated in future as "the ruling group". They form
a group since they possess a solidarity which is essential to
the exercise of their power in the pueblo,[2] and which finds
its institutional expression in the "Movement", the single
political party. They possess common values and common
opinions upon many matters though they are by no means
always in agreement with one another. These are the people
who represent the government to the pueblo, and who
represent the pueblo to the government. From the ambiguity
of this position certain tensions emerge. According to the
situation they may express solidarity in sentiment and
behaviour, either (*a*) with their pueblo against the rival

---

[1] I am indebted for this observation to Mr. George M. Foster, whose book
Empire's Children contains an account of the *compadrazgo* in Mexico.

[2] The words "group" and "class" appear to be much misused. A class is a
number of objects which may be classified through the possession of a common
characteristic. Group, on the other hand, implies a proximity which in sociology one might interpret as solidarity, as for example in the expression "to act
as a group". Yet modern practice allows "a traitor to his class" and "the
£500–£750 per annum income-group". In fact, the terms are used indis-
criminately much of the time, and the assumption that social solidarity is
purely an economic matter passes between them unquestioned. This assumption
may be reasonable in "Middletown", in Alcalá it is not permissible.

3. Gathering Esparto grass

4. The valley below the town

pueblo—"We, the Alcalareños, against those of Jacinas",
as in the power struggle for leadership of the *partido*; or
(*b*) with the ruling groups of other pueblos in the business
of administration and in commerce (this solidarity sometimes
shows a hostile attitude towards their social "inferiors",
sharpened by memories of the Civil War—"We, the enlightened and responsible people, against the uncultured
masses"); or (*c*) alternatively with either or both of these
against the central government or its provincial representatives, as when the whole pueblo co-operates in order to
deceive the visiting inspector, and word is sent in order to
give warning of his approach—"We, the responsible people,
defending the pueblo against the predatory bureaucracy."

Linking pueblos in a different way, though sometimes in
co-operation with members of the ruling group, are people
such as millers, farmers, owners of flocks, dealers, artisans.
These people carry on trade within the restricted area of the
neighbouring towns. They show no solidarity as a group,
since there is no situation in which they are juxtaposed to
any other group. They are, rather, the richer element of a
number of occupational classes, from the remainder of
which they are distinguished neither by manners, speech,
dress nor education. They are part of the pueblo in the full
sense of the word. These people move about in order to
extend their relations beyond the boundaries of their towns,
gaining through such an extension both economic advantages and prestige. In contrast to them, there are those who
go away to seek a living because they cannot get one in their
own home: journeymen to work in the harvest in the plain
on the one hand, and on the other, beggars, doers of odd
jobs, hawkers of anything from lengths of cheap cloth to
religious medallions, some of them widows of the Civil War;
gypsies who offer to clip a horse or find a buyer for a donkey,
the hangers-on at fairs; shoeshines, ice-cream vendors, prosti-
tutes—people who, for one reason or another, have gone
into vagabondage.

CHAPTER III

Occupation and Wealth

(i) Agriculture

In the first two chapters Alcalá was defined in relation to the larger scale structures of province and state, and in relation to other similar communities of its neighbourhood. It is now time to turn to the internal structure of the pueblo.

It is common for authors of sociological studies to employ the concept of "social class" in order to classify the members of a society, and this method seems adequate in dealing with the modern Anglo-Saxon world. In reality, there is considerable variation in the meanings which different authors have attached to this term.[1] But quite apart from the dangers arising from this fact, to accept any of the ready-made theories of social structure implicit in the different definitions would run contrary to the method of analysis of social anthropology. For analysis must always be preceded by description. The questions, therefore, which must be asked are not: "What are the social classes in this society?" and "How are they differentiated?", but: "What social distinctions are recognised in this society?", "In what situations are they evident?" and "What is their significance?" Only by framing the problem in this way is it possible to avoid assuming beforehand that which one seeks to discover, and though in practice certain analytical distinctions must be made in the course of description, it is nevertheless wise to begin by describing those aspects of the society which are most evident, and which can be most unequivocally interpreted, before venturing to use so ill-defined a category as social class.

Social distinctions are discussed in the course of the fol-

[1] Cf. in particular: T. H. Marshall, *Citizenship and Social Class* (Cambridge, 1950).

lowing chapters under various headings, and the first which
I propose to treat is occupation.

The majority of male occupations are connected directly
with the land. The *término* of Alcalá measures a total of some
twelve thousand hectares. Slightly more than half of these
are classified as forest, though this includes both the acorn-
bearing holm-oaks on the high ground (about a quarter of
the total), the pine forests on the mountain and the fine
glades of cork-trees whose naked trunks glow like red velvet
after the *descorche*. It also includes areas of bushes and scrub.
The arable land, a tenth of the total area, is of poor quality
for the most part—of second and third quality according to
the official rating—and it is hard and costly to cultivate on
account of the slope and the frequent boulders and outcrops
of rock. No modern machinery is used in the agriculture of
Alcalá nor would it be feasible to use any save in a few
chosen places. There is no doubt that but for the high prices
of grain on the black market during the post-war years
(1939–50), much less land would be tilled than is the case.
Much of the hillsides are terraced and formerly grew vines,
and the wine of Alcalá is held in good repute; but the phylloxera destroyed the industry, and most of the vine-growing
land was replanted with olives or reverted to pasture. The
soil is suitable for the cultivation of the olive, and many
groves have been planted within the last fifty years. There
are 175 hectares of olives, that is, 13 per cent of the arable
land. Crops are grown beneath the olives in order to take
advantage of the ploughing which the ground must have.

Pasture accounts for 16 per cent of the total area and
another 19 per cent is classed as barren land though there
are few rocks where the hardy goat cannot find a mouthful.
There is a hillside of one hundred hectares covered by esparto
grass, and some more is to be found among the pastures.

The irrigated land covers less than fifty hectares in all,
but its value under the meridional sun is out of all proportion
to its area. Up to three crops a years can be taken off it by
a skilful farmer, and it is here that the most profitable
produce is grown: the fruit crop, walnuts, vegetables,
maize.

The land is divided into properties of all sizes. Altogether there are over eleven hundred properties, though of these two-thirds are of less than two hectares in area. There are a hundred properties of ten hectares or over. Expressed in a different way, two-thirds of the total area of the *término* are owned in twenty-five properties of over one hundred hectares. There are four properties of over 500 hectares, while at the other end of the scale 400 hectares are owned in a total of 800 properties.

There are, it must be pointed out, farmers who own more than one property, and, as will be seen, there are areas where the land-holdings have tended to agglomerate in recent times. Yet there are still today 114 farmers of agricultural lands of more than two hectares.

The smallest properties are agricultural land. Those of medium size are either agricultural or of open pasture or of olives. The large properties are all forest and pasture. There are also lands which are the property of the state. There are the passage-ways for flocks (*cañadas*) which vary in width up to one hundred metres. The grazing there is public. There is a hillside near the pueblo which is common land. The Town Hall owns a property of 800 hectares of pasture and forest which is administered today by the Ministry of Agriculture, though its grazing rights are leased for three-yearly periods by the Town Hall. There were once common lands of far greater extent, but they were put on the market by the state a century ago. In this regard the Spanish Liberals of the nineteenth century achieved the same ends, though in the pursuit of a different ideology, as the magnates of the English eighteenth century.

The produce of these lands is as various as the methods of exploiting them. The livestock raised consists of pigs, goats, sheep and cattle, the latter a hardy half-brave breed, giving no milk and good only for veal in the market-towns or for bull-baiting in the local pueblos.[1] All the people who have to do with livestock, from the owner of a ranch of fighting-

---

[1] The term "bull-baiting" is used in order to distinguish the various bull-festivals of the pueblos from the formal *corridas de toros* in the bull-rings of Ronda, Malaga, etc., for which the true fighting-bull, *toro bravo*, is bred.

bulls in the plain down to the humblest shepherd, are called *ganaderos*.

The large properties of grazing land are administered directly by the owner or by his steward. The owners have flocks, but they also frequently let off pasture for short periods of a month or a few months. They employ *ganaderos* and guards for a salary. Those who stay up in the sierra with their flocks are usually employed on the basis of *cabañería*, a system whereby a reduced salary is augmented by monthly supplies of victuals.

Apart from the large landowners there are also flock-owners who own up to several hundred head but who have no property, or not enough at any rate to suffice for their flocks. Their flocks tend to move more than those of the large landowners and, apart from the general transhumance, their movements are adapted to the condition of the pastures. The irregularity of the rainfall causes this to vary considerably from year to year. These flock-owners are men who work with their own hands, but they also employ a number of men. Several of them have amassed sufficient wealth to buy properties of several hundred hectares. It is one of these who rents the property of the Town Hall.

There are also smaller flocks of sheep, pigs and goats owned by independent *ganaderos*, or by small farmers whose children look after them. They do not employ a man regularly, though they may do so from time to time for shearing or castrating. Every farm and also a number of households in the pueblo keep two or three animals, which supply household needs and graze upon the owner's plot of land or on the neighbouring *cañada*.

The animal from which most money is to be made is the pig. The beasts which are to be fattened for killing are castrated and sent up to the acorn-forests in the autumn when the acorns begin to fall. They stay there for three or four months and are killed during the cold winter weather. There are no flies then, and the risk of the meat going bad is small. These forests are populated not only with the animals of the landowner. Additional animals are accepted both from the herds of the *ganaderos* and also from the individual households, for it is every family's ambition to fatten a pig or two,

since the hams and highly spiced sausages are the traditional
delicacies of Andalusian fare. The method of payment is to
weigh the pig when it goes on to the property and weigh
it again when it comes away, and pay according to the
weight it has gained. While on the farm it is the responsibility of the landowner's *ganadero*, but if it dies it is the owner's
loss. The landowner, equally, gets paid nothing for having
kept it, so that an outbreak of disease upon his pastures may
rob him at the last moment of his year's gross profit. Pigs
are also fattened upon maize in the farms in the valley,
though this is not a general practice. There is less risk of
disease, but it is more expensive. The animals kept for stock
and the young animals cost little to keep: they are fed on
household slops, grazed on the grass on the edge of the roads,
on the passage-ways, or on the properties, and thrown a
handful of maize or peas in the evening. Apart from the
acorn harvest there is rough grazing in the forests during the
rest of the year. Goats and the young pigs are kept there, but
when the pigs come into the woods to be fattened all other
animals must go.

There are other forms of co-operation in the raising of
stock. To have an animal "by halves" (*llevar a medias*
or *llevar a renta*) is one. Goats may be lent by their owner
to a *ganadero* for a specified time. In return, the *ganadero*
takes the milk and also the kids, allowing the owner
one kid per four goats per annum, regardless of their pro-
ductivity. The owner, therefore, gets a small return on his
stock, but he pays nothing; and it is a gilt-edged security,
for the *ganadero* must bear all the risk. If one of the owner's
beasts dies then the *ganadero* must replace it. And the kids
which the owner receives are the best, for he may choose
them himself. They remain with the herd until the end of the
contractual period. A similar custom exists for the exploitation of sheep.

An arrangement based upon the same conceptions is
common in the raising of pigs. The pregnant sow is given to
another party to feed and care for until the piglets are
weaned. In return for this service he receives half the litter.

A valuable product of the forest is its wood. This is made
into charcoal. The owner of the forest may employ a char-

coal-burner to work on his account. But a form of exploitation by halves is commoner. The representative of the forestry commission gives permission for the trees to be felled. These are then marked, and the charcoal-burner moves in. When his work is done he meets the owner's representative and together they weigh it, dividing it into equal shares. It is stacked on the edge of the property nearest a road or track, and then mule- and donkey-drivers come and buy it to take to the big towns.

The cork is cut from the trees every nine years. A dealer or the owner of the factory in Benalurín comes and buys it on the tree. He then brings his men who cut it, weigh it—in the presence of the owner's representative—and cart it away.

Other produce of the non-agricultural land which provide employment in various ways are the timber of the pine-trees, the esparto grass, and the partridges and rabbits.

The agricultural land of Andalusia has largely been held in *latifundia*, ever since Roman times.[1] The complex of dry-farming, with its uncertain yearly returns and fluctuating demand for manpower, may be seen throughout the history of the Mediterranean to have tended to encourage the agglomeration of property, and also of habitations, into large units. The vast expanse cultivated by short-term, town-dwelling labour for a single master is common not only to Betica, la Mancha and Castile, but to much of Italy as well. This type of land-holding is typical only of the plains,[2] and it is rarely found today among the mountains. The soil of the sierra tends to be poorer than that of the plain and is more laborious to cultivate and more subject to erosion. In any case its unevenness makes it unsuitable for large-scale exploitation. There are large properties in the *campiña* of Guadalmesí but they are almost all exploited by tenants in small-holdings or *parcelas*, under the direction of a foreman who represents the owner, as well as himself cultivating a

---

[1] See Julio Gonzalez, *Repartimiento de Sevilla* (Madrid, 1951), pp. 396–436. Also, E. Lévi-Provençal, *L'Espagne musulmane au Xème siècle* (Paris, 1932), p. 161.

[2] P. Carrión, *Los latifundios en España* (Madrid, 1932), quoted by Brenan, *op. cit.*, states that 68 per cent of the land of the province of Cádiz is owned in properties of over 250 hectares.

parcela. Casual labourers unite with the small-holders for the performance of certain tasks in the harvest, when labour forces of over a hundred men take the field on one property after another.

Upon the smaller arable farms of Alcalá these methods of exploitation are not known There are three main areas of agricultural land within the *término*, the chief of which lies in the valley below the town. As has been seen, the farms vary greatly in size. On the lower land, farther from the town, the holdings reach up to forty hectares. The richest farmers own several of these and exploit them directly themselves. Others are owned by people of Alcalá, sometimes people who reside elsewhere, and are let to tenant farmers; more commonly these days, they are owned by the farmers themselves. High prices since the Civil War (particularly on the black market) and a law protecting the rights of tenants —giving them security of tenure and the right of first refusal in the case of sale—have enabled many to buy their farms.

The higher land nearer the pueblo is poorer. Much of it is terraced where the vines once grew. Much has been planted with olives. The holdings here tend to be smaller. There are, however, olive-groves of up to twenty-five hectares.

Another type of agricultural property is the *huerta* or small irrigated farm.[1] There are about twenty of these in the valley. The average size is from one to three hectares, though such farms often include an adjoining patch of non-irrigated land. The area irrigated is determined by the amount of water which is available to irrigate them. Certain springs are the property of the farmer upon whose land they rise, and he can irrigate as much as the water-supply permits. Some patches of irrigation are no more than half an acre where a meagre trickle starts from the ground. But the main water-supply derives from three strong sources on the hillsides at the head of the valley. The water of these is not privately owned, but rights to its use are attached by tradition to certain lands. The water belongs to the millers for

---

[1] The term *huerta* is also used for an irrigated area as in the name "la Huerta de Benamahoma". In the case of a very small irrigated farm or the patches of irrigated land which surround each mill, the term *huerto* is used.

their industry, except for Tuesdays and Saturdays in between
St. John's Day (24th June) and St. Michael's (29th Sept.) or
such other days as the mayor, at the request of the *hortelanos*,
or cultivators of irrigated land, may proclaim. These days of
irrigation are divided up into periods of a few hours during
which each *huerta* receives its water. These periods were
formerly determined by the movement of the sun. When it
was light enough to distinguish which side up a coin lay in
the hand the right of the irrigators commenced. When the
sun's first rays struck a certain farm-house the right to the
water changed hands. When the shadow reached the navel
of the Infant Jesus which stands in the niche in the front of
another house the water must change its course once more.
For the most part these signs were shadows upon the rocks on
the far side of the valley. These rights have, today, become
converted by common consent into the hours of the clock,
but whenever a dispute arises concerning the rule, the old
farmers refer to the traditional *señas del agua*, the signs made
by the sun. The rights are supposed to devolve from the
regulations of the Confederación Hidraulica, which has
jurisdiction over them, but in fact during the period with
which we are concerned, the titles to water-rights were few,
out of date and of doubtful validity. Nobody had bothered
to regularise their water-rights for many years, and in the
meantime both the course of the water and the accepted
practice in using it had changed. It is not, therefore, surprising that the great majority of disputes which arose in the
valley concerned water-rights.

The *huertas* are all farmed either by tenant or owner with
the exception of the largest in the valley, which was exploited
by an employee until 1950 and after that by a system of
share-cropping which will be discussed later. As in the case
of the other small farms, the *huerta* is a family concern. The
farmers live with their families upon the land. Nevertheless,
this does not preclude them from employing a man for a
few weeks at a time when extra help is needed. Equally, at
other times there are hands to spare, and a member of the
family may well go out to work for a few days for a daily
wage. They are at different times both employer and
employed.

Finally, there are a great number of plots of land owned by
people whose main source of income is the work of their
hands—some eight hundred of under two hectares whose
average size is half an hectare. Most of these lie within three
kilometres of the town. The land is usually of poor quality
and there is an area, called *los terrajos*, composed almost
entirely of such holdings and dedicated mainly to the cultivation of the vine. These were distributed from common lands
when the commons were put on the market in the last
century. There has been a tendency for these small-holdings
to fall in recent years into the hands of wealthier people.
The two vintners have been buying them up. Nevertheless,
most poor families still own a plot somewhere or other.

There are 440 labourers and the majority of these men are
employed by the day. Others are employed for a fixed period
at a slightly lower salary, and others yet again are employed
permanently at a further discount (*fijos*). The mean figure of
employment is 350, but this does not take into account the
periods of rain in the winter when work is laid off altogether,
and no one is employed other than the *fijos*, nor does it
include those who go away to work for the harvest in the
plain. Employment by the day is a common feature of
Mediterranean dry-farming, and the general practice in
Andalusia used to be, and still is in many places, to collect
in the central square at daybreak in order to contract for the
day's work. This system is used in Guadalmesí, for example,
but not in Alcalá where the arrangement is made privately,
usually the night before.

Another system of employment is by piece-work. This
system is used for weeding sometimes,[1] and is general in the
harvesting of olives which is paid according to the quantity
gathered. The olive harvest of 1951 was so abundant that
there was a shortage of labour to collect it. Very favourable
terms were offered to induce people to come. One small
farmer even offered to go halves with anyone who would

---

[1] In which instance it is contrary to syndical regulations. Piece-work was
bitterly opposed by the Anarchist movement in Andalusia, which regarded it
as abusive. It is not generally resented today in Alcalá, for it is practised only
in the case of an individual arrangement between employer and employee.
This is called *un ajuste*.

come and pick for him, though the normal reward is one-ninth or one-tenth of the quantity picked.

A variety of other forms of co-operation in agriculture exist which are reminiscent of those already mentioned in connection with pasturing. Plots of land on the large farms of the lower valley, small plots in the *huertas* or in the *terrajos*, are exploited in partnership by two men, whose motives are often social as much as economic. These are called *aparcerías*. The various requirements of the enterprise, land (irrigated or dry), seed, manure, and the various tasks which the cultivation demands, are shared between the two, and the crop is divided at the end. In theory it is the co-operation of two men, each of whom has something to offer, but who lacks either the time or material to venture on the undertaking alone. The man who needs grain to sow seeks a partner rather than pay for it and risk its loss if the year turns out badly; the man who needs labour because he is himself engaged in other work (or expects to be) makes an *aparcería* rather than pay the money of a daily wage. So that the system has the aspect of an insurance policy. The risk is divided between the two participants, and the shared interest induces a keener co-operation than that which wages can elicit. It is nevertheless frequently difficult to see why a man has accepted to exploit his land in this way other than in order to render neighbourly service, repay a favour or cement a friendship. He may well be partner in an *aparcería* upon his own land, and at the same time upon the land of another. Moreover, he may also subdivide his share in the enterprise, bringing in an additional partner.

Another variant of the *aparcería* is the partnership between the landowner and the landless labourer, the former putting up all the capital and equipment and the latter doing all the work. The landowner lends the seed to the enterprise and recovers it before the crop is halved. Yet another form applies to the clearing of woodland and its conversion into arable. *Aparcerías* may be made for a few months for a potato crop, or for the full three-yearly cycle of the land. The essence of this type of arrangement is the freely made contract, and as such its form is always liable to fluctuate. A certain stiffening in the demands of landlords has been noticeable since the war on account of the greatly increased demand for land and the high prices of agricultural produce. In fact, any arrangement, *un convenio*, may be made provided both parties agree. Thus, for example, the large *huerta* already mentioned is cultivated under an arrangement whereby plots of land are given over to different farmers of the valley in return for a fixed quantity of the crop sown, while the ground beneath the olives, which produces only a poor crop, is sometimes given over for nothing for the sake of the ploughing it will receive. If it is a good year the farmer makes a present to the owner of the land of a measure of grain, a gesture evoked by the social code and not by any legal obligation.

It can be seen that money is made from the land in the following ways:

(1) Through ownership only. Rent is paid yearly on St. Michael's Day. The landlord has no responsibilities other than the paying of taxes. Formerly, when tenants were not protected in their tenure and rents were uncontrolled, the landlords were prepared to put money into the land and deal with major repairs, now they tend not to. The traditional forms of contract [1] were clearly designed in order to protect the interest of the landlord and free him from responsibilities. They were normally made for three years (or multiples of three). The rented farms are all agricultural land with the exception of the property of the Town Hall, which is exceptional in every way. All tenancies date from before the introduction of the law which gives the tenants security of tenure, for no one will put a tenant in now that he cannot be evicted save by paying heavy compensation. Today there are more owner-farmers than tenants.

(2) Through ownership and exploitation through an employee, an *encargado*. This is the system on which the large pastoral properties are run. The part played by the owner in the direction of the land varies a great deal. There is the absentee landlord who seldom visits his land; the landlord who lives elsewhere but comes frequently and takes an active part in its management; the resident land-

---

[1] See Zoilo Espejo, *Costumbres de derecho y economía rural* (Madrid, 1900).

lord who leaves to the *encargado* no more than the duty of
seeing that his orders are carried out. The degree of
responsibility with which the *encargado* is entrusted varies.
"Overseer" would be a good translation in many cases.
He works with his own hands and is not differentiated
from the mass of farmers and farm-labourers by any
cultural standard. Few small properties are run in this
way, and in Alcalá it is generally considered unsatisfactory
as a method of exploitation, save on the large pastoral
properties which require very little administration, or
when the owner is a practical farmer who directs the
enterprise himself.

(3) Through ownership and exploitation by the owner's
own hands, together with such additional labour as he
may require. This is the commonest form of exploitation
of agricultural property.

(4) Through ownership combined in partnership in an
aparcería. This has already been discussed.

(5) Through the exploitation of rented property.

(6) Through the work of a man's hands in return for a
daily wage, contracted for the day or a short period, or as
a permanent employee. The wage varies according to the
nature of the work.

(7) Through a man offering his labour and such other
assets as he may possess in partnership.

(8) Through independent action; hunting game either
with gun or more usually by snaring or trapping; picking,
preparing and sometimes working esparto grass, picking
wild asparagus, making *picón*, a kind of charcoal made
from small wood by a simple and rapid process, or working a lime-kiln. These are methods used by those who can
find no work or who prefer their independence. They are
mainly outside the letter of the law since, in the majority
of cases, they involve either poaching (though shooting-
rights are not generally enforced by the owners of property) or pilfering.

The variety of forms of co-operation and also the continual fluctuations in the price-levels, both of produce and
labour, which have already been mentioned, can be seen to
relate, in the first place, to the insecurity which attaches as
much to the role of exploiter as to that of employee (or

formerly to the insecurity of tenure itself). All arrangements
are short-term ones, for no one can have confidence in the
future. Every harvest is a gamble, and the history of Andalusia is one of alternating plenty and famine. Under such
conditions one would hardly expect to find a steadily
balanced system of exploitation such as is usual in countries
of reliable climate and adequate rainfall.

What is more, this instability is visible not only in the
system of exploitation but in the distribution of landed
property itself. In the evolution of land-ownership two
tendencies are simultaneously apparent in the valley:
agglomeration and dispersion. The first owes its existence, in
this instance, to the recent enrichment of the larger farmers.
They have put their profits into land, and where possible
have enlarged their holdings by the acquisition of neighbouring ground, or they have bought other farms. In this manner
a number of the larger properties have been built up out of
smaller holdings in the last fifteen years. The tendency
towards dispersion is caused by the fission of property which
the law of inheritance imposes. The intricacies of this law
need not be examined here. Its general effect—and in this
it is in harmony with the values of family life—is to divide all
inheritance equally among the children of both sexes.
Families tend to be large, and while in some instances the
heirs sell their share to one of their number, in others the
inheritance itself is divided up. In this way a number of
small-holdings have sprung up in the lower valley, where
young men have built themselves a house upon their share
of a larger property and settled down to farm it. A change
in the controls and marketing values or a few bad harvests
might well reverse this situation, for these small-holdings are
uneconomical to exploit. In fact, both tendencies are
inherent in the land-tenure of Andalusia, which might be
described as either stagnant or dynamic from one period to
another, but never as stable.

In *résumé*, this instability finds its most obvious correla-
tions in the uncertainties which surround the exploitation of
land, and in the hazards of the law of inheritance, but
alongside these must be counted the lack of a mystical
attitude towards the land, the value system of a people who

dwell in towns from which they go out to cultivate the earth, but who do not love it.[1]

[1] This characteristic of the agriculture of Alcalá, like many others, is typical of much of the Mediterranean, though it contrasts with the north-west of the Iberian peninsula. Cf. "Amour et labeur ont également manqué à la terre syrienne; le fellah la cultive sans doute, mais comme à regret, et sans que son exploitation sache voir au delà des nécessités immédiates; il travaille pour lui et non pour sa terre; il ne sent pas que celle-ci le dépasse et le prolonge." J. Weulersse, *Paysans de Syrie et du proche-Orient* (Paris, 1946), p. 173.

Cf. also: "Land may in one society be a mere good offered for sale with no more ceremony or ado than the exchanging of one denomination of money for another. In another society, the land may be the common property of a group, may represent spiritual values so closely bound up with the integrity and sanctity of group mores that it cannot be transferred." F. Tönnies, *Fundamental Concepts of Sociology*, trans. Charles P. Loomis (New York, 1940), p. xxiii.

Here land is an impersonal good, and this fact can be related to the values attached in this society to Time and the Past. The people of Andalusia mind more about the present than the past, and this is most visible in their mortuary customs. Cf. J. Pitt-Rivers, ed., *Mediterranean Countrymen: Essays in the Social Anthropology of the Mediterranean* (The Hague, 1963), Introduction.

CHAPTER IV

Occupation and Wealth
(ii) Industry and Trade

IF THE possession of land bestows no social virtue and its cultivation, so far from being a sacred duty or a labour of love, is simply a hard and unrewarding way of making a living, it follows that the distinction between persons according to whether they are engaged in agriculture or not carries no more than a purely practical significance. Occupation is a matter of choice, not of calling, and the nature of a person is not thought to be influenced by his occupation in the same way as it is, for example, by the place of his birth. It is true that the distinction between labourers and herdsmen is the subject of certain generalisations and the basis of not a few jokes. People who work the land sometimes jeer at the uncouthness and lack of ambition of the goatherds who are prepared to spend weeks at a time away in the mountains; while the latter are proud of the independence which their life gives them. Yet in no situation do the two elements confront one another and in no sense are they opposed. Indeed, a great number of people have at one time or another followed both the goat and the plough. In the same way we shall see that occupational distinctions, such as that between the millers and the *hortelanos*, even when they lead to opposition of material interests, are never extended beyond the occupation itself, never become the basis of a cleavage in the community. Neither millers nor *hortelanos* are thought even by the rival faction to be in any way different from the rest of the society. Some irrigate and some mill and both want the water, but there the matter ends.

This conception is the antithesis of the notion of caste, a notion which will also find its place in this study when the gypsies come to be dealt with, but which is not found within the structure of the pueblo. Here, indeed, we touch upon one of the essential values of the pueblo which is the equality, in the sense of the identity of nature, of all those who are born in the same place. Whatever they may do—and precisely because of the lack of such distinctions their versatility is very great—they remain by nature the same. The dichotomy between the agricultural and the urban classes which has dominated English history down to the present day is one which cannot be made. Here everyone, conceptually at any rate, is a town-dweller. How he gets his living is another matter.

An important number of the dwellers in the valley are occupied in exploiting the source of power provided by its waters. These were once, before the advent of mechanical energy, at a greater premium than they are today. The cloth industry owed its existence in Alcalá to the mountain pastures which produced the wool and to the streams which powered its numerous fulling-mills. The technical advances of modern industry, and Alcalá's lack of communications, had already all but ruined its prosperity when the electrically powered cloth-factory was built there in 1938. In recent years, the lack of electrical current almost brought that enterprise to a standstill, so that its owners started another venture, reverting to the traditional technique and rehabilitating one of the old water-worked factories in the valley. Until 1951 the factory in the pueblo worked on an average only two or three hours in the day, and it is still threatened with power-cuts. It employs eight men and six women of various ages. The factory in the valley will employ perhaps half as many when it is working.

The milling industry has encountered fewer difficulties. There are fourteen grain mills in the valley. A few ruined edifices litter the banks of the central stream, and those in the confluent valley whose water-supply enabled them to work in the winter months only, have disappeared altogether. Several of the mills working today were converted from old fulling-mills, though in their total number there are only two more than there were two hundred years ago (according to the census taken in 1752 by the Intendant-General of the Kingdom

of Granada, the Marqués de Campo Verde). The activity
of these mills is continuous and profitable, particularly since
the war. There is an electrical mill in the town which is
restricted by power-cuts to the same hours as the factory. It
is the only mill authorised by the present economic controls.
Nevertheless, even with its restrictions it manages to mill
all the flour required by the rationing system, and a bit more
on the side which is more lucrative to the miller, but gets
him into trouble periodically with the inspectors.

Being officially closed the water-mills are all entirely
devoted to the black market, but grain from the *campiña* of
Guadalmesí keeps them fully occupied. The techniques of
milling have altered little since the Marqués de Campo
Verde's day. All the mills now employ stones imported from
France, or failing that Barcelona, which are harder than the
local granite, but only one has so far equipped itself with a
ball-bearing for its central pivot, a local and imperfect
invention which broke down after a few months. The remainder continue with the traditional brass post-and-socket
bearing. The volume of the mill-stream is not great, and no
mill has more than one stone. Output depends upon the
speed at which the stone can be driven, which again
depends upon the amount of water. During the summer
months the springs diminish and water is also required for
irrigation.

The mill is a family unit and can be worked by a single
adult male aided by wife and children, but the work really
requires at least two grown men. Several millers keep one
permanent employee. One mill is rented and one is exploited
on a system of halves. The remainder are the property of the
millers. The millers are therefore independent men whose
livelihood is made outside the economic structure which
the state recognises, though the illicit nature of their work
is never—and, indeed, in such a society as this, never could
be—a cause for moral reproach. Nevertheless, they are not
lacking in the traditional qualities of their calling. The
millers of Alcalá know all about mixing a little plaster in with
the flour, dampening it in order to increase its weight, and so
on, and their reputation for craftiness rests upon these practices and has nothing to do with their relations with the

official hierarchy. Like the farmers of the valley, they also
have profited by the high prices.

In addition to the flour-mills there are two olive-mills. One
is worked by electricity (though a petrol engine has been
used in recent years to supplement its meagre source). The
other makes its own electrical power from a small dynamo
turned by a mill-wheel. Since olives are milled during the
winter months the miller is not hampered by shortage of
water as much as are the millers of grain during the summer
and autumn. Both these mills are larger and much more
lucrative concerns than the flour-mills and they employ
several men during the milling season.

Since both the owners are persons of influence and will be
referred to later, it is convenient to introduce them at this
point:

The owner of "la Pileta", the mill worked by electricity,
is Don Antonio. He is the son of a former landowner in
Alcalá who was also the chemist of the place. He himself has
studied for the career of lawyer. His father was shot by
the "Reds" together with his brother. Don Antonio has
properties in Jacinas and Seville apart from the olive-lands
and *huerta* of the Pileta, and he himself lives the greater part
of the year in Seville where his children are being educated.
His two spinster sisters live in the family's house in the
pueblo and go down to the Pileta in the autumn for the olive
harvest. The family reunites there for Christmas. The sisters
play a leading part in Church affairs in the pueblo. While
they are in residence in the valley the priest comes from time
to time to say mass in the chapel which is part of the building.
An employee goes round the farms to give notice and those
who wish (and also those who wish for the favour of the
Pileta) attend. The sisters supervise the milling and keep
the count of the loads of olives which are brought in, but the
family is not popular. The majority take their olives to be
milled, at a more favourable price and more promptly, it is
said, in "el Juncal".

This is the name of the other olive-mill which was set up
fourteen years ago in an old fulling-mill. The owner is
"Fernandito Piñas", the son of a tenant farmer of Alcalá. A
bachelor of fifty-five, he is the youngest of four brothers, but

it is he who "has the voice which sings". A story is told that the origin of his fortune was a treasure which a bandit hid upon his father's farm. He was not rich before the war but was a leading personality among the farmers so that he was made Mayor of Alcalá after the flight of the "Reds". He did not remain mayor for long but has since been one of the two chiefs of the farmers' syndicate. He has made much money and bought much land, so that he is now the largest farmer and landowner in the valley. He lives in the Juncal in a modest manner, works hard and follows the way of life he was born to. He does, however, sometimes use the local taxi. He goes frequently to the pueblo and wields great influence in local affairs. He is a man of impressive appearance and old-fashioned manners, courteous but without social pretensions, shrewd and tough in business but charitable and a good employer, on which account he is popular. His heirs are two sisters' sons.

The relationship of these two men to the community of the valley could not be more diverse. To begin with Don Antonio is seldom there. His sisters are in charge of the olive-mill most of the time. This limits the part played by the Pileta in local affairs. It is also limited by the fact that since it is powered by electricity they do not require the water of the valley. Their *huerta* possesses its own spring. It is sometimes suggested that his title to the water is false and that it is really the water of the community. There does not appear to be any justification for this suggestion. The Pileta derives its influence in the valley through property, through its power to employ and to provide an alternative to Fernando Piñas' mill, and through its relationship with the church organisations and the "Movement", the officially sponsored political organisation.

Fernando Piñas is far closer to the community. He belongs to it as a person. He lives there. He also employs more men than the Pileta, and more people take their olives to him. He also has great importance on account of the fact that he has the right to use his water for milling. In the ill-defined condition of water-rights it is not difficult for the *hortelanos* (garden cultivators) to take advantage of the millers, since the latter, on account of the illicit nature of their occupation, cannot go to law. A traditional right exists to irrigate with the *romanientes*, (properly *remanentes*), the water which seeps down the main channel after it has been cut off above. The millers use this to irrigate plots around their mills, but, in recent times, other farmers owning land on the banks of the channel have begun to use this water in order to irrigate land which has no claim to it. *Hortelanos* have tended to extend their hours of irrigation at the expense of the millers. In this situation a key position is held by those who use the waters of the valley for power in a licit manner, the owner of the cloth-factory in the upper valley, and, lower down, Fernando Piñas on the waters of the Juncal. They are able to go to law and can defend their rights, and they therefore become champions of the rights of the millers. When four years ago a meeting was called to discuss a project of employing a water-guard between the millers and *hortelanos*, it met at the cloth-factory. Agreement broke down over the question of the division of the expenses involved. Since then quarrels over water-rights have occurred every summer.

Modern trends have treated the craftsmen of the pueblo less well than the millers and have contributed in ways which have already been mentioned to the general economic decline of the area of the sierra. The destruction of the archives of Alcalá by the Anarchists makes an exact comparison impossible, but it is not rash to surmise that the percentage of craftsmen in the total population is considerably lower than it was, say, one hundred years ago, even without considering those of the wool industry. In the days when cloth-making was at its height, it provided work in various crafts. The fulling-mills, the water-worked looms with their various processes, the washing of the wool, the spinning, the weaving, combined into single buildings as time went on (though the spinning of wool by hand and also hand-weaving as home industries did not disappear until the nineteen-thirties), the dyeing and all the dealing in a trade which was traditional throughout Europe at that time for the wealth which it brought made Alcalá an exceptionally wealthy place for its size. Antonio Ponz[1] noted at the end of the eighteenth

[1] *Op. cit.*

century that in Alcalá mendicancy was unknown thanks to the wool industry. But this is not the only craft to have declined. Soap is no longer made in the pueblo for sale, though many households make their year's supply at the time of the olive-milling. The soap offered for sale in the shops is brought from Ronda, whereas in 1846, according to Madoz,[1] there were two factories in Alcalá. The sugar shortage of present times has virtually ended the manufacture of chocolate. The copper foundry in Peñaloja has closed down and sold out. The blacksmiths of Alcalá no longer make the agricultural tools nor perform more than elementary repairs. Serious repairs are sent to the workshops of Ronda which have oxy-acetylene welding plants. The decline of population has produced a glut of building materials so that the tile-kiln of the area has gone out of business. Now modern building is beginning to employ bricks where none were used before, and reinforced concrete makes its appearance among the plastered granite. These modern materials are imported into the pueblo, which was hitherto able to satisfy all its requirements from its own resources, its tiles and timber and its sand and stone. The plaster-burner still deals with the locality's requirements, and there is a kiln in the valley and another up on the hillside. Lime-kilns are numerous and are exploited by craftsmen either working independently or as employees of the owner of the land where the kiln stands. This, however, is not a whole-time occupation for anyone. The chair industry in Peñaloja, powered partly by water and partly by electricity, continues to work. In Alcalá one carpenter uses electrical power. One in the valley is buying piece by piece the machinery necessary to use water-power.

The craftsmen are independently minded people, though they are by no means so independent in fact as the millers. The builders are employed by the day, and in wet weather they must usually stop work. The carpenters are employed either by the job, by the day or for a longer period. The blacksmiths work by the job in their shop.

The only industry which seems not to have suffered in modern times is the shoe-maker's. Alcalá has a long tradition in this art and men come from other pueblos to get their boots

1 P. Madoz, *Diccionario Geografico-estadistico-historico de España* (Madrid, 1846).

there, the heavy rough hide boots which wear better than the products of the shops of Ronda. Yet the curing of hides is no longer done in Alcalá except sporadically and inexpertly.

As early as 1862 Mateos Gago, a politician of eminence and a son of Alcalá, directed a report to the government pleading that the railway, which was being projected to connect the area of the sierra, should take the path of the valley of the Guadalete from the plain of Jerez to Ronda, giving among his reasons the necessity of bringing transport facilities within range of his native pueblo if its wool industry was to be maintained in prosperity. His plea failed, and the railway was built to Ronda from Algeciras. The gloomy prophecy of this far-sighted man was in due course fulfilled.

The first motor-road reached Alcalá in 1917 from the main Jerez–Ronda road. By 1935 the town was also connected to Jacinas, and another road to El Jaral over the mountains was under construction, though it was not finished until after the war. A local road down the valley to the main road was completed in 1930. Since the war a road was built over the pass to link up Peñaloja with Alcalá. It is not easy country in which to make roads. The sudden and heavy rainfalls on such steep slopes undermine all but the most soundly built and had by 1930 carried away segments of both mountain roads cutting off Peñaloja from its parent. It can now only be reached by car by a roundabout route nearly fifty kilometres in length. Continual work is required if the roads are not to be lost during the bad weather. The roads are a state responsibility administered from the provincial capital, and only within the confines of the towns are they a local charge —which explains, perhaps, why Andalusian roads tend to disintegrate at the entrance to a pueblo. The state-employed staff are mostly men from the area but not necessarily from the pueblo, and a foreman responsible for the *término* lives in Alcalá. The building or improvement of roads is put in the hands of contractors, but extra labour is also employed in the winter by arrangement between the foreman and the mayor, partly for the sake of the roads and partly as a measure to deal with the unemployment.

On weekdays a bus runs from Jacinas to Ronda and

returns in the evening. There is one taxi in the town and no
lorry. The scarcity of transport is general throughout the
country, and the roads are in a much worse state than they
were in the days of General Primo de Rivera. Before the war
Alcalá had three taxis and a lorry. Now lorries come only
occasionally, bringing goods, or collecting the charcoal which
is stacked by the roadside near the large properties.

For the daily needs of the community the form of transport
is the pack animal: horse, mule or donkey. Carts were once
used, though only to transport machinery and such things as
could be moved in no other way. Now there are none. A
system of tracks connects the pueblos of the sierra which
were, before the building of the roads, a state responsibility,
though there were also tracks which were the responsibility
of the Town Hall. Nowadays both have fallen into disrepair,
and where they were cobbled there are now only scattered
stones. A number of mule-and donkey-teams were owned by
members of the community which carried the products
of the sierra far afield. Alcalá, for example, even supplied
Cádiz and Seville with ice, packed snow conserved in pits on
the top of the mountain and carried down on mule-back
during the summer. Today there is only one donkey-team
left, which travels between Alcalá and Jerez. Donkey-
and mule-teams also come from Ronda to collect charcoal
from the properties. Individuals who own a donkey and have
no other work sometimes make up a team and go to Ronda
with a similar load. The high price and high maintenance
cost probably account for the fact that there are not more
teams in the pueblo. The farmers and millers own their own
beasts.

Alcalá receives mail on six days a week provided the bus
does not break down, and the newspapers come from Cádiz
only a day late. A single telephone post is open during the
day-time.

The high cost of transport, whether by motor vehicle or
beast of burden, has an important effect upon the structure of
the pueblo's economy through the inequality of price-levels
which exists from place to place and from time to time.
Buying and selling is an activity which can be very profitable,
and the ambitious small capitalist turns to speculation. There

is no clearly defined limit to the class of people devoted to trade. No social barrier separates those who trade from those who do not, and, except for the largest landowners who have neither the incentive nor the possibility since they do not live continuously in the pueblo, most of those who consider themselves sharp enough indulge in some form of exchange from time to time. Trade, in fact, is a general activity in which some specialise more than others.

To begin, however, with the pueblo's shops: as in all small communities the degree of specialisation is small. The shops are no different architecturally to other houses. There are no show windows. Everybody knows what is sold in which house. The shopkeeper is nevertheless distinguished from the private person who happens to have something to sell by the fact that he pays a municipal tax, the *matricula*, for the right to trade.

The prices in the shops of Alcalá are, on an average, 10 per cent higher than in the shops in Ronda. Not only are there the costs of transport. Manufactured goods are frequently bought from dealers in Ronda or Jerez so that they have in addition to their cost price the percentage which the latter regards as his due. Wines and spirits pay a municipal charge on entering the pueblo. Those who have enough to buy to make it worth their while go to Ronda on the bus to make their purchases, and those who go there for any other reason take advantage of the opportunity. As in many other contexts things are cheaper for the rich. In addition, the bus-conductor makes his position a profitable one by doing people's shopping for them in return for a tip. He himself decides what his tip shall be.

The shopkeepers also act as dealers, buying local produce (e.g. oil, grain, products of the pig), in bulk when the prices are low and selling it later at a much higher price when the scarcity has set in; for the yearly fluctuations are very great, and those who can afford to, buy their supplies for the year in bulk when the price is lowest. This, as much as anything, has enabled the shopkeepers to become as rich as they are. Those who have done well have bought farms.

But there are others who have started a shop in order to supplement other sources of income. The chemist is a professional man holding a state appointment, but he makes more of his income from his shop than from his salary. The former chemist was, in addition, a largish landowner. Other small landowners of a social standing equivalent to that of the professional classes have shops. In El Jaral the Justice of the Peace is a large landowner, brother of the doctor and member of the most distinguished family of the town, yet his wife keeps a shop.

In addition to the general store-keepers there are those who have a small shop or keep a stall in the market; the bakers, who in three out of four cases are the close relatives of millers; the two vintners, who make wine, sell it and also trade in an odd article or two; the barbers and the keepers of bars. While on a smaller scale still, yet also aiding in the distributive system, are persons mainly widows with children, or women who for other reasons find themselves obliged to seek a living, who buy the farmers' produce in bulk when they arrive in the town with it and then resell it, either officially in the market, paying the small charge (5 reales) or privately in their houses. Then there are women poorer still who go round the farms buying or begging produce which they sell in the pueblo. The Civil War has left many such people, widows of men who died on the wrong side and who consequently have no pension, who have a few children or an aged parent to keep. They circulate over all Andalusia, specialising, though not uniquely, in black-market items and contraband from Gibraltar, carrying things in baskets beneath their black shawls from places where they cost less to places where they can be sold for more, "buscando la vida" ("seeking a living"). Their poverty is, in a way, the strength of their position: for if they are caught they cannot pay a fine, all that can be done to them is to confiscate their goods. There are others who gain their living in a more legal but not dissimilar way; the men and women who buy eggs for the shops; and the agents for the shops of the big towns who buy game as soon as the season opens.[1]

There are a number of brokers in the town, ten altogether.

---

[1] This causes the price to rise sharply. Game is caught and sold before the season opens, but the *remitencia* is too conspicuous an organisation to be permitted to function then. It must await the official date.

They buy and sell, contract for one thing and another, but their chief function is to act as agents to arrange sales. They deal in anything from a farm to a goat. Since theirs is a recognised profession they are liable to pay the *matricula*. The Town Hall of Alcalá, unlike that of wealthier Jacinas, has not insisted upon this, and in fact none of them pay. These are the picturesque figures, with their long, forked walking-stick and wide hat, who are seen at all the fairs of Andalusia. Those of Alcalá do not all live up to the traditional image, yet they have the same reputation for good humour and sharp practice as all the world over. There will be more to say about them in the discussion of the technique of bargaining.

The distribution of wealth, as has been seen, is far from equal in this society. Both in terms of spending-power and also of the means of acquiring spending-power there is much variation. The large landowners receive considerable rents in Alcalá without spending more than a few months there in the year, while poor labourers scrape along working seven days a week when there is work in order to feed a large family, dreading the long weeks of rain when no wages are paid and bread must be begged from the baker on credit. They are tough people and they raise healthy children on meagre incomes, but they are proud and perhaps the humiliation of their circumstances pains them more than their material wants. It is a curious fact that the rich towns of the plain with their beggars and their dirty children give the casual observer an impression of far greater misery than the pueblos of the sierra whose economic situation is worse. Yet the economic structure of a society is one thing and the social meaning of the rights which it engenders is another. We are concerned to know, therefore, not only who possesses or acquires or spends (and how and where) but what social values attach to possession, acquisition or disbursement.

There is no doubt that the ideal behaviour is very much opposed to close-fistedness, but lavishness in one direction usually imposes restrictions in another. Here people like to make gestures of generosity towards the friend, the acquaintance and the stranger, and they like to make a show of their generosity. We shall see that generosity is more

than a matter of the individual disposition but a require-
ment of the system of friendship. The accusation of meanness
is very damaging to a person's reputation, for such prestige
as derives from money derives not from its possession but
from generosity with it. Wealth in itself is not, as in much
of European society, an intrinsic merit. Conversely, poverty
implies no inferiority in other spheres than the economic,
and only the inability to respond to generosity places a person
in a position of humiliation, for it exposes him to the accusation of being grasping. That is to say, it is only where
economic inferiority is translatable into moral inferiority
that it involves loss of prestige. It is precisely where all men
are conceptually equal that this translation is able to be
made—because no subordination is recognised which might
exonerate one man from returning the favour of another.

These values are clearly illustrated by the behaviour of
beggars, in which two distinct approaches to the problem are
distinguishable. There is, to begin with, what might be
described as the gypsy technique in begging. This consists in
flattering, fawning, inspiring pity and using any conceivable
line of moral blackmail to extract alms. The implication of
meanness is the chief weapon in blackmail, and it is used not
only directly in the form of a reproach but also behind the
person's back. Thus, when Lola, the old gypsy, comes round
the farms begging she takes from her basket all the things
which she has been given elsewhere and shows them off.
". . . This bread was given me by so-and-so. These tomatoes
they gave me at the mill. And here is the orange which
Fulano gave me—a rich man like him and all he can find to
give a poor woman in need is an orange. Shame upon his
stinginess!" This method is used by habitual beggars,
gypsies and persons who have lost their shame. The approach
of the "honourable" beggar is very different.[1] He is a man
who would be ashamed to beg in his own pueblo, but begs
because he is travelling in search of his living and has run out
of money. He asks for food or alms or work, and he asks for it
quietly and proudly, basing his claim to help upon a duty
which is thought to exist everywhere—that he who has must

[1] An excellent portrait of such a beggar is given by Washington Irving, *The
Alhambra* (London, 1832), Introduction.

give to him who has not. Such a beggar tends to be very shy and to stand at a distance waiting to be asked what he wants. He does not sacrifice his pride willingly and he feels troubled by it in such a situation. At times such people cover up their shyness by a brusque and insolent manner as if to deny that they are asking a favour which they cannot repay, and leave giving no thanks, for shame to utter the conventional "May God repay you" of the beggars.[1]

The idea that he who has must give to him who has not is not only a precept of religion, but a moral imperative of the pueblo. It is visible in the manners of the people of Spain who will not eat in the presence of friend or stranger without first offering their food, a gesture in which this sentiment of the community of humankind is kept alive. Inevitably this "egalitarian" sentiment comes into conflict with the freedom to dispose of his property which every individual possesses. The idea of individual ownership is clear and strong,[2] and the total right of an owner to do what he likes with his property is never questioned. On the other hand, there are a very limited number of things he can do with money inside the pueblo, other than buy property to divide among his children. There are no expensive sports, no regular entertaining in the home, no competition in conspicuous waste. All the houses are whitewashed inside and out. Floors are all tiled. Furniture is more plentiful in the houses of the rich, but there is no great difference in quality. All families, even the *señoritos*, eat the *puchero* (vegetable stew). With his money, a man can put his house in order, buy good clothes for himself and his family, good contraband coffee and tobacco, send his children away to be educated for a career, but beyond that point there is virtually no way of spending money other

[1] For an amplified analysis of the Andalusian beggar see my paper "La Loi de l'Hospitalité," *Les Temps Modernes*, No. 253 (June, 1967).

[2] This is well illustrated by the tenacity with which the rural Anarchists hung on to the idea of the *reparto*, the division of the land into individual holdings in the face of the communistic doctrine of the movement. Cf. Diaz del Moral, *op. cit.*, p. 61; "Y, disfrazado o no con sus falsos motes, *el reparto* ha seguido siendo en todas las exaltaciones campesinas la mágica palabra que ha electrizado a las muchedumbres. No ya solo en las revueltas de la Internacional y en las de 1882 y 1892, sino en las agitaciones anarquistas de principios del siglo XX y en las sindicalistas de los ultimos años, el estado llano de las sociedades obreras, a despecho de los elementos directores y, a veces con el asentimiento de éstos, ha aspirado siempre a distribuírse la tierra en lotes individuales, es decir, a ingresar en las filas de la burguesía agricultora."

than on charity or on excursions to the big towns in search of *el vicio*. It is felt that rich people who go away to spend money are betraying the pueblo, and the reason often given for the economic decline of Alcalá is the departure of a few rich families to the big towns of the plain. Most ways of spending money other than in satisfying the needs of simple living involve going away from the pueblo and are regarded as wicked.

Los ricos, the rich, are always wicked when treated generically. They are responsible for the hardships of the poor. They have perverted the social order through their ambitions. They are the source of corruption. Who the particular *ricos* are is obscure, but they are generally thought of as being distant personalities far richer than anyone in the pueblo. These opinions, although encouraged by the political creeds of the Left are by no means inspired by them, nor are they necessarily found in company with them. They are, rather, part of the value system of the pueblo.

The moneyed people of the place are thought of by many, in many social contexts, as evil. Their fatness is pointed out as a proof of their over-indulgence and idleness. The shop-keepers in particular come in for adverse comment, and the advantages which wealthier people have, particularly with regard to what they are able to do for their children, are bitterly resented. Yet here, already, the sentiment of moral indignation has made way for personal jealousy. It is felt that such advantages are wrong, and yet few will not admit that they would take them if they had the chance.

The values relating to money may be summed up as follows. They are not those of protestant capitalism.[1] The possession of money here is in no way a sign of grace, or a basis for moral distinctions. It is morally neutral. But the ways in which it is acquired or spent are subject to moral judgement. If it is gained at the expense of others, it is ill-gotten. If it is guarded avariciously, if it is spent in self-indulgence, it is evil. If it is gained by intelligence or hard work, if it is spent in meeting moral obligations, then it is good. Money is something which enables a man to be what he wants. It gives

---

[1] Cf. Max Weber, *The Protestant Ethic and the Spirit of Capitalism*, trans. Talcott Parsons (London, 1930).

him power, power to be either good or evil. It bestows
prestige only if it is employed in a morally approved manner.
This clearly leaves the door open to a certain ambiguity. For
the moment I will go no further into the question than to add
that persons who become involved in the system of patronage
tend to regard this as the proper manner of using wealth.
The successful patron, thanks to his wealth, acquires great
prestige within the orbit of his influence and escapes, thereby,
the condemnation which is reserved for *los ricos*.

Nor are the values relating to money those of nineteenth-
century liberalism. Transactions with money are not operations of an impersonal economic law but a form of personal
relationship in which people establish or express mutual
regard through an exchange of goods. We have already seen
in agriculture co-operative ventures which resemble arrangements to take in one another's washing. Articles are not
thought of as having an intrinsic money value, but are
subject to the relationship of the persons who exchange them.
An item is not "worth such-and-such a price" in itself, but
only in relation to a specific vendor and a specific buyer. The
idea that the vendor is bound to sell at a certain price because it is the price that others are asking is not generally
accepted; on the contrary, it is thought right that a wealthy
person should pay more for things than a poor person—unless
the vendor wishes to honour him. A shopkeeper favours an
influential client by making him a special price. Since he likes
to favour all his clients, no one, in the end, is charged the
price advertised in the window. Money payments for services
are particularly liable to fluctuation in this way in a community where many men are employed singly for a short
period or for a specific task. A service performed for money
remains none the less a service and commits the recipient to
moral obligations even though he may have paid through the
nose.

The subjection of economic values to moral and social
values is illustrated in the technique of bargaining. For while
marketing and purchasing fit into the framework of established social relationships, or serve to establish them, the
negotiations with capital values do not. The vendor of an
animal or a property wants to sell it to the person who will

give him the most for it, and he wants as much as he can possibly get, for it is an event which will not recur. On the other hand, to do this involves him in a violation of the moral code. To admit that one has asked an exorbitant figure or offered an inadequate one is to confess oneself grasping or mean and to lose face. Yet not to get as much as one can is to lose money, and be made a fool of. The essential hostility between the two bargainers is not only itself potentially anti-social, it leads to a commitment of pride which makes it impossible for the two to reach an agreement. Hence, the role of the professional *corredor*, or broker, who steers the bargain to a clinch, saving the face of the bargainers through his intermediary position. He, or there may be two of them each representing his client, acts as a friend, pleading, arguing, flattering, lying, using all his guile to induce the buyer to raise his price, the seller to lower his, enabling each to maintain the fiction that he is not really keen upon the deal, that he enters it only to oblige the other. To drop this fiction means to lose the bargain.

There are also, of course, sales between friends, but these are conducted in private and there is no need for a *corredor*. They fit into the scheme of friendship, as a favour which creates or fulfils an obligation. Men are sometimes heard to complain that they have been obliged by friendship to sell something which they had no wish to part with. Sometimes, moreover, this is quite true.

CHAPTER V

Status and Age

ALREADY in examining the values which attach to money we have raised the question of the significance of possessions in differentiating one man from another. This was discussed in terms of prestige. The question of status was deliberately left on one side, though it may have occurred to the reader that the prestige derived from wealth might nevertheless play an important part in determining status and in defining social class.[1] This question is the subject of the present chapter.

We have discerned in the pueblo a strong reluctance to accord superior status to its members who are economically superior, and in the pages which follow the different bases of differentiation will be examined and some attempt made to detect where they give rise to a superiority of status. We must be on our guard against assuming that status will necessarily be recognised by the same attitudes and sentiments as in our own society. Already in the seventeenth century foreign visitors were astonished by the familiarity with which the grandees were treated by their retainers, and the traveller of today is frequently struck by the distinction which the Andalusians, and indeed all Spaniards, seem to make between the personality and the social position of others, a distinction which gives to their manners a particular warmth and delicacy. Nor is it to be detected only in their behaviour towards

---

[1] I use the word "status" in the sense current in modern sociology, as, for example, Professors MacIver and Page when they write: "Status may be based upon differences of birth, wealth, occupation, political power, race, or, as in the case of traditional China, intellectual attainment. Frequently status is determined by a combination of two or more of these factors." (*Society*, p. 353.)

It is well to bear in mind that status is not necessarily a matter of hierarchy, but simply of differentiated social position. Hence the status of a guest. However, for MacIver and Page, it is the criterion of social class where "a hierarchy of status groups" exists (*Society*, p. 348), and the essence of class-distinction is the "social distance" which this hierarchy imposes between its different levels.

foreigners, whose strangeness and whose special status might
be expected to provoke a form of conduct which is exceptional. It is a distinction which is fundamental to the system
of values of this society and which underlies all social behaviour. It might be expressed in various ways, as a respect
for human personality rather than for human rights, or as
the belief in all men's equality in the sight of God, or in the
ultimate futility of the mortal condition, or, at any rate, as
a lack of faith in man's ability to control his own destiny.
This regard for personality is present in the adult's behaviour
towards the child and in the Justice's behaviour to the criminal and in the criminal's behaviour to his victim. It cannot
be expressed in sociological terms, and yet it is recognisable
in Andalusia in every social context.

It will be apparent that a certain status is accorded to
those who occupy official positions in the pueblo. These
people, the administrators and professional men, are first of
all considered, not in relation to the structure of government,
but as members of the community. The high proportion of
outsiders among them has already been noted. With the
exception of some of the schoolmasters, all the professional
men appointed by the state come from another area, and if
they own any property it is not here, nor do they have a
motive to acquire any here since they aspire to be moved in
due course to a more important post. Recent times appear to
have increased the number of outsiders in this class. The
Mayor of Alcalá (and of certain other towns as well) is today
an outsider, a state of affairs which could never, it is thought,
have occurred a generation ago. The doctor and the chemist
are also outsiders today, while formerly both posts were filled
by sons of Alcalá. The yearly salaries of professional and
administrative people, if they have no other source of income, give them a standard of living far below that of the
large landowners, yet they "keep up appearances" with the
rest of the resident wealthy. Members of the smaller property-
owning families also fill certain administrative posts, such as
director of the Monte de Piedad, of the Property Registry,
etc., while other of their members have been taken away
by their careers to distant parts of the country. They are

distinguished from the richer farmers, in several cases considerably wealthier than they are, by education and by the refinement of manners which accompanies it. They do not keep apart from them socially, however, but may be seen together in the *casino* talking at the same table or playing cards.

Who, exactly, comprises what I have called the ruling group, and in what ways are they differentiated from the rest of the community? Other than landowners and the professional people, there are the owners of the larger business enterprises and also the occupiers of municipal office, legal office or those who have influence in syndical or Church affairs—the people in whose hands effective power resides.

Power, however, means much more than the occupation of a post endowed with authority. It means: "the capacity in any relationship to command the service or the compliance of others"[1]—the control of social sanctions. Thus economic power means the ability to apply economic sanctions, to offer rewards in the form of material advantage, or to refuse them, power to employ or sack, to buy, sell, allow credit, quash a fine or to favour materially in any other way. For this reason the owners of large properties are all to be included in the ruling group, though their importance within it, the use they make of their economic power, depends very much upon the individual personality and the circumstances of their lives. Those who do not live in the town cannot play much part in local politics.

Political power means the ability to enforce sanctions which derive, ultimately, from the laws of the state, that is, through the institutions recognised in those laws. These are various and relate to such matters as municipal government, the organisation of Justice, the constitution of the Civil Guard, the syndicates, and so forth.

Power also derives from medicine. The doctor, the vet and the chemist possess power, since, quite apart from the official documents which may require their signature, they have the monopoly of services which people need. In the same way the priest is an important member of the ruling group. He can appeal to the religious conscience of those who are

[1] MacIver, *The Web of Government* (1947), p. 82.

sensitive to such an appeal. He alone has power to perform the rites of the Church.

The members of the ruling group share certain common standards of conduct, the most important of which is their adherence to the Church. These standards are necessary to the cohesion of the group and are never questioned by its members. For power, while it enables those who possess it to influence the conduct of others, makes them at the same time more sensitive to the sanctions of others. An anti-clerical schoolmaster or doctor would not hold his job down for long. A landowner who aroused the antagonism of the other members of the group, particularly the municipality, would find himself at a disadvantage in a number of situations, which will become evident later. Equally, the landowner who antagonises the pueblo can get no good labour. (There have been instances of this in Alcalá.) But the old man who lives in a cave, begs and eats berries, can say what he likes, provided he does not forfeit the charity of all.

The ruling group owes its integration, then, to its structural situation, not to the possession of overt characteristics. It is significant that no word exists in current usage in Alcalá to designate this group of people generically—precisely because they are not a class but a group. When they are referred to it is by the nebulous title "los que mandan en el pueblo" ("those who command in the pueblo"). There is no uniformity among them either of dress, education, birth, wealth or way of life. This is made plain by a consideration of the ways in which the different elements of the community are differentiated.

First, dress. There is a clear distinction to be made between working-clothes and smart clothes. The aspect of the pueblo on a festive day is quite different from its usual appearance. There are few men, then, who do not dress in "urban" clothes: cloth suit, leather shoes, collar and tie. Those who live in the valley keep their festive clothes in their house in the pueblo. They never wear them in the country, but they wear them in Alcalá for special occasions and for courting, and they would not go shopping to Ronda if they could not wear them, for the Andalusian is extremely sensitive in matters of appearance.

The *sombrero de ala ancha*, or wide-brimmed hat, is an article both of festive and also working-dress. It bears a particular association with *ganado* (livestock) and is always worn with the short jacket and tight trousers of cattle herdsmen. But bullfighters wear it in this way for charity fights out of season. It is worn as working-dress by shepherds whom its brim protects both from sun and rain. In wet weather a mackintosh cover is put on. It is worn by many farmers also, though agricultural labourers tend to wear berets or soft hats instead. The landowner also wears it if he goes into the country, particularly if he goes on horseback. Yet it is worn —without a tie for it must never be worn with a tie—on festive occasions by poor people as part of their smart dress, and it is also worn by the sophisticated at fairs and bullfights. (To wear it at the bullfight is the mark of the enthusiast.) The professional and administrative classes do not wear it, for it implies an association with *ganado* which in them would appear pretentious. It is because of the associations of the *feria* (the festival, fair and cattle-market) with the spirit of merry-making that it is the theatrical dress of flamenco singers and dancers.

Apart from the occupational nature of working-dress which distinguishes the manual workers, distinction of the degree of importance of a man is not easily made. Few of the members of the ruling group wear ties every day; the majority do not shave every morning. Some of them wear berets. In general, the distinction which in summer strikes the eye in matters of dress is not between persons of different social category of the pueblo, so much as that between persons of the pueblo and summer visitors. In dress the professional men vary between the fashions of the summer visitors and those of the leading families of the pueblo.

Nor does the female dress reveal any clearer distinctions. As with the men, those who work are clearly distinguished on working-days. But on festive days the young all struggle to array themselves more splendidly than the rest, and some idea can be gained of the economic position of the family from the quality of their clothes. Hair-styles are hardly significant, unless the tightly waved *permanente* be taken to mark a lack of sophistication. No women ever wear hats. For church all wear the small black lace *velo* in which a certain variation can be detected as to size and quality. Elderly women all dress in black. Just as for fairs men don the wide-brimmed hat of the *ganadero*, so girls put on the spotted and flounced cotton dress of the gypsies. But, today, at the fair of Alcalá almost all the girls who do this are summer visitors— with the exception of a few small children whose adoring parents wish to show them off.

There is certainly no lack of display, and the general standard of dress reached is indeed quite remarkable, considering the material possibilities of the people of Alcalá. The idea of display is formulated in the verb *lucir*, meaning literally, to shine, thence to distinguish oneself or to show something off. There is often a Cinderella who will not go to the fair because she has nothing to show off, and will be put to shame and made pitiful in front of her friends. But the motives for showing off are not those which might be deduced from the "theory of a leisure class".[1] The display is not directed towards the object of differentiating oneself from others considered of inferior social standing, and economic differences do not give rise to differences of style. In the small society where everyone is known personally there is neither advantage nor need for visual differentiation as in the anonymous society of the city. Here display aims at a different target, that of personal aesthetic triumph, the conquest of admiration and the humiliation of one's equals.

The variation of speech and accent from one pueblo to another has been mentioned already in Chapter I. There is no variation in accent between persons of different social position other than such as may be ascribed to education. All the upper classes of Andalusia speak with a strong regional accent. Education means the elimination of a number of "rusticisms",[2] but the word "education" means a great deal more in this community than book-learning, and refinement of manner and speech are things which may be found

---

[1] See T. Veblen, *The Theory of the Leisure Class* (New York, 1922).

[2] Among the wealthy of the large towns are to be found those who affect a vulgar mode of speech in order to stress their affiliation with the country, landed property, bullfarms and old-established riches.

quite independently of schooling. This, however, is a matter which cannot be objectively assessed, nor is illiteracy something which can be measured statistically, though such statistics are to be found in the municipal register and statistics of illiteracy of the country are published. Over and above the completely and self-confessed illiterates are those who read and write with more or less fluency. The total figure, though it represents only those of the adult population of Alcalá who have no pretensions to literacy, is worth examining. Illiterates are found above all in the higher age categories. The percentage among the over-sixties is very high. Looked at from another angle the element which shows the highest figure is that of old-fashioned farmers, for the reason, perhaps, that they were more frequently raised upon farms too distant for them to attend school.[1] Contemptuous reference is often made to the lack of education of the farmers of the lower valley, the richest area of the territory, and of the wealthier flock-owners. Illiteracy is not therefore confined to the economically weakest element of the community, and does not appear to handicap the man who farms a single farm.

These country-dwellers were not entirely denied the possibility of education, for the profession of ambulant teacher, *maestro rural*, is an old-established one in the sierra. Men whose qualifications extend little beyond a cursory knowledge of the three R's visit the distant farms to give the children lessons, and gain thereby a wage barely greater than that of a labourer. Today in Alcalá there are five men who make their living in this way. If there are reasons to suspect that their pains do not always lead to success, the existence of such an institution does, at any rate, testify to the desire and respect which the people of Alcalá have for the accomplishments of the mind.

The consideration to which a career entitles a person is far greater than that which mere wealth can evoke. Within the framework of the egalitarian values of the pueblo it supplies

---

[1] I am by no means convinced that the assumption made here is justified, i.e. that illiterate people are those who were not taught as children to read and write. It is quite possible that some who had acquired these arts at twenty had lost them again through lack of practice by the age of sixty.

a reason for respecting a person in himself and not merely on account of what are regarded as fortuitous circumstances, that is to say, his possessions.

People assert that the courtesy title of *Don* is the privilege of those who hold a university degree, who have a "career". In practice the use is heavily influenced by other criteria, such as age, wealth, appearance and occupation. Thus, very few unmarried men are addressed as *Don*, until they reach full middle-age, the exceptions being a young doctor, and a young lawyer who is the Secretary of Justice. All four schoolmasters are addressed as *Don*, but not the young man of twenty who is schoolmaster in the school in the valley. The priest is *Don*, but his brother who lives with him is not *Don*. By no means all the ruling group are *Don*. Of the two Justices of the Peace, one is rarely, the other never, *Don*. But the corporal of the Civil Guard is sometimes *Don*, a gesture of deference to his authority.

The circumstances in which the title may or may not be used are of great significance. There is all the difference between addressing a person directly and referring to him to a third party. Who this third party is, is also important. Official occasions again demand a distinct mode of speech. In daily life all other categories are heavily influenced by the respect which is felt for a person on account of his character. A reluctance to refer to some of the resident landowners as *Don* behind their backs is noticeable, even though they may be persons of age holding important administrative posts. The largest resident landowner called "el Señorito" is usually called *Don* if referred to by his name, but his son, a young man of twenty-six, never, either directly or indirectly. He is called by his Christian name like any other member of the pueblo.

While the title is freely accorded to those who are considered to merit it (and the professional men are so considered regardless of their popularity), a great deal of resentment is directed against those who like to be called it without the full conformity of the pueblo. The family of a young and able business-man furnishes a case in point. His father is commonly called Don Rodrigo, and the family first came to live in the pueblo eight years ago. On one occasion

a craftsman and his friend, a small farmer, were overheard
discussing him: "He's no more *Don* than I am." "What is his
career I'd like to know?" "He's nothing but a silly old fool
who gives himself airs." "If he is Don Rodrigo then we're all
Don, I am Don Andrés and you are Don Manuel." When
questioned about the son they firmly asserted that he would
never be called *Don*. Some of his employees refer to him as "el
Señorito Pepe", but otherwise no one calls him anything but
Pepe. He is married to a member of one of the leading
families of the pueblo and has considerable social ambition.
It remains to be seen whether the craftsman's assertion will
be disproved. When asked whether Fernando Piñas was
called *Don* when he was Mayor of Alcalá they replied
that some addressed him like that, but only with their
tongue in their cheek to curry favour, for in those days
there were many in need of his favour. Today nobody
calls him *Don*. This, though he is one of the leading
personalities of the ruling group, and one of the largest
landowners.

The reason why such people can never be accorded the
title is because they are felt to be no different from others.
They are part of the pueblo. This is the point at which the
identity of the two distinct meanings of the word is demonstrated. As has already been stated, the pueblo is at the same
time the members of the community and also the people in
the sense of *plebs*. If a person is raised to the status of a career
he no longer belongs entirely to Alcalá but to the wider
community of the educated.[1] People no longer feel equal with
such a person. He is no longer judged by the same standards.
He is different. The title of *Don* is used, we may say, to
express recognition of this difference. But this difference has
nothing to do with blood, it is a question of a degree of refinement acquired through up-bringing and education, which
involves him in a different world and makes him a different
kind of person.

The title is also used in all official contexts, in legal documents and on envelopes or on the town hall notice-board,
for any adult person. The state denies its competence to

---

[1] Cf. Blasco Ibañez, "La Bodega" (Valencia, 1905); the Anarchist preach-
er is addressed as "Don Fernando" by the workers.

determine who is or is not to be called *Don* by calling everyone so. Or, expressed from the point of view of the pueblo,
when a person enters into relations with the world of "official-
dom" he becomes a temporary member of the community
of the educated.

A word of prime importance to the question of social
distinction is *Señor*. Like the title *Don*, it is a term which
denotes respect or "social distance". In general, it is used as
a term of address to a stranger, or by children to adults, or
when receiving an order, or pompously for emphasis: "Si,
Señor!" ("Yes, Sir!"). It is also used to address and to refer
to God. Its original meaning is *seigneur*. In everyday use it
indicates a person unknown or unnamed, or, as a specifically
descriptive term, a person-worthy-of-respect. Within the
pueblo it is used as a title for elderly persons-worthy-of-
respect. It is prefixed to the Christian name in the same
manner as *Don*. Whereas the title *Don* is given to a person of
full social maturity, but differentiated from the pueblo by
status, the title *Señor* is given to members of the pueblo whose
maturity is past, and who have retired from active work.
There is no strict property qualification, but it is accorded
more freely to the successful old farmers than to people who
live in the pueblo. One must be a "fine old boy" to be given
it. Indigence, drunkenness or any serious moral shortcoming
disqualify one completely. The feminine form *Señora* appears
to be bestowed a little more freely. In such contexts it is
used by persons of superior social status with a nuance of
condescension.

The diminutive of this word has different connotations.
There is, to begin with, *Señorita* meaning "Miss", but *señorita*
is at the same time the feminine of *señorito* and as such it may
be used to refer to a young married woman. *Señorito* is used as
a term of affectionate respect with reference to or in addressing the young adult of superior status. Servants use it.
Employees sometimes use it. Gypsy beggars use it to any
person dressed in urban dress, for the attribution of youth
flatters. Using it carries an implication of subservience. It
can mean the most important person in a place, the boss,
provided he has the necessary status. As such it comes to be

the nickname of "el Señorito", the largest resident landowner, the son of a former cacique.

It is a term which easily becomes sarcastic, so that it may
mean not only a "person worthy of respect" but also a
person with social pretensions. Used to denote a social
category it means the well-to-do without necessarily implying
any respect. "The *señoritos* of this place", I was once told in
a town of another province, "are a rotten lot. They are
always putting their servant-girls in the family way, and
won't pay a decent wage to anybody." In this sense, as the
propertied people, it was used as a political weapon by
the Left, which coined the word *señoritismo*, the oppression of
the have-nots by the haves. The communist underground
propaganda discourses insistently on this theme.

In the widest sense it means a person who is not obliged
to work for his living, who wears a collar and tie all the time
and keeps his shoes clean. But it has not for that reason lost
its use as a term of respect. Maria la Castaña, the widow of
a small tenant farmer, can tell a real *señorito* when she sees
one from one of those fellows who are just trying to look like
one—"and there's a lot of them about these days!"—you
can tell by the way they behave to people, she maintains. Do
they have to be born *señoritos* in order to be real *señoritos*?
She is not sure, but they have to be brought up as real *señoritos*
otherwise no amount of money can make them what they
are not.

How the behaviour of real *señoritos* varies from that of
those who do not deserve the appellation is not easily said.
The criteria are necessarily subjective, but an inclusive view
approximates to the following:

(1) The *señorito* has education and manners. He is not
"rough".

(2) He is generous with money, even care-free. Meanness is the hall-mark of the *nouveau-riche*, it is thought, and
this view is expressed in the saying:

> "Ni pidas a el que pidió
> Ni sirvas a el que sirvió."

> "Neither beg of him who begged
> Nor serve him who once served."

(3) He looks after his dependents and uses his influence to protect them. He willingly accepts to be patron to them.

(4) He does not tolerate humiliation nor accept to be put under specified obligations to people who are not also *señoritos*. He knows how to be friendly, *simpatico*, and to talk with people on an equal footing, yet without relinquishing his status. He will drink and joke with his social inferiors but he will always insist upon paying. He uses the second person singular towards his dependents "with whom he has confidence" and provided they are of his generation or younger, but he does not allow them to use anything but the third person to him.

(5) His family does not observe all the customs of the pueblo (e.g. in the naming and upbringing of children).

It can be seen that ideally the distinction between the *señoritos* and the pueblo is very clear. In practice, of course, it is not in the least so. There are many marginal cases on which judgements vary. The *señorito* who is thought not to be a real *señorito* is nevertheless treated as such on the surface. Even "el Señorito" comes in sometimes for a piece of adverse comment behind his back and is compared unfavourably with the summer visitors. It is hard to find the personification of an ideal in someone who is always there.

Brenan has observed that the anti-clericalism of the Anarchists was in part inspired by the feeling that the Church had betrayed the ideals of Christianity.[1] Analogously, anti-*señorito* talk often rings with a nostalgia for the betrayed ideal of aristocracy.

How far do these facts assist in answering the questions put forward on page 34?

The distinction between pueblo (*plebs*) and the *señoritos* has been made. Otherwise the pueblo has been treated as a culturally homogeneous whole. Is such treatment justified? To begin with, it has been shown that there is no "hierarchy of status groups". There is a differentiation of status relating to upbringing and education and this is, by and large, what is called a distinction of social class, but this is not clearly defined nor does it correspond to similar differentiations in

[1] *Op. cit.*, p. 191.

political power or wealth. There are certain cultural variations whereby *la gente fina* (fine folk) are differentiated from the pueblo, but these relate to territorial horizon as well as to standard of education. The pueblo recognises that the indigenous *senoritos* are less *finos* than the fine folk of the big towns. In their cultural standards the intermediate position of the *señoritos* of Alcalá, devolving from their dual association with the pueblo and with the upper class of the province, is manifest. Within the pueblo they tend to conform to the cultural standards of the pueblo, which are limited in material matters such as housing and food and which in matters of dress, or recreations, offer them no incentive to differentiate themselves. When they go away, on the other hand, they tend to conform to the standards of those whom they regard as their equals.

When the word pueblo is used it means all those who belong to the pueblo except where it is used in juxtaposition to the *señoritos*. When there is an assembly all the pueblo including the *señoritos* are there by right. There are no recreational societies, no associations [1] which have membership, no formalised groups. The cafés and bars tend to have their clientele but they are by no means exclusive, and if a customer is habitual it is because of convenience of location, taste for the company or for the particular wine sold there. During the festivals the mayor and his friends make a point of holding their reunions in a different establishment each time in order that the profits of the occasion shall not go all into one pocket. The need to form exclusive groups is not felt, and indeed such a segmentation would run contrary to their feeling of what the pueblo is. Co-membership of the pueblo provides an adequate basis for social relations with any other member. Other than that accorded to the "authorities" there is no precedence, overt or tacit, of the nature of status. In the processions the children go first, followed by the women, rich and poor intermingled without distinction. The authorities follow the priest, though without any determined

---

[1] There were political parties before the Civil War, but they cannot be said within the pueblo to have corresponded to status groups. An exception is the *casino*, whose relationship to the ruling group differentiates it from the pueblo (*plebs*). The religious societies are in no sense corporate groups. They never meet.

order. The men follow. There are no fixed places in church. Where the pueblo divides up, it divides along the lines of sex and age-differentiation only.

There is one exception to this. Upon a certain day in the year the pueblo differentiates itself—geographically—into the upper half of the town and the lower half. This day is the Monday of Our Lady of Carmen which is celebrated by a bull-festival.[1] A bull is let out into the streets with a long rope tied to its horns, and the young men of the pueblo run in front of it showing off their bravery. A group of youths clings to the far end of the rope, making it fast to the iron bars of the windows, so that when the bull turns and charges them they can escape by fleeing into the house or by climbing clear of his horns. A traditional rivalry exists in this connection between the young men of the two halves of the town, which is demonstrated in the endeavours of each faction to take the bull to its quarter and keep it there as long as possible. The two factions are called "Jopones" and "Jopiches", the augmentative and the diminutive of the word *jopo*, a tail or penis. The Jopones are those of the upper town and pride themselves on being tougher than the Jopiches, perhaps because of the greater number of shepherds among them who are supposed to be rougher than the rest, perhaps because the majority of the *senoritos* live in the lower town. The distinction does not correspond to any clear division. For though there is an implication that it was once based upon the rivalry between the rich quarter and the poor quarter—and in the centre of the poor quarter was the *Asamblea*, the traditional meeting-place of the workers—rivalry itself implies a relationship of equality, and an account of the festival written at the end of the last century indicates that difference in wealth between the two quarters was not significant. The antagonism between the two quarters once extended into everyday life, and the struggle for possession of the bull may be supposed to have grown up during the period when feeling was most violent. The terms are still used today to describe a person of one quarter or the other, but, save among the

---

[1] "Un toro a la cuerda." Such festivals took place until recently in a number of other Spanish pueblos. Louis Dumont, *La Tarasque* (Paris, 1951), p. 195, describes a similar festival in Tarascon, France.

children, the rivalry is gone. The pueblo is much smaller than it was formerly, and the antagonism never possessed anything like the seriousness of inter-pueblo feeling.

Geographical proximity, neighbourhood, is the principle according to which fission takes place because it is the principle on which integration is based. There is no "corporate consciousness" attaching today to any unit smaller than the pueblo. Many facts are related to this truth. Here one only will be mentioned. Apart from the economic instability which is endemic, the inheritance law makes it impossible for the family's standard of wealth to be maintained with any regularity by the children. The economic unit breaks up on the death of the father if there are more than a few children, so that the family cannot be said to possess much permanency as a property-owning institution. (The *señoritos*, in that standards of class are here involved, face the greatest difficulty with regards this problem. Their families arc noticcably smaller than the farmers'.) A certain amount of marriage takes place between farmers' families with the motive of maintaining property, but they show little sign of developing a corporate consciousness. They feel superior, but only on account of their wealth—personally superior to those who are less wealthy, but the comment of one person on another is never related to class, because the conception of superiority derived from membership of a class does not exist in the pueblo.

At the same time there are possibilities that children of the pueblo will acquire superior status. The two daughters of one not very large farmer go to school at a convent in Ronda where the children of *señoritos* go. They are his only children. The son of one very small farmer is being educated for the priesthood. Attempts were made to find a patron for the clever young boy of a miller so that he could have further education. There is an intelligent young man who owns a herd of goats with his brother but hopes to make a career for himself in the secret police. A change of status, as opposed to making money, whatever the means, involves leaving the pueblo and seeking a place in the wider society of Spain. Many have succeeded in this as the pages of Spanish history will testify, but many fail. And among the failures must be counted those,

not to be found in pueblos such as Alcalá, whose fidelity to
their ambitions is maintained even after its economic foundations have collapsed. The gentleman, too proud for manual
work and too poor to eat, dates from at least as far back as
the poor squire of Lazarillo de Tormes.

This description has been written so far from the point of
view of the pueblo (*plebs*). Seen from that of the *señoritos* of
the pueblo it is a different picture. It has been shown that on
one side they are part of the pueblo and on the other they are
not. The world to which this second side belongs is far more
attractive to them, and that is why many have gone to live
in the big towns where social life has more to offer a person
who has money to spend. Where the forces of the pueblo do
not operate, attitudes of "competitive class feeling" emerge.
Display begins to take on the function of social differentiation. The summer visitors are mostly aware of their superior
social status or of a status which they themselves feel to be
superior to the leading families of Alcalá. They are richer,
they live in more important places, they take a holiday for
the summer. "There are only", one of them said, "three
families of this pueblo whom you could call 'society'."

At this level a word makes its appearance whose meaning
is not understood by the majority of the pueblo—*cursi*—it
means socially pretentious, affecting a refinement (and thereby claiming a social status) which one cannot justify. This
word is the weapon with which the upper-class families of
Spain have, during the last century, defended themselves
against the claim to equal status of those whom they regarded as their inferiors. The social setting where this word
appears exhibits resemblances to the "open-class structures"
described by modern American sociologists; appearance
kept up at great cost in order to qualify for a social status
which can barely be afforded. Pío Baroja, in *Las noches del
buen retiro*, describes a Madrid family who shut up their house
in the summer in order that people should think they had
gone on holiday. Yet even though resemblances exist it

---

1 This "social mobility" is expressed in an Andalusian saying:

"el, tendero	"He a shop-keeper
el hijo caballero	His son a gentleman
el nieto pordiosero."	His grandson a beggar."

would be a mistake to assume that the systems are identical and that the feelings and motives of the middle classes of Andalusia are the same as those of any other part of the world. We are not concerned here to fit the data provided by Alcalá into the definitions derived from the study of other societies, but rather to formulate our own principles of social structure which shall have validity here, and these can only be discovered by considering matters such as status within the totality of human relations. Without an examination of the reciprocal interaction of the members of the different status levels and how they combine within the same society, the nature of the system necessarily remains obscure, and so far only the outward characteristics of status and social class have been discussed.[1] In order to define the relationship of pueblo to *señoritos* in structural terms, it will be necessary first to examine the categories of sex and age which cross-cut the distinctions of status, and then to describe the political structure of the community.

The title *Don* is not given to young men, I have said, and the title *Señor* is given only to the elderly. Middle-class society tends to use the title *Don* towards its elderly and respectable members in the same way as the pueblo uses *Señor*, but the two forms of address are not otherwise similar. Yet both are expressions of respect. Respect, however, is shown in a diversity of situations and must first of all, if all the uses of these titles are to be explained, be distinguished as "respect for undefined standing" and "respect for superior standing". Undefined standing demands respect since it is potentially superior standing. Hence the official use of *Don*. The unknown person is called *Señor* and is referred to as "Señor So-and-so" because his standing is not recognised

---

[1] Cf. T. H. Marshall, *op. cit.*, examines the current definitions of social class and concludes (p. 106) : "I prefer to stress the institutional character of classes and to think in terms of a force rather than of groups."

It is perhaps a mistake, in any case, to attempt to formulate a definition of social class which shall have validity in any society, since only in relation to the total social system does a social class come to possess its particular characteristics. Put more precisely, the institutions of a society are functions of the total social structure. A biology which sought to furnish a definition of the foreleg which would be equally valid for the horse and for the lobster is obviously absurd. In sociology such methodological errors are less apparent.

by both speaker and listener. The title might be said to
express the "social distance" dependent on the status of
stranger. Since each is stranger to the other the title is used
reciprocally. "Formal language" is everywhere respectful because it aims at maintaining, or establishing, this kind of
social distance. One can see, then, that social distance in-
dicated by the form of address *Señor* may be related to:

(*a*) Non-membership of the category formed by acquaintanceship, by means of which status is recognised.
(*b*) Superior social status, as to employer or *señorito*.
(*c*) Superior standing in the hierarchy of age, the child-
adult relationship or the adult-elder relationship.

It is a commonplace of social anthropology that full adult
standing is only attained with marriage and parenthood.
Here, the married and unmarried are not separated formally
on any occasion. Certain activities are thought to be proper
to unmarried people, but it is common to discover a married
person among the group, or vice versa. "Standing derived
from age" is not formalised, and, though marriage certainly
affects a person's standing, the variation of age at which
people marry and the existence of bachelors of advanced age
make any such formalisation impossible.[1]

The standing of full adult of the pueblo is not superior to
anyone but the children and youths. Full membership of
the pueblo entitles to nothing more than equality. Therefore,
the idiom of manners is generally very informal. Persons of
both sexes use the second person singular to one another, and
the respectful third person is reserved only for the parents and
persons of greater age.

Respect for the parents is strong, and children always
address their parents in the third person, save among the
modern-minded *señoritos*. Boys do not smoke or drink in the
presence of their fathers. The respect for the elderly derives
partly from their similarity with the parents, but also from
the respect which the younger person paid to the elder when
he was still a child. If they work together, which necessarily

[1] Boys do, in fact, sometimes marry before going to do their military service
though this is not well regarded. Among the *señoritos* they must wait until they
have finished their "career", i.e. the studies for it, before they think of marriage.

entails a relationship of equality, then the respect paid to the elder tends to disappear. But by the time a man has reached full adulthood (around the age of thirty) the parents and their contemporaries are verging on retirement. Retirement in this community of, traditionally, poor tenant farmers and day-labourers means becoming an economic drag on the family and an idler who no longer fits directly into the network of reciprocal services, but also a person who is privileged not to work. It means on the one hand a fall in practical importance, and on the other, the attainment of the state of fulfilment for which his life has been lived. These old men and women who have successfully reached elderhood and have retained the respect of the pueblo, become the guardians of tradition and the old-fashioned ways, and are called "Señor Juan" or "Señ' André". Their loss of material importance is compensated by a gain in moral importance. They incarnate the goal which everyone would reach.

Status differences are defined, then, by various criteria and are appreciated in different ways by different people in different situations. Many factors enter into the establishment of the degree of prestige necessary in order to be called *Don*, but what is particularly significant for our understanding of the nature of status in this society is the importance in relation to it of age. This cross-cutting of the status category by the age category reveals that social status differentiates a person from the pueblo, not from birth, not even when he reaches manhood, but when he reaches the age to play an effective part in the affairs of the pueblo. The difference between the quality of respect derived from status in Alcalá and in the conservative peasantry of northern Europe, in western France for example or in western England, is already clear to anyone acquainted with the latter. I suggest that the quality of respect attached to status deriving from a monocratic social structure, such as the feudal system, differs from that of Alcalá on account of the uniqueness of the patrician in the locality. The lord of the manor is a symbol of the whole community, the *señorito* is not. He is not a being differentiated by nature and by his unique relationship to the community, but only by accomplishments and circumstances.

CHAPTER VI

The Sexes

(i) Courting: the values of the Male

THE CATEGORIES discussed so far have not taken into consideration the dichotomy of the sexes. The analysis of this facet of the social structure comprises in the first place the institutions and behaviour in which they are differentiated, and in the second the institutions and behaviour in which they are united.

As soon as they can talk children become conscious of the sex to which they belong. Their membership of one category or the other is continually stressed in speech. Their behaviour is applauded or condemned by reference to rules expressed in generalisations upon the correct conduct for little boys or little girls. "Little girls don't do that", "What a pretty little boy!" etc. The identification of the individual child with one sex or the other is reinforced at every point by adults who see the child not only as he is but also as the man or woman he will become. Children are encouraged from an early age to imitate adults of the same sex. The small girl follows the mother or elder sister about the house with a small broom in her hand while she is still too young to be of any effective assistance. At four years old, the little boy may already be seen pasturing a piglet which he controls by means of a string attached to its hind leg. By the time he is nine he goes out with his whip and *zalea* (sheep-skin) to spend the day pasturing animals. When the child plays in the street it is with a group of his own sex. When at six he goes to school it is to a boys' or girls' school taught by an adult of his own sex. The school in the valley is an exception to this since there is only one teacher, but it is a rare exception, for elsewhere the schools are all situated in the pueblos. Education, whether in school or at home, separates the sexes, for the tasks which the child will perform, the norms of behaviour to which it will submit, and the values which it will adopt, differ according to sex. Most tasks are the prerogative either of man or of woman, and there are few examples of persons who undertake those considered to be proper to the other sex. The only occupation which is pursued equally by both sexes is that of shop-keeping.

The role of women, as in all societies, centres upon the home. All work to do with the home, the care of children and clothes is theirs. Of the animals, only chickens and rabbits fall within their province. Girls may sometimes be seen pasturing goats, but this is only because the family is poor and there is no male child of the appropriate age. The *matanza*, the killing of the household pigs, shows a clear differentiation of the roles of the two sexes. It is something of a celebration and relatives who no longer form part of the household are often present. Some skill and experience is required in killing, and, if no member of the family possesses it, a son-in-law or uncle, known for his ability in this respect, may be invited. This would avoid having to employ a professional "matador" (meaning in this instance, "pig-killer", not bullfighter). The men prepare the *patio*, light fires to heat the water, rig up the sling, catch the pig, hold it down upon the table, and the matador cuts its throat. The blood is collected in a basin which it is the task or privilege of the lady of the house to hold and stir. When the pig is dead, the men clean the hair and dirt off with scrapers, while the women serve them, pouring the boiling water on to the carcass. The men then sling the animal up by its hind legs, and the matador butchers it. The role of the men ends when they have borne the meat into the house. There the women clean it and make sausages and prepare the meat in other ways. The men perform one other task, the preparation of the hams. Though this is not clearly defined as men's work, it requires a certain amount of knowledge, and the matador supervises the pressing of the veins in order to extract the blood. If this is not done properly, the hams will go bad. The hams are the most valuable part of the pig and are sold for money, though one may be kept for the use of the household. The money recovered in this way serves to finance the next

year's pigs. This division of labour is not governed by any
recognised rules; indeed, any attempt to discover a formulated rule of conduct meets here with the response, all too
frequent in this society: "Each one does as he thinks fit", or
"Each family has its way of doing it"—"Cada país su ley y
cada casa sus costumbres", the saying goes ("Each country
has its law and each house its customs"). Men's and
women's tasks devolve "naturally" from the conception
which people have of what men or women do best. No taboo
steps in to prevent women from scraping or men from making
sausages, and they may well be asked to assist in the role
normally filled by the opposite sex, if another pair of hands is
needed. They would not thereby be thought to be "effeminate" or "unfeminine", it would simply not be expected
that they do it very well, and, since they have not been
brought up to do it, the expectation would be justified.

In Alcalá women do not normally work in the fields for
hire, though it is common in the plains of Andalusia for girls
and even elderly women to go out in parties to weed upon
the large farms. They are most commonly seen there working
separately from the men. It is said that once the women
worked in the fields in Alcalá because there was more work
than there is today. There are today only four women in
the pueblo who go out for hired work. On the other hand, it
is quite frequent for wives or daughters of poor families to
help in work upon the family plot of land, weeding or
harvesting, or sowing the seed. Women are most commonly
seen working in this way in the *terrajos*, and the spraying and
harvesting of grapes is mainly women's work. There is one
form of work, however, in which a great number of women
take part, and for gain: the olive-harvest. This takes place in
the autumn when the men are busy ploughing. It is paid as
piece-work. Teams are formed among families and friends,
four or five people in each, including children of almost any
age. One at least must be a man or growing lad, for his role
is to climb into the trees and beat the branches with a slender
pole. The women and children collect the olives from the
ground.

When women desire to make money, either to supplement
their husband's income or because they have no husband,

they do so by performing other women's work for them:
domestic work, sewing, fetching water, looking after children; or by petty trading.

These generalisations, even were they one hundred per
cent accurate, would describe a differentiation which is
purely ideal. The realism of these people quickly admits
exceptions. Necessity forces people into activities which they
do not undertake from free choice. There is a girl who works
with her father and brothers at the heavy work of picking
esparto grass—"as if she were a man". And yet she remains
in all other ways entirely feminine. "What a shame!"
people say, "for she is a pretty girl and look at her hands
now. They are like a man's."

It is not only occupation which differentiates the sexes. In
recreation the same dichotomy is maintained. Women do not
go into cafés but stay in their houses where they visit one
another. Women do not smoke. The rich people of the big
towns differ from them in these ways, and the families of the
señoritos once again demonstrate their intermediate position.
Though they are never seen smoking, they will on feast-days
make up parties of both sexes at a table outside the *casino*.
For the women of the pueblo the shops, the fountains and
above all the wash-house or the stream-bank, where washing
is also done, are meeting-places, so that being in the pueblo
all day they do not have the same incentives for social
reunion in the evening, quite apart from the household duties
which attend them on the return of their menfolk from work.
The extreme cleanliness in regard to clothing, which is
characteristic of Andalusia, is not unrelated to the need for
someone from each household to go daily to the wash-house,
if the family is to keep well informed upon the issues of the
day.

In relation to religion the sexes are again separated. In
festive processions they walk apart. The funeral is followed
normally only by the menfolk once it leaves the church The
seating in the church reflects the same division. Men, un-
accompanied by their wives, stand at the back, while the
women and those who stay beside their family, sit on the
seats in front. Some men prefer to remain apart from their
womenfolk and to stand with their own sex at the back.

A spirit of solidarity exists between persons of the same sex in the face of the other, which is illustrated in the sympathetic attitude of women towards a woman whose husband causes her distress or among men towards a man whose employer, a lady, is difficult. Generalisations of a critical nature concerning the opposite sex are often made when persons of one sex are gathered together, or in mixed gatherings when someone wishes to adopt a tone of humorous raillery towards the other sex.

The behaviour of the unmarried people during the evening *paseo* (stroll) accentuates the solidarity of the sexes, though not in such a way that can easily be reduced to generalisation. Groups of up to five or six girls walk together with arms linked. The boys eye them as they pass or walk in twos and threes behind them. Sometimes a boy is attached to the end of the line of girls by virtue of a specific relationship to one of the girls, brother or fiancé. But in general, fiancés walk by themselves in pairs on the road at the entrance to the town.

Yet this solidarity does not exclude either quarrelling or fighting among themselves. Occasional fights among women break out, usually at the fountains where, particularly in the summer when the water supply is less plentiful, it may be necessary to wait for some time in order to fill a pitcher.[1] Fights cannot take place between the sexes, except of course within the institution of marriage, though quarrelling occurs over money and business. When Diego Perez' *aparcera*, a woman who owned two hectares of cultivable land, defaulted on her obligations, he took her to law. Had it been a man he would, he asserted, have beaten him up instead.

There are few situations in which persons of different sexes collaborate outside the family. A good deal of chaff passes where groups of young people of opposite sex confront one another, but there is no *camaraderie*. Friendship is essentially a relationship between persons of the same sex. So, a man visiting a friend on a farm may often be seen to shake hands with the male members of the family and not with the

[1] The fights arise over the order of precedence which is "first come, first served" unless a person renounces her right, yet it is typical that people in this society seldom form queues; they are far too much alive to the presence of others to need such a demonstrative method of maintaining the order.

female. For to do so might be to demand an intimacy with the family which he did not possess.

The only person whose position in relation to the sexual dichotomy is somewhat mitigated is the elderly woman. When past the age of sexual attraction her behaviour tends to become freer as regards the other sex. Widowhood brings, for the first time, full legal and economic responsibility as well as the greater influence which she enjoys within the family. Her role in business is more active, though she is not in general reckoned by men to be any good at it. The word *viuda* (widow) is common in the titles of business enterprises in Andalusia. At this age a dominance formerly dormant is apt to appear. There was even one old woman who used once to play cards and drink wine with the men in the café. She was considered eccentric and disgraceful, but nothing was done to prevent her.

To attempt to define the standards of behaviour between the sexes in terms of prohibitions and obligations would be difficult. Conversation is free and no subject is taboo, provided it is not discussed indelicately in the presence of the opposite sex. The restraints in behaviour proceed from the conceptions which the situation brings into play. In the organisation of conduct, not only in situations where a member of the opposite sex is present, a primordial importance attaches to the ideal types of either sex. It would be tedious to attempt to enumerate the moral qualities attaching to manliness or womanliness for in general they are the same as in our own traditional culture: "Knights are bold and ladies are fair." Courage and strength are emphasised as male attributes. Beauty and frailty are for women. The saying: "El hombre como el oso, mientras más feo más hermoso" ("Man like the bear, the uglier the handsomer") expresses this aspect of manliness, while the grace of the women in carriage and gesture reveals the value which is given to delicacy and beauty in the feminine ideal. The fact that moral judgements are expressed in terms of beauty and ugliness, the idiom of the feminine ideal, is a point whose significance will be brought out later.

The quintessence of manliness is fearlessness, readiness to defend one's own pride and that of one's family. It is ascribed directly to a physical origin and the idiom in which it is expressed is frankly physiological. To be masculine is to have *cojones* (testicles), and the farmyard furnishes its testimony in support of the theory. Castrated animals are *manso* (tame), a castrated ox is not dangerous like a bull. A castrated dog, it is thought, will always run away from an uncastrated one. A man who fails to show fearlessness is lacking in masculinity and, by analogy, castrated or *manso*. While it is not supposed that he is literally devoid of the male physiological attributes, he is, figuratively, so. That part of his person does not possess the moral qualities properly associated with it.

The bullfight is an occasion when the full figurative force of this conception is displayed. The bull which is *manso* is booed from the ring. The dead bull which has shown courage is applauded as his carcass is dragged out. The bullfighter, even though he may be lacking in skill and grace, is not despised as long as he is still able to show that he has valour. Yet if he fails or fears to kill the bull he is utterly disgraced. For the essence of the bullfight is the ritual revindication of masculinity and if this value is debased then the whole human species is defiled. The virility of the bull has not passed into its slayer. The champion who took the ring to redeem through his bravery the sacred quality of male pride has failed and the crowd greets him with contemptuous fury.

The terms relating to this conception are heard not only in the bullring but continually in everyday life. Thus, for example, in a quarrel concerning water-rights, one *hortelano* (garden-cultivator) said to the other, who had given him offence by repeatedly failing to relinquish the water at the appointed hour:

"Estaré en el cau' a la hora de cortar y si tienes cojones ven." ("When the hour comes to cut off your water and send it down to my *huerta* I shall cut it off myself [the place where the water is changed lies inside the other *hortelano's huerta*] and try to stop me if you dare!" Literally: "If thou hast *cojones*, come!") It is a challenge to fight. The implication is that if the other does not come, it is either that his antagonist is right and he admits that he must cut off his water at that hour, or alternatively that he has no *cojones*, that is to say that he is lacking in the full social personality of an adult male, and is a person who can be overridden with impunity. In fact, by the time the challenge is issued there is already a dispute of some standing. The challenge is intended to settle the question of water-rights neither by law, nor by an appeal to force, for it settles nothing if the other *hortelano* comes and they fight. To be beaten in a fight does not prove lack of courage (any more than the bullfighter is disgraced if he is carried wounded from the ring. He is only disgraced if he is physically able, but lacks the courage, to kill the bull). The challenge is intended to settle the matter, because the *hortelano* stakes his social personality on the issue. The other man knows that he is in the wrong in fact and under those conditions he will not come, for if there is a fight the matter is likely to be brought before the law and his fault will be displayed; but having failed to come, he cannot then continue to steal his neighbour's water without admitting that he lacks masculinity and was too frightened to uphold his rights openly, that he is a sneak-thief. The challenge served therefore to force a renunciation from the other *hortelano* of his claim. The social significance of the conception in relation to the political structure—and a later chapter will discuss this—resides in this: that a man who loses his masculinity forfeits his standing as a full adult male and through this loss of prestige he loses his value in the system of co-operation.

The word which serves literally to translate manliness (*hombría*) also contributes to the same conception:

"The modern race is degenerate," said a friend once, "in the days of our grandfathers there was more manliness than today." To be "muy hombre" is to have an abundance of that moral quality of honourable masculinity, and, through it, to command the respect of one's fellows.

Other words which might be discussed if the length of this chapter permitted are: *soberbia* and *orgullo* which express the idea of excessive self-regard, and *amorpropio* and *honor*[1] which are intimately connected with manliness. *Pundonoroso* (meticulous as regards honour) is a popular epithet for bullfighters.

Clearly, such a conceptual evaluation of sexual virility

---

[1] Cf. Pitt-Rivers, J. "Honour and Social Status" in J. G. Peristiany, ed., *Honour and Shame; the Values of Mediterranean Society* (London and Chicago, 1966). For a general discussion, see my article "Honor," in *Encyclopedia of Social Sciences* (New York, 1968).

leads to a certain proclivity to justify masculinity literally, and the moral precepts taught in education tend to be outweighed by the desire for such justification. Success with women is a powerful gratification to the self-esteem of the Andalusian. The appreciation of feminine beauty and the attitude of ready courtship which it inspires are expressed in the *piropo*, a word which means literally a ruby and also means a compliment paid to a lady. It is a tribute paid disinterestedly to one whose presence is a source of joy and, theoretically at any rate, without any ulterior motive. It may be paid publicly to an unknown lady as she passes down the street, for it requires no response from her, and the freedom and charm of such a custom has done much to recommend the cities of Andalusia to the pretty tourist. Opportunities for this kind of *piropo* barely exist in the pueblo where everyone is known, but an appreciation of feminine attractiveness is nevertheless not scant in Alcalá. The restraints upon the sexually aggressive behaviour of men derive, it appears, from sanctions of a social nature rather than from the prohibitions of the individual conscience. However, before considering them we do well to turn to the institutions and behaviour in which the sexes are united.

There are situations in everyday life in which the category of sex is overruled by the categories of age or social status. The respect due to age or official position may go far to obliterate the significance of the criterion of sex in a specific situation. The employees must obey the employer. The patients must visit the doctor. Persons of different sex are grouped together in juxtaposition to a person distinguished from them by another category. But we are concerned here to examine the relations between the sexes in situations where the difference of sex is prerequisite to the relationship of the participants.

The only institution which binds the sexes together is the family. Primarily through marriage, but also through all the relationships established by it. The form of the individual family is continually changing in time, but we may take as its starting-point the moment when the young person abandons the companionship of his own sex and family, and seeks to establish an individual relationship with a person of the opposite sex and another family.

As the children grow up through adolescence the segregation of the sexes takes a new turn. The interest in the opposite sex, unrelated hitherto to structural issues, begins to offer the possibility of a lasting attachment which will alter the standing of the couple radically. The boy deserts the "dirty-story-telling" group of his fellows to go courting his girl. Typically, the farming families of the valley, in contrast to wealthier families of the pueblo, tend to form attachments of a serious nature as early as fifteen to eighteen years, and to regard each other thenceforward as *novios* (sweethearts), in all the structural implications of the term. *Novios* are boy and girl who will eventually be man and wife. The *noviazgo* (courtship) is the prelude to the foundation of the family. It is characteristically long in this society, always of a few years' duration, though the length depends on the age of the participants and also on their economic position. Yet it should not be regarded as a time of delay necessary for the establishment of the economic foundations of the family, though it fulfils that function. It is, rather, a steadily developing relationship which ends in marriage. The degrees of seriousness which attach to the term and give it at times a certain ambiguity derive from the fact that it covers all the stages of courtship from acquaintance to marriage. The dog which deserts the farm at night in search of a bitch is said to go "buscando la novia" ("searching for a *novia*") and the word may even be used as a euphemism for a married person's lover. But the term does not imply sexual intimacy when referring to an established relationship between boy and girl. It is thought proper to "respect" the woman who will be your wife.

The first step in the formation of this relationship is made when two young people leave the group in order to talk to one another alone. They sit together or go for a walk apart at some reunion, and this establishes a tentative beginning. If this behaviour recurs then people say that they are "talking to one another". The expression is important for it sums up an aspect of the *noviazgo*. It covers all the period of informal relations, extending from the first stage up till the "demand for the hand". During this time the relationship deepens but it is not yet irrevocable. Andresito, speaking of his former *novia* said: "I spoke with her for twelve years and at the end

she turned out a whore." This period of twelve years was
exceptionally long owing to the fecklessness of the speaker
and his inability to follow with one job for any length of time.
When finally it became evident that he would not marry her,
he laid the blame on her.

The idea of this talking together is that the *novios* get to
know each other really well. The swiftness of the men to enter
a sexual relationship of no structural importance contrasts
with the care and delay with which they enter into matrimony. But the nature of this talk, though it inevitably varies,
has a particular quality associated with courtship and which
serves to forward the purpose of that institution. Its purpose
is to bind the emotions of each to the other so securely that
the attachment will last a lifetime. The word *camelar* expresses
this kind of talk. It means—and it is above all the man who
does the talking—"to compliment", "to show gallantry to",
"to cause to fall in love". It is subsumed that adulation is
what causes people to fall in love, and this theory is found in
the secondary meaning of the word: "to deceive with
adulation". In this way the nominal form *camelo* comes in
the end to mean: "nonsense", "line-shooting", "a tall
story", "a tale.which no one but a fool would be taken in
by". It is generally asserted that the essential attribute for
success with women is knowledge of how to talk to them. The
Don Juan must know how to deceive women with words.
However, in the case of courtship, this knowledge is put to
the service of matrimony. Love is an essential to a happy
marriage. And this is not only the opinion of romantic
señoritas. Andrés el Baño, a hardheaded and intelligent small
farmer says: "You can see clearly which marriages were
made for money. They spend their whole lives quarrelling.
Sensible people marry for love." "How is a man to spend all
his life working for a woman if he has no *ilusión* for her?"
For it is admitted that love, like all terrestrial delights,
is an illusion—to fall out of love is *quitarse la ilusión*. But
in marriage it is a necessary illusion. Each person knows
that he or she is not in fact the most wonderful person in the
world, but through *camelos* one can be made to feel it and to
feel the same about the other. The attachment formed by
this mutually inspired self-esteem bridges the gulf of sex-

differentiation and forms the bond on which the family is built.[1]

Courting takes place traditionally, in Andalusia, at the *reja* (the grill which covers every window), and sentimental numbers in the music-halls and the romantic postcards sold on news-stalls portray a *novio* so ardent that only iron bars can safeguard the purity of his love. The reality is less theatrical, of course. In summer the *novios* can go for walks together in the immediate vicinity of the town. To stray too far, to be out after dark, excites suspicious comment in the pueblo. Men who work and are away until dusk must do their courting after nightfall, and upon Thursdays and Sundays, the days for courting, boys will walk five or six miles, even after the day's work, in order to keep a rendezvous with a girl. Courting takes place at the girl's home. In Alcalá the doorway is used rather than the window. The visiting *novio* stands on the threshold to talk to his girl while she stands within. The girl's family pay no attention to the couple. If the father comes out he pretends not to notice the *novio*. Formerly it was considered an affront to the father to be seen by him courting his daughter. The suitor would retire while the father was in sight, but today he separates slightly from the girl and lets go her hand. To hold hands is considered proper behaviour for *novios*, save in the presence of a member of her family.

When the couple decide to get married, the *novio* makes a formal call upon the father of his *novia* in order to ask for her hand. His mother calls upon her mother. The girl's father is supposed not to answer but finally to allow himself to be persuaded by her mother. When the request is granted the young man hands over a sum of money[2] to the girl with which she is to buy the requirements and furniture of the house, and the wedding day is fixed—usually for a date three or four months ahead. The *noviazgo* then enters upon its final stage and although it remains theoretically repudiable, it would by now be extremely difficult for the *novio* to escape.

---

[1] The word *ilusión* is most commonly heard in the sense of ambition or hope, but it is also used with conscious cynicism as a euphemism for "lust".

[2] In the case of farming families working as a centralised economic unit the money is provided by the parents. This fact certainly contributes to the length of courtships in the valley.

The parents have been brought in who will become linked in the relationship of *consuegro* (co-parent-in-law). The money has been paid. From that moment onwards the marriage is assured. But until the demand for the hand the ties which bind the two together are purely personal. The longer an engagement lasts the stronger becomes the obligation to marry, the worse a repudiation would appear if there were no excuse for it but faithlessness. The danger is above all one for the girl, because once a long engagement is broken off it may not be easy for her to find a second suitor. The girl who has had other *novios* is not sought after in the same way, for the pride of the second *novio* must, to a greater or lesser extent, be sacrificed if he is to follow in the footsteps of another. If his *novia* were not a virgin it would make him a retrospective cuckold, but even if this is not believed, she would nevertheless be a less attractive proposition than previously. Girls whose first engagement is broken off tend to marry less easily subsequently.

It can be seen, then, that a girl of, say, twenty-five, whose engagement falls through after a long courtship is in a difficult position. If she has beauty or the prospect of inheritance, she will have no difficulty in finding a new *novio*. But if not, then she may have missed her opportunity. Andresito's *novia* remained a spinster. The moral feelings of the pueblo supply a powerful sanction against such faithlessness, for it involves the other members of both families. But *noviazgos* are in danger above all when boys go to work elsewhere for a time, and thereby escape the sanctions of the pueblo. They sometimes do not return but break with the *novia* of their home town and marry in the place where they are working, where they may never admit having had a previous *novia*, and where in any case the matter will have little importance.

In the face of this danger for which, should it materialise, the society offers no redress, one is not surprised to find the supernatural coming into play. There is a wealth of folklore which relates to finding and holding *novios*, and much of the practice of the *sabia* (wise woman) is devoted to resolving this problem. The girl whose *novio* begins to look at other girls with interest, visits her less regularly or writes to her less frequently, in short, gives her reason to believe that her hold over him is weakening, may go to the *sabia*. For the *sabia* has power to discover whether he still loves her or not, and is also able to perform love-magic in order to secure his constancy. She uses her love-magic, in this context, in support of the social order. The love-magic which she is able to do for men is thought to be employed for a more sinister purpose, which will be discussed in Chapter XII.

CHAPTER VII

The Sexes

(ii) Marriage and the Family

THE NATURE of the relationship established in courtship changes fundamentally with marriage. Here ends the free, personal, purely emotional bond. Marriage is part of the overt structure of the community. Ties are created not only between the *novios* but between persons who were previously linked by no more than common membership of the pueblo, if by that. Other ties are weakened by the formation of these new ones. A new pattern of social relations emerges. The system of naming serves well as an introduction to the structure of the family.

The young woman adds her husband's patronym to her own names. Let us say that he is: Manuel Castro Barea, and she: Ana Ruiz Menacho. Then she becomes: Señora de Castro, or (her official form of address) Señora Doña Ana Ruiz Menacho de Castro. The pueblo will continue to call her Ana Ruiz without her husband's patronym.

The dual surnames are composed of the patronym of the paternal and maternal grandfathers. In the same way, the children of this marriage will bear the surnames Castro Ruiz.

Within the pueblo, but not among the families of the *señoritos*, the children will be given Christian names in accordance with those of the grandparents; so that if Manuel Castro Barea is the son of Andrés Castro and Maria Barea, then the first child of each sex will be named (after the paternal grandparents) Andrés and Maria. The second child of each sex will be named after its mother's parents. The grandchildren are regarded as the descendants of one pair of grandparents as much as of the other, and this accords logically with the fact that they will have an equal claim upon the inheritance of both.

The law regards the family formed by this marriage as a single unit with, in many aspects, a single legal personality.[1] The wife becomes subject to her husband's tutelage, for in the eyes of the law he is the representative of this single personality. The wife, if she is over twenty-one years of age, will have become *vecina* (neighbour) of the pueblo. On her marriage she ceases to be so but becomes instead *casada*, the wife of a *vecino*. She also loses the right to control her worldly property, though she can prevent her husband, who administers it as he wishes, from disposing of it. Yet she cannot buy or sell property without his consent. The property of both is regarded as a single unit which the husband controls.

Neither are likely to have any property from the parents while the latter are still active, though the new couple may be given charge of a farm or mill belonging to one of the parents. If any dowry is given, which is rare, it represents either an advance of the share of inheritance of the girl's parents, or a free gift on their part. To make such a gift to one's child is called *mejorarle* (to improve him). As a general rule property does not pass until death.

The people of Alcalá feel very strongly that every family should possess its own house, and to marry without setting up a separate home is regarded as a make-shift arrangement. The poorer people are the more insistent upon this need for independence, and the economic advantages which might accrue from forming a larger family unit are offset by the desire to be free of the tensions which make family life impossible where there is more than one family in a house. "Cada uno en su casa" ("Each one in his own house") that is the only way to live peacefully. "Casada casa quiere" ("housewife wants house"), the saying rubs in the point. For while a joint family might collaborate in spending money, they cannot collaborate in making it, where each man's income derives from a daily wage. The husband must rent a house for his bride, and with the housing situation as at present it is not an impossibility even for the landless day-labourer. On the farms of the valley where family relationships are made clearer by geographical distance and

[1] Viz. Civil Code, Title IV, Chapters I and II.

conservative tendencies, it can be seen that the marriage of a child of either sex involves, or should involve, his withdrawal from the family unit. The modern custom, followed only by some is for parents to pay the sons who work upon their farm a daily wage once they are fully grown up, in order that they may start to prepare to found a family. But on some of the farms they keep the family finances integrated until a son marries, when he must have his daily wage to keep his wife. He may keep her in the pueblo in a house of his own (rarely in the parents' house even though they seldom go there) while he goes down to the valley every day to work. He may set up house in the valley or even build a house there, or he may also bring her to live with his parents or, more frequently, go himself to live with and work for hers. He may work for her parents and keep her in a house in the pueblo.

An old tradition of the farmers, followed by few nowadays, ordains that the elderly parents keep the daughter or daughter-in-law to live with them for the first year of her marriage. In one family where this is followed, the son works elsewhere and visits his parents' farm on Sundays to see his wife. At the same time the farm is worked by a son-in-law, the husband of an elder daughter who has a large family and lives in the pueblo. Hence the elderly parents live on the farm with one son-in-law and one daughter-in-law while their seven children all live elsewhere. Living with the old people there is also one grandson, the son of the son-in-law, and a boy-employee of fourteen years. The object of keeping the daughter or daughter-in-law with the parents is to assist the newly married couple to set up a home, for in this way all the husband's pay can be saved. The wife lives for nothing with the old people and in return she does the housework and looks after them. This arrangement is clearly only possible while she has no children of her own, and this may explain why it is an arrangement for the first year of marriage only.

In general, sons-in-law get on well with their wife's parents, and there are several farms where they live and are employed in preference to a son. The virtual avoidance between father- and son-in-law while the girl is courted ends with marriage, and gives way to an easier relationship than that of the father with his own sons, who must preserve

a stricter respect for him than must his sons-in-law. The
daughter-in-law, on the other hand, very seldom gets on well
with her husband's parents once she has a family of her own ;
and even before that her relationship is always formal and
sometimes strained. She is a virtual stranger to his parents
when the son marries her, for she has remained with her parents while her *novio* came to court her at their house. Little
by little, he has adapted himself to the ways of her parents'
house. He has made friends with her brothers.[1] After the
demand for her hand the avoidance of the father has lapsed
and he has been invited into her house. She has had no such
opportunity to become acquainted with his parents, and
when she comes to them it is not to ask a favour, but as the
established wife. Parental love is warm, and it is through her
that the parental tie is loosened. In such a situation, rivalry
between a man's wife and his mother for his chief regard
seldom fails to produce sparks. Living in the same house they
must collaborate more closely than the men-folk in the fields,
and for this reason a mother always prefers to have her own
daughter to work for her who is used to her authority and
the ways of her house.

An Andalusian saying points out the tendency to matri-
locality.

"Tu hijo se casa	"Your son gets married
Y pierdes a tu hijo	And you lose your son
Tu hija se casa	Your daughter marries
Y ganas otro."	And you get another one."

In the determination of locality, the moral and legal
equality of children regardless of their sex, combined with
the unity of the married couple, create a situation where the
emotional tensions inherent in family life assert themselves,
and the identification of the woman with the home overrides
the principle of patriliny.[2]

[1] Not straight away. The father formally ignores him, and for some time he
is regarded with suspicion by the brothers. The family requires to know whether
his intentions are serious or not. Antonio, son of Andrés el Baño said of the boy
who had already courted his sister faithfully for four years : "Hasta ahora se ha
portado bien con nosotros" ("So far he has behaved well towards us"). But in
time this suspicion gives way to friendship.

[2] The participation of the maternal grandparents through surname,
Christian names and property, in the lives of their daughter's children must not

This pattern of relations is also illustrated in a subsequent stage of the evolution of the family. Elderly parents, no longer able to work and look after themselves, are dependent upon their children to keep them. But it is noticeable that the children with whom the parents choose to stay are, in a slight majority, daughters rather than sons. It is only surprising that the disproportion is not greater, for elderly widowed mothers are seldom happy in their daughter-in-law's house. This sacred duty which requires poor people who work hard to devote part of their income and much of their time to the care of aged parents is generally respected, though it is said that before the initiation of the old-age pensions scheme old people were more often abandoned than today. Dutiful children are the insurance against a wretched old age or one spent in an institution in another pueblo. Parents who do not give their children proper moral "education" will be faced in old age with shameless children who neglect them. Respect for parents is not based upon authoritarian rule. Children are punished very little and are never expected to emulate their elders prematurely. They learn through imitation and are encouraged much with kisses and applause, for the love of children is great here. It is enormously senti-mental and demonstrative in comparison with that of Northern Europeans, and neither mother nor father, brother nor sister is ever either stiff or emotionally restrained towards them. At the same time, the identity of the child with its parents is continually stressed in its relations with other youngsters in the pueblo, so that the child's social personality is defined in relation to its parents. Children are always known as the children of so-and-so. In the advance of age the material tie between children and parents grows weaker, but

be confused with matriliny. It is the mother's patronym which she gives to her children, not her matronym. In so far as this society is lineal at all it is patri-lineal. The lineal principle, however, is incompatible with the social structure of the pueblo and has little importance there. In the tradition of the aristocracy, patrilineal descent was, of course, important, and was found together with a whole number of structural elements which contrasted with those of the pueblo; a monocratic relationship to community through the *senorío* (lordship) and a system of inheritance through the *mayorazgo* (entailment), which maintained the unity of property preferentially in the male line. It is noteworthy, however, that the majority of Spanish titles pass through the female line in default of a male line in the same degree of kinship.

the moral tie remains full of vigour. Within a community which knows no other principle of grouping, and where other relationships tend to be unstable and kinship ties are weak, the strength of the family stands out in solitary relief.

The statement that kinship ties are weak requires to be justified. Where kinship is associated with political structure, locality or economic production, one is accustomed to find that the extensions of the elementary family are endowed with structural importance. Enough has already been said to make it clear that this is not the case in Alcalá. People are seldom able to give a comprehensive account of their families further than their first cousins. Property alone provides an incentive to strengthen the ties with persons outside the elementary family.

The law of inheritance greatly influences the structure of the family, and the diversity of the traditional laws of inheritance of the different regions of Spain points to an equal diversity in their family structure. There is no regional tradition in Andalusia in the matter of inheritance. Its law is the law of Castile. When the property-owner dies his property is divided in half. One half is subdivided equally among all his children, the other goes to his widow for the duration of her life after which it also is divided among the children. During the widow's lifetime the division does not often take place, but when neither of the parents remain and the grandchildren are already fully grown it becomes necessary, in the interests of family independence, to make the partition. In fact, the way in which the property will be split up is usually foreshadowed in the arrangements which are made for its exploitation when the owner becomes too old to control it himself. Where the property is composed of several distinct holdings they are divided amongst the children, possibly with certain monetary adjustments, or with adjustments to the extent of the properties. In other instances, however, either it is impractical to divide the property or the heirs are unable to reach an agreement upon its division. The property then remains intact. If the joint owners fail to agree regarding its exploitation it is very often sold, so that the price may be divided among them. However, where they agree well enough, it is often regarded as preferable to retain the property intact in joint ownership and hope that time provides a solution. This, it frequently does. The property is run by one or more brothers and brothers-in-law on behalf of all. Little by little the other participants are bought out and the property remains in a single pair of hands, to face the same problem once more in the next generation. Where, for example, a brother is tenant in another farm or follows a different occupation such as artisan, he is well content to allow this to happen: but rivalry is common between brothers and sisters for ultimate possession of the inheritance. The joint ownership works well enough on occasions, though quarrels regarding its administration and profits tend to arise. In the third generation, that is to say when members of the second generation start to die, the difficulties become too great if they all leave children. Before anything can be done, it is necessary to reach agreement in a varied group of uncles and cousins and this is neither easy nor is it efficient. At this point people are glad to sell their interest and put their money into something else. Finally, a solution to the problem of inheritance is provided by the marriage of first cousins. Where families are not too large, the property is sometimes held together, or rather reunited by a marriage in the third generation. There is, however, nothing resembling a customary obligation to do so, and Andrés el Baño, for example, considers that such marriages ought not to be allowed. It is rather an arrangement which ambitious parents make in order to avoid having to split an inheritance. The number of descendants and the nature of the property determine the advantages of such a marriage, and where the farm is small and there are many grandchildren the advantages of cousin marriage are not great.

The relationship of first cousin is an equivocal one. Cousins are conscious of belonging to the same family for they have common grandparents whose inheritance they share, and yet at the same time they are not in any way interdependent. There is no specific code of behaviour for them. If they are brought up in close contact with one another, then their family association provides the basis for firm friendship. But cousinship in itself does not involve any rights or obligations Nevertheless, upon this uncertain ground, relations of genuine affection spring up, not only between cousins of the same sex but often, stressing membership of a common family, between *primo* and *prima*. This relationship is what might be called fraternal, but at the same time there is no absolute prohibition upon sexual relations between persons so related. Such a relationship is not incestuous, though marriage between persons so related requires a special dispensation. When José-Maria Perez took his cousin la Castaña to Jacinas on the back of his mule he claimed to be acting in a spirit of fraternal co-operation, but that did not prevent the evil tongues of the valley from attributing quite another motive for their journey. The label of cousinship is used sometimes to conceal the true nature of a relationship. Thus in the parish register a number of entries of *primo* or *pariente* (kinsman) denote a relationship which is nothing of the kind.

The ambiguity relating to the word *primo* explains its curious slang use. "Foolish or incautious", says the dictionary. The sense might best be rendered by the colloquialism "mug". The cousin is the prototype of the mug, for he puts faith in the strength of kinship ties and is soon deceived. "We are all brothers", quipped a witty fellow to his drinking-companions, "but not *primos*."

We can now see cousin-marriage in its true light. It is a way to reinforce the disintegrating family unit, and where property is involved there is a strong motive to do this. But it can also be explained in terms of sentimental affinity. The country families are considered slightly odd and unsociable by the pueblo—a fact which is seen in the exaggerated accounts of their lack of education and uncouthness. This reason is frequently given as an explanation of cousin-marriage. Shy children raised on the farms frequently form attachments to their cousins in a way that those raised in the hurly-burly of the pueblo do not. Cousin-marriage, though not specifically a characteristic of the tenant and owner farmers of the valley, is more frequent among them than in the pueblo.

A second type of marriage which possess a certain similarity with cousin-marriage is marriage between pairs of brothers

and sisters—similarity, that is, in the circumstances which
favour it. For this type of marriage should be regarded as
marriage between affines, and just as cousin-marriage can be
viewed as the desire to strengthen the link between blood-kin,
so this appears as the desire to strengthen affinal ties. Two
families united hitherto by a single marriage are thenceforth
united by two. There are three instances of this in the valley
and but one in the pueblo itself.

In summing up, we can see that the lack of mutual rights
and obligations outside the elementary family, the lack even
of occasions on which the unity of the extended family is
expressed, for cousins are not bound to be asked and are
not always asked to weddings, makes of kinship a facultative
rather than a firm bond. It is an excellent basis for friendship, but it is not in itself an important element in the structure of this society. Among the country-dwellers, marriages
are favoured which reinforce this basis, for they need to co-
operate on a more permanent footing than those of the
pueblo. One might say that the nature of the exploitation
of the land in small-holdings produces a tendency to extend
family ties. Yet in the absence of the institutions and values
which might support such an extension, ties between kin
cannot be regarded as important.

Two relationships remain to be discussed. First of all
affinal ties. The identity of the matrimonial couple and the
husband's responsibilities in formal matters bring him into
very close contact with his brothers-in-law, and one very
often finds strong friendship between men so related. This is
not the case with their parents though these are united in a
relationship which bears a special name, *consuegros* (co-
parents-in-law). Parents have, in fact, little influence over
their children's choice of a spouse. (One might well marry
to please one's parents, but one could hardly pursue a courtship such as I have described in order to please them.) United
by the institutions of marriage and baptism, and by their
common relationship to their grandchildren, *consuegros* are
equally divided by jealousies in relation to the latter. They
tend to be formal and mutually critical rather than warm
with one another.

Contrasting with the wary and distant relations of the co-parents in law is the relationship between *compadres* (co-parents literally, meaning co-godparents). Godparents are chosen friends of the parents who enter into a formalised friendship with them through their marriage or the baptism of their children. On the occasion of a marriage, a pair of godparents are chosen (*padrinos de boda*), usually a married couple from the close kin of the groom. A married elder brother and his wife is the conventional choice. These, according to one tradition, are also the godparents of the first child (*padrinos de bautizo*). Those of the second child will be chosen from among the relatives of the wife. There are many divergent ideas on the choice of *padrinos*, which need not here concern us. The relationship of godparent is a kind of spurious kinship involving obligations towards the child or in the marriage festivities. The *padrinos* are responsible for the costs. Far more important however, is the relationship which it creates between the parents and the godparents. This is called the *compadrazgo*. In order to become *compadres*, either the would-be *compadre* offers himself or the father invites him to be a godparent to his child. It is a bond of formal friendship more sacred than any personal tie outside the immediate family. Its seriousness is stressed by the fact that, in the popular conception though no longer in the Canon Law, it creates an incest taboo—you cannot marry your *compadre*[1]—and also by the mode of speech which *compadres* are obliged to adopt in talking to one another. Save when they belong to the same elementary family they must use the third person, even though they have spoken to one another in the second person all their lives. The explanation given for this is that "*compadres* respect one another". This respect does not involve a stiff or formal attitude; on the contrary, they speak to each other with great ease, but each is under the obligation to do for the other whatever he asks of him.[2] The *compadre* is an honorary mem-

---

[1] There are also frivolous derived forms of *compadrazgo* such as the *compadres de carnaval, madrina de guerra,* between whom marriage is permissible and frequent. For a more detailed study of this institution, see my paper "Ritual Kinship in Spain," *Transactions of the New York Academy of Sciences*, Series II, Vol. xx, No. 5 (1958).

[2] Technically, co-parents-in-law (*consuegros*) are also *compadres* and address each other in the third person, but their relationship is usually very different in feeling. People do not refer to their *consuegro* as my *compadre* unless the latter relationship exists in its own right.

ber of the elementary family, but he is at the same time free
of the trammels which bring dissension among kin. In the
changing kaleidoscope of friendship the *compadrazgo* is an
irrevocable tie of mutual trust, stronger than that of kinship
because it owes its existence to the free consent of both parties. A young *señorito*, explaining his quarrel with his married
sister, said: "It is ridiculous that a man should be bound to
people through kinship. To your mother and father, yes, you
have obligations, for they have brought you into the world,
but what is a brother, sister or cousin? I recognise ties with
no one save the friends of my choice."

The *compadres* may or may not be relatives. It is usual for
the first few children to be "baptised" by members of the
family. Very frequently the parents of both husband and
wife wish to "baptise" one of their grandchildren, and in
this way the relationship of father-in-law to son-in-law is
overlaid by that of the *compadrazgo*. In the same way it serves
to reinforce ties with members of the family. However, it is
also entered into with persons who are not relatives. These
may be neighbours or they may equally be friends who live
in another pueblo. There are certain advantages in having a
compadre in another pueblo, though the danger of losing touch
with him if one ceases to be able to go there is also to be considered. Finally, there is the powerful *señorito* who is *padrino*
to the child of a poor family. In this case, the relationship of
compadre is not stressed so much as that of the munificent
padrino. "Don Fulano is *padrino* to that family for he has baptised one of their children." This establishes him formally as
their protector, but, without any such ritual tie, the word is
also used to mean any powerful person who is prepared to
patronise (*empadrinar*) a poor man or to use his power to protect him. "El que no tiene padrino no sirve pa' na' " ("He
who has no *padrino* is no use for anything"), said a dejected
poor man, whose application for a plot of ground in a new
colonisation scheme had failed. A popular saying expresses
the same idea: "El que tiene padrinos se bautiza" ("He who
has *padrinos* gets baptised"). There are also *padrinos* who offer
themselves at the suggestion of the religious associations in
order to encourage poor people to celebrate their relationship with the rites of the Church. Certain of them cannot

afford to get married though they live together as man and wife. The *padrino* pays for the religious ceremony and gives them a present as well.

The significance of this institution will only be seen clearly in conjunction with the institution of friendship which is discussed in Chapter IX and from which it differs in that it is a permanent relationship which cannot be renounced.

A certain diversion from the theme of this chapter has been necessary in order to treat of kinship coherently, and to show the limits of its influence as a principle of grouping and how it creates ties between the sexes. It is not intended to convey that where there are ties of kinship or affinity people do not give weight to the difference of sex. Marriage, the nodal point of the system, is founded precisely on this difference. A man reaches his full manliness in fatherhood; a woman in motherhood attains her full social standing. The change which marriage brings in the relationship of *novios* is reflected by changed attitudes. Marriage marks the end of romantic love, the beginning of the preparation for parenthood. This transition is reflected in the nostalgia of married people for the days when they were *novios*. "That is when everyone is happiest."

The change of attitude is not always complete. Few are the men who do not retain something of the boy, and there are opportunities for many members of the pueblo for justifying their manliness while away from home. But the fleeting infidelity need not detain us. We are concerned with pre-marital and extra-marital relations within the community.

It is generally conceded that girls' morals are not what they used to be. Babies are not infrequently born to the unmarried *novia*. Provided that her *novio* will marry her there is no harm done and no great shame attaches to her plight, at any rate among the people with no "social pretensions". The sanctions of public opinion are strongly exerted to force the boy to honour his obligation to marry her. Salvador was father to his *novia*'s child while he was still writing to another *novia* whom, he maintained, he preferred but who lived elsewhere (he had met her in Jerez during his military service). His widowed mother, a very forceful character, went to the family of the girl and demanded that the baby should be named after her, as was her right if the marriage were to take place. As both grandmothers were called Maria a happy ambiguity prevailed, but soon afterwards the mother made a demand for the girl's hand on her son's behalf and paid some money for the setting up of the house. When the child was nearly eighteen months old they were finally married. The delay was partly due to the fact that his elder brother had to get married first. In most cases the parents of children born prematurely marry. However, in another case the *novio* rebelled, said the father of the child was not he but his uncle, and there was a very ugly row which would have ended in the courts had not the papers been mysteriously mislaid in the Town Hall. The child had no father, took the same surnames as its mother, and its uncle was *padrino*.

In neither of these instances was the courtship really well established. In other cases, as we have seen, poor couples set up house together without the formality of a marriage ceremony and raise a family. During the years before the Civil War many families abandoned the rites of the Church, but in the eyes of the pueblo this is not important. If they live together faithfully and raise a family then they are married. "I don't know whether they are married by the Church, but they are a married couple", is how the matter is explained. Today many pressures are brought to bear in order to get them married. Both the Church societies and also the Town Hall use their influence. In certain cases, the need to register the child in order to get it a ration-card at the time of weaning is seen to be the conclusive moment. It is then said that: "Les echan las bendiciones" ("The marriage is sanctified").

No doubt on account of a pregnancy, there are a number of couples who marry very young, some even before the boy has done his military service. While, in addition to these cases, it sometimes happens that young *novios* wish to force the issue and run away together, establishing themselves in a house in the pueblo—very often in a house belonging to parents who are farmers in the valley. Sometimes the parents react by recovering their daughter and, if she is still under their tutelage, bringing the forces of Justice into action against the young man; but in other instances they accept the *fait accompli* and attempt to enable the young couple to set up a home and get married.

In short, the situation presents no grave problem as long as the parties are unmarried. If, on the other hand, they are either of them married and are not content to observe discretion but set up house together, then the pueblo finds itself threatened in one of its vital structural principles. Its reaction will be described in a later chapter.

The lack of recognised obligations between kin within the pueblo can be contrasted with those which exist between fellow-townsmen, whether they be kin or not, outside the pueblo. The term *naturaleza*, meaning literally birthplace, but hence the pueblo to which a person belongs by origin, expresses this in formal contexts, and the significance of this has already been mentioned. A person who goes away requires an acquaintance in the place to which he goes who will accept responsibility for him, and a close relative is obviously the ideal host in this situation—brothers, brothers-in-law, uncles, *primos*; but failing a relative then a fellow-townsman is the person who assumes this responsibility. When women go abroad they usually put up at the house of an Alcalareña even though they may not claim friendship with her previously. The lack of structural obligations within the pueblo can be related to its completeness as a community, in the sense that the relationship of fellow-townsmen to fellow-townsman requires no amplification and admits no exclusion in the context of daily life. Away from the pueblo, in another place, this same sense of community between fellow-townsmen is what the obligation rests on.

CHAPTER VIII

The Sexes

(iii) The Values of the Female

IT IS now possible to discuss the values attaching to womanhood. We have seen how the tasks of the community are
distributed between the sexes and have observed the
importance of the role of the male sex in relation to the legal
structure of the state; man's pre-eminence, that is to say, in
formally conducted social relations. On the other hand, we
have observed that women play a predominant part in the
home and, on that account, in the structure of neighbourly
relations. And this may be allied to the fact that the women
are in the pueblo all the time while the majority of men must
leave it in order to work. The male social personality has
been related to the conception of manliness. The feminine
counterpart of the conception, which expresses the essence
of womanhood, is *vergüenza*, or shame. In certain of its aspects
only, for the word has first of all a general sense not directly
related to the feminine sex and it is this which must first be
explained.

It means shame, the possibility of being made to blush. It
is a moral quality, like manliness, and it is persistent, though
like manliness or like innocence, which it more closely
resembles, it may be lost. Once lost it is not, generally
speaking, recoverable, though a feeling remains that it is only
lost by those whose shame was not true shame but a deceptive
appearance of it. It is the essence of the personality and for
this reason is regarded as something permanent.

It is closely connected with right and wrong, since its
presence or absence is detected through an ethical evaluation
of the person's behaviour which is thought, in fact, to be
determined by it, but it is not synonymous with conscience.
It is, rather, its overt or sociological counterpart. The social

5. The Day of the Bull

6. Corpus Christi procession

anthropologist possesses no technique for examining the motivations of the individual conscience; but, fortunately for him, people are disinclined to let pass without comment behaviour on the part of their fellows which they would feel guilty to indulge in themselves, and are even willing sometimes to decry publicly that which they would do themselves if they had the chance, and believed they could do without it being known. The code of ethics to which *vergüenza* is related is that which incurs the moral stricture of the community. To use Marett's distinction, it relates to "external moral sanctions" not to "internal moral sanctions" or conscience.[1] Thus, to do a thing blatantly makes a person a *sin vergüenza* (shameless one); but to have done it discreetly, would only have been wrong. This, then, is the difference. Shamelessness faces the world, faces people in particular situations. Wrong faces one's conscience. Let me now try a definition:

"*Vergüenza* is the regard for the moral values of society, for the rules whereby social intercourse takes place, for the opinion which others have of one. But this, not purely out of calculation. True *vergüenza* is a mode of feeling which makes one sensitive to one's reputation and thereby causes one to accept the sanctions of public opinion."

Thus a *sin vergüenza* is a person who either does not accept or who abuses those rules. And this may be either through a lack of understanding or through a lack of sensitivity. One can perceive these two aspects of it.

First as the result of understanding, upbringing, education. "Lack of education" is a polite way of saying "lack of *vergüenza*". It is admitted that if the child is not taught how to behave it cannot have *vergüenza*. It is sometimes necessary to beat a child "to give him *vergüenza*", and it is the only justifiable excuse for doing so. Failure to inculcate *vergüenza* into one's children brings doubt to bear upon one's own *vergüenza*.

But, in its second aspect as sensitivity, it is truly hereditary. A person of bad heredity cannot have it since he has not been endowed with it. He can only behave out of calculation as though he had it, simulating what to others comes naturally. A normal child has it in the form of shyness, before education

[1] R. R. Marett: "The beginnings of morals and culture", in *An Outline of Modern Knowledge* (London, 1931).

has developed it. When a two-year-old hides its face from a
visitor it is because of its *vergüenza*. Girls who refuse to dance
in front of an assembled company do so because of their
vergüenza. *Vergüenza* takes into consideration the personalities
present. It is *vergüenza* which forbids a boy to smoke in the
presence of his father. In olden times people had much more
vergüenza than today, it is said. Another polite form illustrates
this aspect of shame. To be shameless in this sense is to be
descarado or *cara dura* (hard-faced), and this is a far more
serious matter than to be "thick-skinned", the nearest
expression in English to it.

It is in this second sense, as a moral quality innate and
hereditary, that the term *sin vergüenza* reaches its full force
as an insult, that the epithet used to a man's face is tantamount to insulting the purity of his mother.

The value attaching to a word depends upon the situation
in which it is used. The humorous use of *sin vergüenza* is
common, particularly in reference to infants and pets. The
affectionate father pinches the little boy's cheek and tells him
adoringly that he is one. This is not only a form of humorous
inversion but also a statement of a truth: the child is not old
enough to understand the values of society and therefore a
sense of shame in relation to conduct is not demanded of it.
It amounts to telling it that it can do no wrong. As it grows
older the term will acquire more weight. The first situation
in which it will hear the serious use of the expression is in
relation to its excretory habits. This is the first situation in
which a sense of shame is required. Other forms of conduct
will become reprehensible in those terms as the child grows
up. But the humorous use recurs whenever the indulgence
associated with childhood is evoked: whenever, for example,
middle-aged men feel boyish.

It will hardly surprise the reader to learn that *vergüenza* is
closely associated with sex. While to cheat, lie, betray or
otherwise behave in an immoral manner shows a lack of
shame, sexual conduct is particularly liable to exhibit shamelessness, and particularly in the female sex. Lack of shame
exhibited in other behaviour is, as it were, derived from a
fundamental shamelessness which could be verifiable if one
were able to know about such matters in the person's sexual

feelings. It is highly significant that the more serious insults which can be directed at a man refer not to him at all but to a female member of his elementary family and in particular to his mother. Personal reproach, while it refers to a man's character or actions, is answerable, but when it concerns a man's mother then his social personality is desecrated. At that point, if he has manliness, he fights. Up till that point matters can be argued. A man must make a living for his family, and this will lead him into conflict with other men. To fail to meet his family responsibilities would appear more shameless than to take advantage of people for whom he was not responsible. A certain licence is conceded to the male sex, so that a man is not judged so severely either in matters relating to business or in his sexual conduct, where the need to justify his manliness provides an understandable explanation of his shortcomings. "Men are all shameless", women say. The essence of his shame will be seen in his heredity, however. And therefore a reflection upon his mother's shame is far more vital than a reflection upon his own conduct. By extension, any reflection upon his sister's shame is important to him since it derives from his mother's. The whole family is attained by the shamelessness of one of its female members.

Just as the official and economic relations of the family are conducted in the name of its head, the husband, who has legal responsibility for and authority over its members, so the moral standing of the family within the community derives from the *vergüenza* of the wife. The husband's manliness and the wife's *vergüenza* are complementary. Upon the conjunction of these two values the family, as a moral unity, is founded. From it the children receive their names, their social identity and their own shame. Shameless behaviour on the part of their mother—marital unfaithfulness is the most serious example of this, though one form of shamelessness implies the others and is implied by them, since *vergüenza* is something which either one possesses or one lacks—brings doubt to bear upon their paternity. They are no longer the children of their father. He is no longer father of his children. The importance of a woman's *vergüenza* in relation to the social personality of her children and of her husband rests upon this fact. Adultery on the husband's part does not affect the structure of the family. This is recognised in the law of the land in the distinction which it makes between adultery on the part of the husband or wife. A husband's infidelity is only legally adultery if it takes place in the home or scandalously outside it.[1]

A wife's *vergüenza* involves a man, then, in quite a different way to his mother's. Her unfaithfulness is proof only of her, not of his, shamelessness, but it defiles his manliness. In a sense it testifies to his lack of manliness, since had he proved an adequate husband and kept proper authority over her she would not have deceived him. This much is implied, at any rate, in the language which appears to throw the blame for his misfortune on the deceived husband himself. In English, the word "cuckold" is thought to derive from cuckoo, the bird which lays its egg in the nest of another. Yet the word refers not to him who plays the part of the cuckoo, that is, the cuckolder, but to the victim whose role he usurps. The same curious inversion is found in Spanish. The word *cabrón* (a he-goat), the symbol of male sexuality in many contexts, refers not to him whose manifestation of that quality is the cause of the trouble but to him whose implied lack of manliness has allowed the other to replace him. To make a man a cuckold is in the current Spanish idiom, "to put horns on him". I suggest that the horns are figuratively placed upon the head of the wronged husband in signification of his failure to defend a value vital to the social order. He has fallen under the domination of its enemy and must wear his symbol. He is ritually defiled.

The word *cabrón* is considered so ugly that it is never mentioned in its literal sense in Alcalá. Even shepherds refer to the billy-goat of the herd by the euphemism *el cabrito* (the kid). Yet, figuratively, the pueblo uses the word in a wider sense than is general. It applies there to both the cuckold and the cuckolder, to any male, in fact, who behaves in a sexually shameless manner. It will be noted in the rhymes quoted on page 172 that the horns are attributed to someone who was neither cuckolder nor cuckold but had left his wife and children in order to set up house with another woman.

---

[1] Viz. Criminal Code, art. 452, also Civil Code, art. 105, § 1.

The best translation of *cabrón* as the pueblo uses it is "one who is on the side of anti-social sex".

While the greatest importance is attached to female continence—and the Andalusion accent upon virginity illustrates this—incontinence in the male has been shown to carry quite different implications. Sexual activity enhances the male prestige, it endangers the female, since through it a woman may lose her *vergüenza* and thereby taint that of her male relatives and the manliness of her husband. Yet *vergüenza* in a woman is not synonymous with indifference or frigidity towards the opposite sex. Quite the contrary, it is the epitome of womanhood and as such finds itself allied in the ideal of woman with the beauty and delicacy which are most admired. The sacred imagery of Seville or the Saints of Murillo illustrate this point abundantly.

The avoidance previously noted between the girl's father and her *novio* can now be explained. Until the young man marries her and thereby becomes a member of her family and therefore a person concerned in her *vergüenza*, he represents a threat to it and through it to that of her family. The avoidance may be seen to relate to the ambiguity of his position as, at the same time, both the potential future son-in-law and also as a threat to the family's *vergüenza*.

In the juxtaposition of these two conceptions, manliness and *vergüenza*, there are two possible bases of interrelation: one social, the other anti-social. In marriage, the wife's *vergüenza* ratifies the husband's manliness and combined with her fertility proves it. Through his manliness he gives her children, thereby raising her to the standing of mother and enabling her to pass her *vergüenza* on. The instincts implanted by nature are subordinated to a social end. But if these instincts seek satisfaction outside marriage then they threaten the institution of the family. Extra-marital manifestations of female sexuality threaten the *vergüenza* of her own kin. On the other hand, the male attempt to satisfy his self-esteem in a sexually aggressive way is also anti-social but for a different reason. If he approaches a woman who has *vergüenza*, he involves her in its loss and through that loss in that of another man's manliness, a husband's or a future husband's. Within the community of the pueblo this cannot but be a serious matter, and Chapter XI will show how the pueblo reacts to such a threat. Expressed in moral terms, *vergüenza* is the predominant value of the home. It involves restraint of individual desires, the fulfilment of social obligations, altruism within the family, personal virtue and social good. Masculinity, on the other hand, unharnessed to female virtue and the values of the home which it upholds and economically supports, means the conquest of prestige and individual glory, the pursuit of pleasure, a predatory attitude towards the female sex and a challenging one towards the male; hence social evil and personal vice. According to the values of the pueblo it is only a force of good as long as it remains within, or potentially within, the institution of marriage.

The value system expressed in these conceptions has been treated so far as if it were common to the whole of the society of Alcalá and uniform throughout even a far more extended area. Yet this is hardly to be expected. Anyone acquainted with the social history of Europe will have observed the variation in the customs relating to sex, both from one country and also from one period to another, but above all from one social class to another within the same country and historical period, while on the contrary certain values are characteristic of a particular class throughout European history. The "immorality" of aristocracies is traditional, while, to take an example from a different class, the attitudes in relation to sex defined by Freud have been declared to be valid only within the middle-classes of Protestant or Jewish cultures. In fact, generally speaking, there is a difference in attitude not only between the sexes but also between the Andalusian *señorito* and the pueblo (*plebs*). It cannot be said to amount to a serious difference in values so much as a difference in the opportunities to implement or defy them. Men with more money and greater freedom of movement have more opportunity to indulge their masculinity in what would, within a community, be an anti-social way. If the behaviour of the *señoritos* conforms less strictly to the morality of the pueblo, it is because they escape the full force of the moral sanctions of the community. They demand, at the same time, a stricter mode of conduct from their womenfolk. On account of the social prestige which they enjoy, they feel themselves entitled to justify their masculinity in relation to the opposite sex, even though this involves them in conduct which they regard as morally wrong. It does not involve them in loss of shame as long as their womenfolk are not involved in any way. The sanctions which hold the anti-social manifestations of sex in check cannot depend upon the public opinion of the pueblo in cases where the pueblo would never know anything about it, but only (apart from conscience) upon a particular concern for other social personalities which is expressed in the word "respect". A young man who came to the pueblo as a summer visitor explained once that while friendship with an attractive girl was virtually impossible on account of the desire which the young man would have of making a conquest, there were, nevertheless, certain relationships of trust which obliged him to avoid placing himself in a situation where he might be the prey to temptation. These relationships of trust were created by the respect which he had in the first place for the girl's husband or *novio*, secondly for her father, and thirdly for her brother. If one were not acquainted with the persons in question then there was no obligation to refrain from gallantries. There was, however, one final exception and this was when one felt respect for her of the kind which one might have towards one's wife, or such that one might wish to make her one's wife.[1] In effect, these restrictions virtually exclude any young woman who is regarded as a social equal, and in this way the manifestations of anti-social sex are projected outside the circle of local upper class society.

It is possible to see now that the conceptual basis of sexual behaviour is the same in the society of the *señoritos* of the large towns as in the pueblo, only the background of sanctions against which it is brought into play differs. The community not the system of values is different. When a wealthy summer visitor attempted to persuade a young girl of the

1 The respect is of course for her *vergüenza*. To achieve her conquest would entail the loss of her *vergüenza*, which would involve one in a relationship with her male relatives incompatible with that between affinal kin. In a slightly different way a man is said to lack "respect" for his wife if he indulges in extramarital adventures.

pueblo to allow him to set her up as his mistress in a flat in
Seville, he was frustrated. The religious associations under
the leadership of the wives of the *señoritos* of the pueblo packed
her off to a convent.

If the essential values of manliness and *vergüenza* are
similar throughout the social structure of the pueblo, there
are, nevertheless, certain points at which differences of status
and *naturaleza* cut across the values relating to the sexes. The
social relations of the family are conducted in different
spheres by the husband or the wife and these are relatively of
greater or lesser importance according to the position of the
family in society, its relationship to the community or to the
state. The position of the administrators' wives furnishes an
example. Their husbands have a function to fulfil which gives
them a basis for their relationship with the pueblo. But the
wives, on the contrary, coming mostly from the big towns,
find themselves restricted by their conception of social class
and their *naturaleza* and by the fact that they participate in
few of the activities which unite the women of the pueblo.
They tend not to establish deep friendships except with one
another, to stick much to their houses, and to bemoan their
fate in having to live in such an outlandish place as Alcalá.
Several who come from Malaga, Jerez or Cádiz spend much
of their time there with their parents. The position of the
señoritos' wives is not the same. They play a leading part in
Church affairs and are attached to the pueblo, apart from
their membership of the community by birth, through their
work in organising the Church brotherhoods, and the various
other functions in which, officially or unofficially, women
intervene.

In brief, the significance of sex in a society comprises
much more than what is termed the division of labour. The
sex of a person determines his position not only in regard to
the organisation of productive or useful labour but to all
activities, and not only in regard to activities but in regard to
the values which influence conduct.

In this society it can be seen that men are entrusted with
authority, with the earning of money, the acquisition of
prestige—(a woman taking her status by and large from her

husband), with relations of an official character, that is to say, with institutions recognised by the law of the land—in consequence of which the sanctions which the law exerts apply more effectively to them, that they spend a greater amount of time outside the pueblo and the home, that they are permitted a more aggressive attitude in sexual behaviour, and that they gain prestige through qualities of strength and above all courage.

Conversely, women are entrusted with the maintenance of the home and all that it means, are more continually in the pueblo, and are more susceptible to the sanctions of personal criticism or gossip in the dissemination of which they play a more important part, as they also do in religious observances. A greater reserve is required of them in matters touching sex, and they are thought to be the repository for the whole family of the quality of shame upon which the sanctions of morality operate. They gain admiration through beauty and delicacy, but physical courage is not required of them.

These differences, by no means comprehensive, are seen to vary in relation to social status according to the relative importance in their lives of forces exterior to the pueblo, or of forces deriving from the personal contacts within it. Thus, illiterate people are more dependent upon personal contacts than are those who can read for themselves the notices in the Town Hall and the provincial newspaper while, to give another example, people who employ a servant, in that the womenfolk no longer go to the fountain or the wash-house, are relatively less dependent upon it. The distinction will also be seen to be significant in relation to the institutions which are described subsequently.

CHAPTER IX

Political Structure

WHEN I first entered the casino I was asked to meet "el amo de Alcalá" ("the master of Alcalá") and it is common to hear the expression "el amo del pueblo" in reference to the mayor. In the town his word is law. He is the "delegate of the government",[1] appointed, the town having less than 10,000 inhabitants, by the provincial governor. He is not paid, but his appointment is an order which may not be refused. He must have the civil governor's permission if he is to be absent from his post for more than fifteen days, and he must inform the provincial capital if he is to be absent for more than twenty-four hours. The post is of indefinite duration. The symbol of his authority is the rod, and until the establishment of a post of the Civil Guard (as little as eight years ago in the case of Benalurín) the mayor of the pueblo bore the sole and direct responsibility for public order.

The mayor is assisted in his duties by the town clerk, a civil servant, member of a professional corps, appointed by the Ministry of the Interior, and only in very rare instances a son of the pueblo. He is the person who knows the law and runs the Town Hall. There is a town council of six members, elected, two by the "vecinos cabezas de familia" (neighbours, the heads of households), two by the syndicates, and a further two by the four already elected from a list presented by the civil governor. These elections excite little interest and in fact the mayor has more or less whom he wants. From among their number he appoints two to be his lieutenants.

In Chapter I we were concerned with the moral unity of the pueblo and the ways in which it was differentiated, culturally, from other pueblos. In the overt political structure this unity is emphasised no less. The competence of the

[1] The form of local government derives from the *Ley de Regimen Local*, 1950. With reference to the opening paragraph of this chapter, cf. arts. 59–67.

municipality extends over such matters as: urban planning, the administration of its properties and the common lands, measures relating to hygiene, rural and urban police, transports, marketing, including the establishment of monopolies in its favour, the levying of certain forms of taxation, instruction, culture and social assistance. These responsibilities are met from a budget of about a third of a million pesetas. About half this sum is derived from property owned by the municipality. The other half is made up from octrois, a tax upon the killing of beasts, a percentage of various taxes formerly owned by the municipality but now the property of the state—these taxes are collected in the pueblo by a tax-collector who is the employee of the state and an outsider, but who lives in the pueblo—compensation paid by the state for other taxes which it has recently appropriated, and subsidies for unemployment benefit. In addition, the mayor's powers include a number of emergency measures such as that which entitles him, in times of hunger, to levy a special contribution for the support of the unemployed, or alternatively, in such circumstances, to allot men in need of support to the different households of the community where they must be fed and given a small wage for the support of their family until the time of crisis is over. It is also customary for him to decide upon a minimum for each householder's contribution to certain charities. The municipality's outgoings consist of: wages to its servants, the up-keep of public buildings, including the law-court; public works; the financing of public functions such as the yearly fair; taxes of the state upon the properties of the municipality; public debt; public assistance (apart from that of the health insurance scheme) either direct or in the form of free medicine, treatment and burial for the indigent—about four times as much is spent upon this as is received for the purpose in the state subsidy; down to 5,000 pesetas set aside to meet the expense of receiving a state official should one happen to pay Alcalá the honour of a visit.

The hamlet of Peñaloja is administered integrally with Alcalá. The mayor of Peñaloja is appointed by the mayor of Alcalá and has no powers except as his representative. The other pueblos of the *partido* are entirely independent of

Alcalá. In this instance the mayor of Alcalá is also the deputy to the provincial council, and as such he represents the pueblos of the *partido*.

The law recognises four forms of co-operation between municipalities, called *mancomunidad* or commonwealth. Only two of these are illustrated in this *partido*: *Agrupación forzosa*, the obligatory sharing of the services and expenses of the institutions of the law by all the municipalities of the *partido*: and *agrupación facultativa* which municipalities are free to engage in by mutual agreement. Alcalá possesses such an alliance with Benalurín in regard to the services and expenses of the vet. The vet of Alcalá is thus also the vet of Benalurín.

The doctor and the chemist are directly dependent on the municipality. They receive a salary paid by the municipality in virtue of their role in the social services. In the doctor's case the greater part of his income is derived from his private practice, and in the chemist's case his shop. They cannot be considered purely as servants of the municipality, but they are obliged to co-operate with it in many matters; and though their appointment does not depend on the mayor, they are in no position to oppose his policy.

Mention has already been made of the rural schoolmasters who give lessons on the farms. The "national schoolmasters", members of the corps to whom public education is entrusted, are very different. Theirs is a "career" and appointments are made by the state, with the agreement of the municipality by whom they are actually paid. Of the five schoolmasters of Alcalá only two are sons of the pueblo. One is from Benalurín, and the remaining two are Andalusians. Of the four school-mistresses only one is of the pueblo. These schools, situated all in the town save for the single mixed school in the valley, educate the majority of the children of Alcalá. Certain poor families of shepherds need the services of their children with the flocks and would prefer not to send them to school, but pressure is brought to persuade them to do so. There is much talk of the disgrace of illiteracy on the part of the political leaders and the present regime has devoted great efforts to education. The education is, although free of the organisation of the Church, much concerned with religious teaching, for the rulers feel that their failure to ensure the religious education of the working-classes was responsible for the Civil War. Most people recognise that education will be an advantage to their children,[1] and one may sometimes encounter a compromise between the demands of the present and the hopes of the future in the shepherd boy who sits on the hillside doing his sums. The families of the landowners and professional men normally send their children to the local school when they are small and to a convent-school in Ronda for their later education.

A certain anomaly may be detected in the position of these servants both of municipality and state: the schoolmasters, town clerks, secretaries of the Town Hall or of Justice. They are, on the one hand, members of a professional body to which they owe their professional status, and, on the other, members of a local body. These two sometimes divergent ties are resolved in the system of appointments. A member of the corps may be appointed to fill a vacancy, but he may then prefer not to discharge the duties himself but to put in a substitute approved by the municipality, also a member of the corps, paying him a percentage of the salary (or even the whole salary—for the effect of devaluation has brought hardship to these people, and they can barely live modestly upon their earnings if they have a family). He may then devote himself to other matters or he may equally take on the job of substitute in a place more to his liking. Thus the mayor was until recently a substitute schoolmaster who held an official post as schoolmaster in another part of Andalusia. His wife, a schoolmistress, held her post in Alcalá "by right". The owner of the post may at any time oblige his substitute to relinquish it to him in order that he may fill it in person. When the owner of the mayor's post returned this happened, but the latter, having become deputy of the *partido* to the provincial council, already had plenty of work on his hands and was very ready to abandon it. In the same way, the town clerk of Alcalá is substitute for a Catalan who prefers to live

---

[1] The great emphasis which the Anarchist Movement laid upon education may be recalled in this connection. There is a tendency among the poor families to deride the state education saying that they teach the children nothing but a lot of religious nonsense.

in Barcelona. He, himself, "owns"[1] the post of town clerk in a nearby pueblo.

There are other servants of the state who exercise their function in the pueblo but are less directly dependent upon the municipality: the state tax-collector, the administrator of posts and telegraph, and so on. They, nevertheless, require to collaborate closely with the municipal authorities, and their common dependence upon the provincial capital ensures this.

The executives of the municipality include the clerical staff, the rural guard, the municipal guards, the *alguaciles* (the officers of Justice), the cemetery-keeper, etc. They are all sons of the pueblo and are purely dependent upon the municipality which even has freedom to dress its guards in the uniform of its choosing. They execute the will of the municipality in all the sphere of its competence. They are persons endowed with authority. The rural guard must see that pigs killed upon the farms, as well as those which are brought to the slaughter-house of the pueblo, are declared and pay the tax; he must verify matters which are brought before the courts. The guards have powers of arrest and a responsibility for public order within the pueblo. In the case of any serious outbreak of violence, however, they send for the Civil Guard. They collect the octrois and they enforce the Town Hall's regulations regarding the markets. They are responsible for seeing that people do not avoid paying their taxes and that the census returns are filled in correctly. They perform these duties with a zeal tempered by human understanding, for they are not the anonymous representatives of the state, but members of the pueblo known by everybody since their childhood. The fact that they are called by their Christian names and nicknames, in contrast to the Civil Guard who are known by their surnames, illustrates the difference in the relationship of the two organisations to the pueblo. They are not moved by a desire to see that the law is carried out to the letter but rather that the wishes of the mayor are obeyed. To give an example, the tax upon business enterprises is only paid by those of importance, for the municipal guards are prepared to turn a blind eye to poor people who try to make

---

[1] A post is said to be held *de propiedad* by the official incumbent.

their living by trading or baking. But from time to time the mayor decides that things are getting out of hand and sends them round to close down the unlicensed businesses.

The essence of the political doctrine which inspires the present government of Spain is to be found in the syndical organisation. The "party", founded in 1934, proclaimed itself from the first "national-syndicalist", and, in contrast to British trade-unionism, which grew from the need to unite the workers in order to give them the power to protect their own interests, it envisaged a system of syndicates which would include both employers and employed and would fill the role, in the desired state, both of labour organisation and unique political party. It claimed to incarnate the destiny of Spain. The party grew to power quickly during the Civil War, and, although many compromises were imposed upon it by the demands of the times, it succeeded in maintaining, within the national movement, the supremacy of its ideas in regard to labour. These ideas grew up, not like those of the Andalusian Anarchists in the agricultural towns, but in the capital and industrial cities. Their application in the social structure of Alcalá presents a strikingly different picture to that which may be seen in some other parts of Spain, and even of Andalusia. This is not the place for such comparisons. We are concerned only with the office of the secretary of syndicates in the pueblo of Alcalá, and the central provincial headquarters which issues regulations relating to wage-levels, price-levels for controlled agricultural produce, and which provides a court of appeal to which disputes regarding employment may be taken. These disputes are first of all heard in the office of the secretary of syndicates in the pueblo before a court comprised of two members of the Sección Economica (employers) and two members of the Sección Social (employees), where, as a general rule, they are settled.

The grain-control, the Servicio Nacional de Trigo, is also operated in the pueblo through the syndicate—as are all the controls of agricultural produce. The office of the syndicates, in collaboration with the Town Hall, apportions among the farmers the share of the grain which the pueblo is required to produce. This grain is paid for at a controlled price. The

black-market price sometimes soars to as much as four times
this figure. The system originally demanded that an agreed
area should be sown with wheat on each farm, and the
farmer was then required to declare his crop. The prevalence
of the return which asserted that the crop had been "totally
lost" induced a more down-to-earth method of raising the
required amount. After the harvest a list is published on the
Town Hall notice-board stating what each farmer's contribution to the grain service is, and, after that, how he provides
it is his own business. The syndical chiefs are responsible for
this list. A varying number of other kinds of produce is also
controlled in a similar way, though there is no obligation to
cultivate specific crops. Inspectors arrive in the pueblo from
time to time to supervise the collection of produce or to attempt
to discover irregularities in the observance of the orders
relating to these and other matters under the jurisdiction of
the Syndical organisation.[1] Their visits are feared and
resented by the whole pueblo, whose reaction to them has
already been mentioned in Chapter I. Yet they are treated
as guests should be treated. They for their part tend to be
reserved in their behaviour. (One refused, on one occasion,
to touch the glass of wine which had been placed before
him.) Upon their arrival or knowledge of their approach
word is sent to the valley where the millers prepare to receive
their visit. This involves stopping the mill, sweeping up the
flour and hiding it and the grain. Each mill is sealed with a
wire which runs round the stone from the centre to the outer
edge and is fixed with a metal seal. This is removed while the
mill is in use but must be replaced for the inspector's visit,
for it testifies that the mill has remained idle. These operations require considerable time and cannot be carried out
in under an hour, so that from time to time a miller is caught
red-handed. The inspector in due course reports the matter,
and a fine is imposed by the provincial headquarters and in
due course published. Upon certain occasions, however, the
inspector can be persuaded to be lenient provided he is

---

[1] An account of the activities of an inspector is to be found in G. Brenan,
The Face of Spain (London, 1950). In order to simplify, the distinction between
the "inspector" and the "fiscal" is overlooked and both are here referred to as
inspectors.

7. A *sabia* reciting an oration

8. An old gypsy

approached in good time. Once the fine is published there is nothing to be done. It must be paid.

The law-court of the *partido* is situated in Alcalá. A dispute enters the realm of law when a denunciation is made to the Town Hall. The disputants are then summoned before one of the Justices of the Peace accompanied by their *hombre bueno* (literally "good man"). There are two J.P.s. One is the owner of the cloth-factory, the other the owner of the cinema. The *hombre bueno* is any person of the litigant's choice, a friend whom he can trust to present his case well. The J.P. hears both parties and reasons with the *hombres buenos*, who reason with those they represent. Slowly the truth is thrashed out and the J.P., in the majority of cases, persuades both parties to agree. He has no power to impose decisions and if the parties do not agree he can only take a summary of evidence and refer the matter to court.[1] "I am a Justice of the Peace," says one, "my duty is to make peace. Only if I fail, does the matter go before the judge." Court proceedings involve a great deal of delay and a great deal of expense. The J.P.s have, in criminal accusations, a slightly greater competence. They are able to award punishment for such minor offences as gambling or abuses of municipal regulations. They can impose a fine up to the limit of 500 pesetas, or they can sentence a man to a day's work mending the street under the supervision of the Civil Guard.

A strong distaste for formal justice, a distrust of it and a preference for an equitable arrangement are to be found in the sentiments of the whole pueblo including those of the legal authorities. A good illustration of these was provided by the following incident. A poor man gained a living for himself and his family catching game by various methods licit and illicit. One night returning to the pueblo his gun exploded by accident and cost his neighbour her eye. It was out of season, and he had no gun licence. He was arrested

---

[1] The role of the *hombre bueno* can be compared to that of the *corredor* in bargaining. He defends the pride of the litigant and enables him to withdraw from his position, not in answer to the threats of his adversary, but in answer to the pleading of his friend. There is an element of bargaining in such a situation which is offset by the J.P.'s exposition of the law and his warning of what is likely to happen in court.

and held by the Civil Guard. But after the case had been
examined by the J.P., people in authority began to ask themselves what useful end would be served by sending him to
prison. He was a man of good character. The mayor, the
J.P. and the judge discussed the matter. The priest put in a
plea for lenience, and it was agreed that if the culprit paid
2,000 pesetas compensation to the woman who had lost her
eye no further action would be taken. The woman was a
widow who depended for her living upon sewing. If the man
went to prison he would not be able to earn anything to pay
compensation to her, and in addition his family would be
left without means of support. The man had no money, but
the director of the agricultural bank, the Monte de Piedad,
was persuaded to advance him the amount on the guarantee
of two guarantors whom the regulations of the Monte de
Piedad require, and who, not without a certain amount of
difficulty, were found. The case did not appear before the
court. This solution was regarded by all as far better than
any that the law was capable of providing.

A case in which litigation arose will be examined in more
detail in a later chapter, and it will be seen once more that
ethical considerations influence the course of formal justice.

The authority of the mayor is exerted through the municipal guards. The persecution of offenders against the law of
the state, the criminal code, is in the hands of the Civil Guard.
In fact, no clear distinction between municipal and national
authority can be made in everyday life. The Civil Guard
takes action at the request of the mayor, for, as I have pointed
out, a high degree of co-operation exists between the rulers
of the pueblo. The Civil Guard is commanded by a corporal
who has a section of eight men. They live in a house in the
pueblo with their wives and families. It is called, both officially and by the pueblo, the barracks.

The Civil Guard was raised originally in 1844 in order to
combat the bandits, and was subsequently of great importance
in the repression of the Anarchist risings which became frequent in Andalusia during the latter half of the century. Semi-
military in character and organisation, they became noted for
the roughness of their methods, and were not beyond em-

ploying on occasions the celebrated *ley de fugas*, a pseudo-legal
method of disposing of unwanted prisoners. They were much
hated by the pueblo, and this fact was influential in the
course of the Civil War in Andalusia. The first thought of
the Anarchists when they came to power was to settle old
scores with them, so that in the towns of Andalusia they were
forced willy-nilly into common cause with the rebellion. In
the capitals they frequently remained loyal to the Republic.

The greater part of their time is spent in patrolling the
countryside, and while there were still bandits in the
mountains around Alcalá their life was not only hard but
perilous. They go always in pairs and always armed.
Superficially their relations with the pueblo are amicable.
There are sons of the pueblo who have joined the force and
who return to visit their families while on leave; for not all
their strength is recruited from the sons of former members,
but it is recognised that it is not possible to contract relations
of lasting friendship with them. For even though an understanding is necessary with them if their good will is to be
maintained, at any moment their orders may require them
to violate the obligations of friendship. The farmers generally,
but particularly the millers who are open to denunciation for
milling at any moment, require to be on good terms with
them, and it is customary for them to receive clandestine
presents of flour or grain from time to time. Their position in
the pueblo can be seen to consist, like that of the municipal
guards, in a compromise between their personal relations
with members of the pueblo and their duty to co-operate in
implementing the will of the authorities. But whereas the
municipal guards are sons of the pueblo and are concerned
with the municipal authorities only, the Civil Guard are
outsiders, members of a state organisation, and while they
co-operate with the mayor they are under the orders of
their officer in Jacinas. Ultimately they need answer only
to him.

Finally there exists a kind of home guard, the *somatenes
armados*, raised originally in the time of General Primo de
Rivera and composed of persons in whom the present
regime has confidence. They do not meet as a body but are in
possession of arms in their homes, and may be called upon

to assist in the operations against the bandits, or to respond to any other call for armed force which may be made.

The place of the Church within the social structure is a matter which cannot be ignored, even though it is not my intention to discuss religion. In Andalusia the Civil War might be likened to a religious conflict, in that the most important criterion of political action was allegiance or opposition to the Church. The names upon the memorial tablets and the roofless churches bear witness to this fact. In the pueblos of the countryside, in contrast sometimes to the big towns, the persons whom the Left put to death were priests, persons who had been connected with the Church such as sacristans, and pious persons particularly among the professional classes. It must be remembered that in fact the majority of the pueblo strongly disapproved of shooting anybody. As a rule people were put to death, not publicly in the pueblo as in the account given in Hemingway's novel, *For Whom the Bell Tolls*, but secretly at night, a mile or two from the town. In many instances those responsible were not members of the pueblo at all but political or militia chiefs from other pueblos or the big towns.

This situation of pro-clerical rulers and an anti-clerical pueblo is the reverse of that which saw the birth of anti-clericalism in Spain a century and a half ago, and this reversal is one of the conundrums of Spanish history. Brenan suggests that the effect of disestablishing the Church and sequestrating its lands was to throw the clergy into the arms of the propertied class who made political use of it, and thereby provoked opposition to it among the landless labourers.[1] In so far as it is possible to abstract a sequence of cause and effect from the multiple conditions of social history, this explanation has not been bettered. Yet one must not overlook the fact that a similar evolution has occurred in other countries of very different political history. It must be stressed, in any case, that anti-clericalism is not necessarily the outcome of loss of religious faith, and to make such a supposition here would be to misplace the problem. In Alcalá strong anti-clerical opinions and faith in the powers of the

[1] G. Brenan, *The Spanish Labyrinth*.

saints, and particularly of the Blessed Virgin, are able to go
hand in hand. This ambivalence, whose significance must
be left to later pages, is not directed uniquely to the institution of the Church though it is most marked in regard to it;
it has already been shown to exist in regard to the *señoritos*.

The question of faith is not relevant to an examination of
the political structure. What is relevant is the uniqueness
of the institution of the Church in relation to social life. The
Church alone can baptise, marry,[1] bury, celebrate the patron
saint of the pueblo and the seasonal festivals and punctuate the
calendar with the saints' days round which the folklore hangs.
There is one priest of Alcalá and four churches of which
one was burned in the Anarchist rising of April 1936. There
are five religious brotherhoods devoted to the cult of different
saints, whose members are recruited from the pueblo.
Subscriptions are extremely low, from 1 to 2 pesetas per
annum in four brotherhoods, and 11 pesetas in the fifth
case. The wives of the *señoritos* play a leading part in these
organisations. Their functions are the organisation of
religious festivals and charity. Of greater influence is the
Catholic Action Committee which exerts itself in all matters
touching religion, particularly in using pressure to get the
rites of the Church observed by the poor, and to have
immoral diversions such as modern dancing prohibited or at
any rate discouraged. Missionary work is done by the ladies
of the Catholic Action who go round the houses of the poor
while the men are out at work and endeavour to persuade
the women to go to confession. This causes resentment
among anti-clerical husbands. "They go round in pairs—like
the Civil Guard," a man once complained. They also do
good works, arranging for the care of the indigent and in-
firm.

In all the organisations connected with the Church
women are much more active than men. The pueblo (*plebs*)
looks upon religion as women's business, and men play little
part in it save when encouraged or constrained to do so. They
require no more from it than the fulfilment of its rites, and
attendance, both in church and also in religious processions,

---

[1] Civil marriage outside the Church was introduced by the Republic and
abolished by the present government.

is predominantly feminine. Among educated people this is not the case. On the other hand, men of the ruling group tend to consider more the political implications of religion, and to them anti-clerical is synonymous with "Red". In general, the attitude of men towards the Church is determined by political and social considerations; for these, as has been shown, are men's not women's business.

The institutions which compose the political structure all depend upon a small number of persons in the pueblo. These are the core of what I have designated "the ruling group". The central figure is the mayor and all except the Church depend directly upon the co-operation of the municipality. The mayor is, by virtue of his position, also the local *jefe del movimiento*, the head of the "national movement", the amalgamation of political parties of which the chief of state is the supreme national head. As such he has authority over the secretary of the syndicates, and also over the "Movement's" members, who comprise all of the ruling group. However, manners mean much to the Andalusian and it is not an authority which is constantly invoked. The mayor gives himself no airs. He appears, not as a hierarchical head separated by his authority from his subordinates, but simply as the key figure of the group. The group, as an actual reality rather than an abstract concept, is visible in the *tertulia*, the group of friends sitting round a table, and it is generally recognised that the realities of local politics are to be sought not in formal declarations in official contexts but in the informal talking among friends. The priest holds a *tertulia* on summer evenings outside the church. The mayor holds one sometimes in the town hall at the end of the morning, but he is more frequently seen sitting with one group or another in the *casino*.

The *casino* is the last, and perhaps the most important, of the political institutions of the pueblo. It is a club possessing some one hundred and twenty members, that is to say roughly all those except day-labourers, small tenants and artisans but including some habitual summer visitors. It is a club in the sense that it has entrance fee and subscription, but it opens its doors to strangers, and during the fair, for

example, is much like any other café. It is the meeting ground
for the men of the ruling group, their friends and all those
who are slightly well-to-do. Here cards and dominoes are
played ceaselessly, and occasionally chess. In summer there
are tables outside under the trees in the square, but there are
also rooms at the back and upstairs. When important private
business has to be discussed, a meeting takes place in one of
the rooms, but this is rarely. Where everything depends in
fact upon private understandings there is a prohibition upon
secrecy. To retire with someone for private conversation
arouses comment and the worst is always suspected. So the
affairs of the pueblo are discussed casually and in public,
but with infinite tact. When something important has to be
said men go for a walk together to the end of the street.

The *casino* is called the Circulo de la Unión for it was
formed by the fusion of the old liberal and conservative clubs.
These clubs sprang up in Andalusia in the nineteenth
century and were a necessary part of the system of *caciquismo*.
Their union (and two have given way to one in all the smaller
pueblos) illustrates the change which overtook the pueblos
on the break-up of that system. After the general strike of
1917 the Conservative and Liberal parties combined in
coalition against the threat of revolution—a revolution which
eventually materialised. The balances have shifted, and their
descendants remain bound together in the face of the pueblo
and in their dependence upon the power of the state. The
advances in the techniques of political control, of communications and of transport, and the economic interdependence
resulting from them have lessened the distance between the
local community and the central government, but at the
same time have accentuated the difference between their
cultures. Today the *señoritos* are culturally less part of the
pueblo, more part of the regional middle-class. The regional
middle-class has moved further to the centre. Much of their
political power has passed into the hands of professional
administrators. The conflict, inherent in all authority, has
broken out and been resolved, in the case of present-day
Andalusia, in favour of the central state which has drawn
more directly under its political control the leadership of
the local community. That this development has not been

followed throughout the whole of Spain a glance at the country's history suffices to reveal. Where the integration of the local community has held fast, the conflict has developed at a different structural level (notably in the agricultural communities of the north). It was not fortuitous that the growth of a revolutionary working-class movement and the growth of the nationalist separatist movements went forward hand in hand.

CHAPTER X

Friendship and Authority

THE INSTITUTIONS through which the pueblo is governed were discussed in the last chapter. Yet in order to make plain how government is carried out we must examine one further institution, that of friendship, and the way it interlocks with the structure of authority.

The egalitarian values of the pueblo are one of the themes of this study. Where all men are equal conceptually, the basis of their co-operation can only be reciprocal service ; a voluntary reciprocity dictated by the mutual agreement of the parties, as opposed to the prescribed reciprocity of ranks. The spirit of contract, not the spirit of status, determines their dealings. Such a spirit has already been observed in the system of co-operation in agriculture. Only one relationship outside kinship is ordained by the values of the pueblo rather than by the free will of those concerned and that is the neighbour. The supremacy of the geographical principle of social integration has been mentioned already, and this evaluation of proximity as a social bond provides the moral basis of neighbourship. Neighbours are thought to have particular rights and obligations towards one another. Borrowing and lending, passing embers,[1] help in situations of emergency, discretion regarding what they may have chanced to discover, compose the obligations into which neighbours are forced by their proximity, but it must be stressed that the relationship of neighbour is never a formal one.[2] It is a

---

[1] Cooking is all done with charcoal. A charcoal fire is easily lit by placing an ember from another fire in the bottom of the grate. To light it otherwise involves much more trouble.

[2] As for example in the Spanish Basque village (cf. J. Caro Baroja, *Los Vascos*), where in the funeral procession the coffin is borne by the heads of the four nearest houses, each one having his appointed place. In Alcalá neighbours also bear the coffin, but there is no rule as to which neighbours. It is borne by anyone who offers himself or by a relative. If no one steps forward for this labour then it becomes a service which must be paid. To be borne to one's grave by hired hands is indeed a sign that one has died unloved.

matter of mutual necessity, a relationship into which good people enter willingly. The pueblo rings with accusations, behind the victim's back of course, of being a bad neighbour. "If only one could choose one's neighbours. . . ." To be friendly is the duty of a properly brought-up person towards anyone while he is present, but a neighbour is always present. He might be described, then, as a friend whom circumstances impose upon one.

Friendship, properly, is the free association with a person of one's choice. It implies a mutual liking (*simpatía*), but, as we shall see, this aspect of it is sometimes put at the beck and call of its other aspect; mutual service. To enter into friendship with someone means putting oneself in a state of obligation. This obligation obliges one to meet his request, even though it involves a sacrifice on one's own part. One must not, if one can help it, say "no" to a friend. On the other hand accepting a service involves him in an obligation, which he must be ready to repay. Hence the necessity for mutual confidence. One must have this as well as *simpatía* for a friend. This much is true of friendship anywhere. What is noticeable in Andalusia is the lack of formality which surrounds it (save in the single instance of the *compadre*). No formal declaration, no ritual initiates it; one enters it through offering or receiving a favour. The instance of the inspector, who refused wine, "who wished friendship with no one" illustrates this point. He would not risk entering into reciprocal obligations which might interfere with his duty. Whether in fact friendship exists or not is frequently in doubt, hence the continual declarations of it, the reproaches for "lack of confidence", the praise acclaiming "a good friend". Hence also the subtle manœuvres intended to test it.

For friendship to be real must be disinterested. The language echoes the point continually. People assure one another that the favour they do is done with no afterthought, a pure favour which entails no obligation, an action which is done for the pleasure of doing it, prompted only by the desire to express esteem.[1] On the other hand, the suggestion that

---

[1] This assurance is also used by all the traffickers in the idiom of friendship who surround the tourist, so that "sin interés ninguno" ("with no thought of interest") comes to mean by inversion "I am not charging you anything, but I expect a tip."

someone's friendship is "interested" is a grave one. Honourable people fight shy of accepting a favour which they will not be able or will not wish to return. The other may wish for one's friendship in order to exploit it. Yet having once accepted friendship one cannot refuse to fulfil the obligations of friendship without appearing oneself the exploiter, for one has entered falsely into a tacit contract. This implication which forfeits a man his shame is used frequently by the exploiters of the principle of friendship.

For the fundamental conception of friendship contains a paradox. A friend is, according to the definition given above, someone whom one likes and admires and wishes to be associated with for that reason. The association is established through a favour which expresses one's *simpatía*. If the favour is accepted, then the bond of friendship is established. Mutual confidence supposedly comes into existence. One is then entitled to expect a return of favour. For favour is at the same time both personal esteem and also service. The word *favor* possesses, like the English word, the meanings of, at the same time, an emotional attitude and also the material gesture which might be thought to derive from this. The former can only be proved by the latter, hence the double meaning of the word. Friendship which is interested is not true friendship since the bond of *simpatía* is missing—in its place is vile calculation. The paradox, then, is this : that while a friend is entitled to expect a return of his feelings and favour he is not entitled to bestow them in that expectation. The criterion which distinguishes true from false friendship flees from the anthropologist into the realms of motive. Yet he may observe that this paradox gives to the institution of friendship the instability which has been noted. The friend who fails one ceases to be a friend. The bond is broken. The way is left clear for a re-alignment of personal relations.

Therefore the element of sympathy is all important. If the friend is deeply attached then he will be true. He will remain with one and sever his friendships with the rival camp. Such a friend is the ideal. He has honour and manliness. But without actually forfeiting his honour he may through skilful evasion manage to maintain his friendships with both sides. These people are famed for the skill with which they dissimulate their feelings. Outsiders who come from other parts of Spain to Alcalá complain of the "indirectness" of the Andalusians. "You never know where you are with them. They will never tell you anything to your face. They will always be charming to you and then behind your back they will betray you." But this histrionic capacity does not mean that they have not strong feelings which they take pleasure in expressing. Hence the importance of gossip. People spend their time discussing how X spoke of Y, how he looked when Z's name was mentioned. Friends inform each other who speaks well and who badly of them behind their back. Every conversation is determined by the relationships of the members of the audience. In this way the process of re-alignment is carried on. Yet there are also true friendships, founded upon affection and esteem, which approximate to the ideal and endure a lifetime. Only they are few. For the struggle for life too easily brings in what one might call the reversed principle of friendship, where considerations of interest dictate the expression of esteem.

The practical utility of such a system is very great. It is a commonplace that you can get nothing done in Andalusia save through friendship. It follows then that the more friends a man can claim the greater his sphere of influence; the more influential his friends are the more influence he has. Friendship is thereby connected with prestige, and boastful characters like to assert how many friends they have, how extensive is the range of their friendships. So while friendship is in the first place a free association between equals, it becomes in a relationship of economic inequality the foundation of the system of patronage. The rich man employs, assists and protects the poor man, and in return the latter works for him, gives him esteem and prestige, and also protects his interests by seeing that he is not robbed, by warning him of the machinations of others and by taking his part in disputes. The relationship of *padrino* and *hombre de confianza* is a kind of lop-sided friendship from which the element of *simpatía* is by no means excluded, though it may happen that, owing to the paradox already discussed, the appearance of friendship be used to cloak a purely venal arrangement, a rich man using his money to attain his ends.

There appears to have been a change in the evolution of *caciquismo* of which the system of patronage was the core, from the first type of patronage to the second. In the early period *cacique* appears to have meant no more than a person of local prestige, and one finds a young man in a novel of Juan Valera[1] boasting that his father is the *cacique* of the pueblo, yet by the end of its course it has become a term of opprobrium meaning a briber and corrupter, the employer of the *matón* (bully).[2]

There are many situations in which the *patrono* or *padrino* is of value.[3] He is not only able to favour his protégé within the pueblo. It is, above all, his relationship to the powers outside the pueblo which gives him value. For example, a *patrono* is required to sign the application for an old-age pension, testifying that the applicant was once employed by him. Many such applications are signed by persons who never in fact employed the applicant. He who can find no one to sign gets no pension. The *padrino* can give letters of recommendation to people who will do favours for him, who will protect his protégés.

The story of a dispute in the valley can be used to illustrate the values of friendship and authority in action. Fernando Piñas, who has been mentioned already, is a wealthy miller and farmer, a syndical chief, and, though in his way of life a member of the pueblo (*plebs*), he is a close friend of the mayor and a person of local consequence. Thanks to his friendships outside the pueblo he is able to *empadrinar* the victims of the

[1] J. Valera, *Pepita Jimenez* (Madrid, 1873).
[2] Cf. Pío Baroja, *Cesar o Nada*, translated as *Caesar or nothing* (New York 1922).
[3] The power of patronage in former times was certainly greater than it is today. Zugasti (Julián Zugasti, *El Bandolerismo* (Madrid, 1876)) explains the power which it had in relation to the law during his governorship of the province of Cordoba.

The copla of Curro Lopez, a bandit of the first half of the nineteenth century, written while he awaited his execution, speaks of the influence which a powerful patroness once had:

"Ya se murió mi madrina	"Now my madrina has died
La Duquesita de Alba	The dear Duchess of Alba
¡Si ella no se me muriera	Had she not died on me
a mí no me ajusticiaran!"	They would never condemn me to death!"

(Quoted by C. Bernaldo de Quiros y L. Ardila, *El Bandolerismo* (Madrid, 1931.)

fiscalía. The miller who is caught milling tells his friend Fernando. Fernando is friendly with one of the inspectors. He choses an occasion to see him and plead the case of the miller. The inspector, it must be remembered, is entitled to a percentage of the fine. But friendship can arrange such matters.

His neighbour, Curro, is a craftsman who lives on a small irrigated *huerto* which is his own property. He is the son of a miller, and after his father's death his step-mother sold the mill which lies within the huerto to Fernando Piñas. This occasioned a quarrel, for Curro hoped to buy it from her and claims that he had the money to do so at the time. In any case, Fernando Piñas refused to let Curro buy it back once it had been sold to him. Today it is run by Alonso, who exploits it on a profit-sharing basis with the owner. Alonso and Curro are next-door neighbours and friends. The watercourse of the valley called El Rio and that called the Arroyo del Chaparral unite in the garden of Curro. Fernando Piñas' olive-mill called "Molino del Juncal" is placed upon the Arroyo, but his grain-mill, occupied by Alonso, is situated lower and is served by both waters. From that point the channel descends, passing through a series of mills and *huertos*. The first mill is owned by Curro's first cousin and *compadre*, Pepe. Curro is friendly with all the millers for he is a fine workman and specialises in work on mills. Some way farther down is the *huerto* of Manuel el Conde (the Count), an independent very small farmer, a recognised authority on agricultural matters and a close friend of Curro's.

Situated immediately above Curro's *huerto* is an improvised acre of irrigation on the property belonging to the wife of Juanito Sanchez who farms it. This is one of the *huertos* which have been made during the past ten years "con agua robada" ("with stolen water") and which have no title either in the eyes of tradition or the law. It takes the spare water from the main stream. Curro's *huerto*, on the other hand, is an old one with as good a title to its water as any in the valley, and he has resented the appearance of this new one which threatens in a dry year to leave him short of water.

I can offer no assurance of the accuracy of the facts in the story which follows, quite apart from the deliberate changes made in the interest of discretion. The facts were

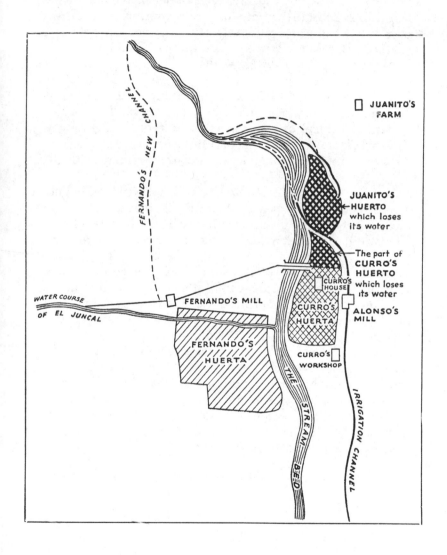

selected first of all by my own range of personal contacts and friendships, secondly by my own judgement as to what was true and what was significant. This was not easy for it is characteristic that everyone tells a quite different story. "Is it not possible to know the truth in such cases?" I once asked in despair. "Very rarely," I was told, "for where money is concerned there is no such thing as the truth. He who has the money is always right." This, as will be seen, is a somewhat cynical exaggeration, but it typifies the view of those who regard the actual state of society as evil. They are by no means only those whose sympathies remain with the "Reds".

If there is little prohibition in this system of values against taking liberties with the truth, there is a very strong one against passing gossip whether it be truth or falsehood. The word *alcahueta*, which in the dictionary means in its primary sense a procureuse, is used in Alcalá in the derived sense of a *correveidile*, a "run-see-and-tell", a gossip. It is a term of heavy moral reproach, for it means a defaulter in the obligations of "neighbourliness", one of the most important of which is discretion. Gossiping is shameless behaviour, and the accusation of it even couched in euphemistic terms may provoke a violent quarrel. Yet the strength of opprobrium which attaches to it does not suffice to ensure people's silence but only to make them careful about what they say and to whom, for it is an offence only against the person betrayed. In the eyes of the person to whom it is told it is a sign of confidence; to the teller it affords a pleasure which is hard to resist. Hence the rhyme which says:

"No hay Sábado sin sol	"There is no Saturday without sun
Ni mocita sin amor	Nor young girl without love
Ni viejo sin dolor	Nor old man without pains
Ni forastero que no sea de buena gente	Nor outsider who is not a good fellow
Ni viejo que no haya sido valiente	Nor old boy who has not been a hero
Ni campana sin lengueta	Nor bell without a clapper
Ni vieja que no sea alcahueta."	Nor old woman who is not a gossip."

The issues involved in this story were ones which, for obvious reasons, could not be spoken of save in confidence, and the difficulties of the field-worker under such circumstances may, to some extent, excuse the incompleteness of his information. However, it must be remembered that this is not the analysis of a point of law but of conflicting human relations, and the emotional attitudes which are provoked are therefore as relevent as the hard facts. (I make no attempt either to condone or condemn the actions of the participants, nor the moral values, nor the legal system involved.) This is what happened:

A dispute arose between Fernando Piñas and Juanito when the former sent men to put the stream bed of the Rio in order at the point where the channel leads off to Juanito's *huerto*. The land belongs on one side of the stream to Fernando and he asserted that water was being lost there. (Frequent repairs are required if this is not to happen.) This water does not affect his olive-mill which stands on the Arroyo, but it must be remembered that he also owns the mill of Alonso and has an interest in its exploitation. Each miller is responsible for the stretch of channel immediately above his mill. Fernando's men repaired the channel by cutting off the corner and bringing the water down a slightly shorter course on the near edge of the stream-bed which is some thirty metres wide at that point. This left Juanito's *huerto* high and dry, and he complained bitterly, but since he had no title to water he had poor grounds for complaint. His wife and daughter went down to the edge of their land on the stream-bank and threw stones at the men working. Fernando asked for protection for his men, and a pair of Civil Guards were sent to restore order. Juanito's wife then refrained from throwing stones, but kept up a flow of brightly coloured abuse for some time before retiring. No one supported Juanito for it was in the interest of all that the channel should be repaired and shortened. Curro, in spite of his enmity with Fernando, admitted that his action was correct in this instance. He was, in fact, delighted to see Juanito's *huerto* eliminated, though he remained distrustful of Fernando. Not without difficulty, Juanito made a new channel for his *huerto* and continued to irrigate it.

The following year Fernando's real objective is revealed:
he intends to divert the waters of the Rio from a point some
400 yards above Curro's *huerto* and bring it down to join
forces with that of the Arroyo above the mill of the Juncal.
The power of the mill would thus be doubled. But Juanito's
garden once more loses its water. However, in the meantime
Fernando has come to terms secretly with Juanito, and a
contract has been signed between the two, for part of the
ground over which Fernando will make the new watercourse
belongs to Juanito's wife. This contract was not made easily.
Fernando offered a good price for the field in question or
offered to exchange it for land elsewhere, but both offers
were refused. The final contract gives him no land in possession but costs him as much as if he were buying Juanito's
huerto.

With his flank secured, as it were, Fernando sets his men
to work in the autumn to build the new channel. He does
not build it out of concrete straight away but makes it in an
improvised manner to try out not only the technical factors
in the scheme but also, perhaps, the reaction of his neighbours.

The person whom, apart from Juanito, this change in the
flow of water affects, is Curro. The upper end of his *huerto*
is too high to be irrigated by the channel of the Arroyo,
which now carries both streams. About three-quarters of an
acre loses its water and it is thought that the fruit-trees
planted there will die. The millers down below are also
concerned, for it appears likely that for technical reasons
they will lose water (meaning power) for their mills.

There is an outcry, led by Curro, but Fernando reassures
the millers, explaining that they will not lose but gain water
since he is going to build the channel in concrete, and the
water will come down quicker and with less loss in the channel
than in the stream-bed. (This is true.) It is also likely that
this latest development comes as no surprise to a number of
millers whose reactions have been secretly tested in advance.
Very soon only two millers continue to support Curro, one of
them Pepe, his first cousin and *compadre*. Curro makes a
denunciation to the Town Hall and is told that he must
serve notice on Fernando to the effect that his garden is

being damaged by this action. Curro sends Manuel the Count and the brother of Alonso. The latter fails to appear at the rendezvous and Manuel goes alone. Fernando makes an offer of compensation which Curro proudly refuses. It appears to have been a not ungenerous offer, but Curro asserts that he is not asking for alms but wishes only to keep intact the *huerto* which is his patrimony. After this Manuel no longer supports him. His attitude towards Fernando has always been somewhat ambiguous. On the one hand he proclaims himself Fernando's disciple and is on terms of friendship with him, while on the other he enjoys speaking evil of him with Curro and sympathising with the latter in his ancient grudge. Now that the test case comes he deserts Curro and sides with Fernando. Curro complains bitterly of his falseness adding certain assertions regarding his family life which reflect gravely upon his moral character. There appears to be no foundation for these assertions, which concern his future intentions as well as his past, but they effectively demonstrate his fundamental shamelessness.

Curro then goes to the pueblo with Pepe and asks the corporal of the Civil Guard to have the work stopped. The corporal says that he cannot take action in such a matter, being a civil matter, without the instructions of the mayor. Curro next goes to the mayor who says he is not competent to take action without instructions from the Hydrographic Commission in Seville. He considers rallying his supporters and going by night to destroy the work which has been done, and set the river back on its course. But in spite of all his warnings of the growing power of Fernando and his assurances that once he has both waters he will become all-powerful and will crush them all, the millers make no response and even his second supporter, a miller, begins to dissociate himself from Curro. Curro now has only his *compadre*, Pepe. Alonso remains on friendly terms but says openly that Curro's demands are exaggerated. Curro is bitterly disappointed and talks of leaving the pueblo and going to work in Algeciras. He proposes selling the *huerto* to a friend, saying that he would sell it him for a moderate price but that Fernando should not have it for a million pesetas. He insists at some length with his friend. Alonso overhears this conversation and goes to tell Fernando. This satisfies Fernando that he is winning the dispute. In due course the news that Alonso has informed to Fernando reaches Curro and gives him further reason to complain of the falseness and cowardice of mankind. After this Alonso no longer comes to sit in Curro's patio.

Curro is at this time working upon some repairs in the mill of the Pileta and he takes his problem to Don Antonio. The previous year has seen bad relations between the Juncal and the Pileta. Fernando Piñas has been charging a more favourable rate for milling and has captured trade from the Pileta. He has been raided by the chief inspector and caught with contraband oil, and has incurred a heavy fine in consequence. Popular opinion attributes the action of the inspectors to the instigation of Don Antonio. Curro's personal ideas and his family tradition are very much at variance with Don Antonio's, yet he is confident of finding an ally here. He contrasts the education and refinement of Don Antonio with the brutishness of his enemy, and quotes a former summer visitor of high social position as saying that Fernando was "unworthy of the capital which he possessed", and had been a turncoat in the war.

Don Antonio offers sympathy and gives advice to the effect that he make no attempt to do anything more in the pueblo but go straightaway to the Hydrographic Commission in Seville, for in the pueblo "everyone listens to Fernando". It becomes evident, however, that Don Antonio, while he would be glad to see Curro successful, is not prepared to become involved in any way himself. Curro therefore goes to a lawyer in Ronda of whom he has heard to take advice and prepare his case. The lawyer looks into the matter and says there is a good case. There is no need to go to Seville, for it is against the law to divert a watercourse without the proper authorisation.

Fernando is meanwhile continuing the work and, confident that he has the situation in hand, is spending money on it. He has not found it possible to take the water by the route originally planned and has had to take it from farther upstream and blast a piece of rock. Juanito has noted this but

makes no move to support Curro in his protest. Fernando is
satisfied that he has the support of the valley and that he
will be able to square the Hydrographic Commission afterwards. This is the way things are done, he says. First you do
the work and then you get permission to do it. Otherwise
they would keep you waiting for ever. As for his antagonist,
Curro, he has nothing but scorn for him:

> "I have no wish to humiliate the man, but he has an
> envious nature. I have offered to pay compensation or to
> buy the land, but he will not listen to me. He guards an
> old grudge against me and will not live like a good
> neighbour. Moreover his grudge was groundless in the
> first place for the mill belonged not to his father but to his
> step-mother by inheritance from her parents. She was
> very good to him and treated him like her own child if not
> better, but he was ungrateful. When she wished to sell her
> mill why should she not sell it to me instead of keeping it
> for her step-son? He envies me my wealth, but I have
> worked hard to get it. If he wishes to get wealthy he should
> do the same. I am up at seven every morning and busy
> straightaway, but his workshop does not open till eleven
> o'clock and some mornings not at all, for he is engaged in
> plotting and in going to visit lawyers to see whether he
> cannot take advantage of me. He is a fool. He should
> spend his money on his wife and children and not on
> lawyers or the poor little things will find themselves with
> no bread to eat. But what can I do about that? They are
> not my children, they are his."

Curro, meanwhile, is encouraged by the lawyer's opinion
that he has a good case and exults in the humiliation which
he is going to inflict on Fernando. He is by no means fully
confident, however, and comes to see a friend in search of
encouragement. The friend gives his sincere advice: to distrust
lawyers and use the strength of his legal position in order to
exact generous compensation from Fernando. He warns him
that the result of going to court may well not be favourable
to him, and that a court-case based upon the extremely uncertain water-rights of the valley is liable to provoke trouble
for everyone and make him very unpopular. Even though he
might win the case he might stir up such a fuss that he could
not subsequently get legalisation for the water-wheel which

he is installing for the machinery of his shop. Curro does not appreciate this line of argument for he has made up his mind to fight. His point of view varies from: "Let us see whether there is Justice in Spain!" to "Now Fernando is going to have to pay all the wrongs he has done me in the last ten years!" He is scornful at the idea of receiving alms at the hands of Fernando. All he wants is his rights. If Fernando wants to climb down he can pay 25,000 pesetas (about three times what the land is worth to buy)—that is only a small part of the money he is going to make with the extra power in his mill. He can well afford such a sum if he wishes to have the water which belongs to another.

The case is tried in Alcalá. Curro loses and must pay all the costs including Fernando's. His plea is dismissed on the grounds that he had given previous permission for the work to be done and consequently had renounced his right to damages. This permission was said to have been given at a syndical meeting of the water-users in the town hall. Curro denies that the subject was ever raised in his presence at that meeting. Testimony was given by two leading figures in syndical affairs. Curro maintains that one of them was not even present at the meeting in question. The witnesses were not cross-examined, and Curro believes that his lawyers were bribed by the other side. He complains privately to the judge afterwards who says: "What can I do? I can only give judgement according to the law and on the evidence which is presented." Curro thereafter agrees that it is not the judge's fault if Justice has gone astray.

Curro is now outraged, humiliated and ruined. He says he must sell the *huerto* to pay his debts and will not stay longer in Alcalá. In fact he sells a house he owns in the pueblo which is let and borrows money from the Monte de Piedad, a loan secured by the faithful Pepe. In spite of the quarrel and the court's decision he still hopes that Fernando will pay his own costs and is galled by the latter's refusal. As regards damages Fernando says, not to Curro but to others, that he will wait and see how much Curro's *huerto* does in fact suffer, and will give him compensation then. Curro's lawyer accepts a slightly reduced fee in view of the lack of success of the suit.

Fernando has defended his position. "Now that fellow

does what he likes in the valley," says Curro. "Now he has the water he will extend his *huerta*. The one he has was built up illicitly, and who is going to question his rights now they have seen what has happened to me." Curro considers the possibility of an appeal and of taking the matter up in Seville but decides against it. He attributes his failure chiefly to the dishonesty of his lawyers who dissuaded him from going to Seville in the first place, and subsequently betrayed him in failing to cross-examine the witnesses in the case in Alcalá. Six months later he feels better about it and jokes sourly that he thought he had caught Fernando out but the latter turned out to be too cunning for him. He may be as rough as a donkey, but for cunning subterfuge there is no one like him, Curro says.

Fernando's position is not as impregnable as all that. During this time the wife of Juanito has returned to the charge. Her contract with Fernando though generously paid has not been observed strictly, and her husband, acting on her behalf, has brought a case against Fernando for breach of contract and damage to her property. Curro and his *compadre* "el Ranchero", ("the cottager") are *hombres buenos*, and it may be a bitter satisfaction to Curro that this time Fernando is defeated. The case is tried in Alcalá, and Fernando must pay damages and costs.

The pueblo is glad to see the powerful man defeated, but the action of Juanito does not inspire any admiration nor is there much sympathy for Curro. His old grudge is well known, and it is generally recognised that he was out for revenge more than for anything else. The corporal's analysis of the situation reflects a generally recognised aspect. He says that the wife of Juanito is a lady who thought that she had found "a breast to suckle her", i.e. a situation out of which she could get something for nothing. She did in fact find it but Curro, who thought that he had found the same, missed it. On the other hand Fernando, although his power is resented by the pueblo on principle, is respected for his ability and his general conformity to the moral standards of the pueblo. The law and morality are not the same thing. Yet no one is sorry for him on account of his exploitation by Juanito, either. It is up to him to know how to manage these

things. As one of his admirers remarked: "That will teach
him to think that he can do everything in the pueblo. He will
be sorry that he didn't go to Seville and fix things properly
before he started, for he could have done so. He has friends
there."

Fernando's power depends upon his position in syndical
affairs and as a former mayor of Alcalá, upon his being
able to get things done, upon his influence with people and
upon their allegiance to him. He is at the same time a
member of the ruling group and also of the pueblo (*plebs*),
(just as the mayor is at the same time part of the local community and also a member of the provincial deputation). If
he were to lose the valley's allegiance to him he would among
other things be of no further use to the mayor, therefore he
cannot antagonise the valley. As has been pointed out
already, he is invaluable to the millers as their spokesman and
defender during the difficult times. He wants the water, but
it is not only contrary to law to divert it, but, far more
important, contrary to the tradition of the valley. On the
other hand it damages only two people, and he is willing
to compensate them generously. It may be significant also
that, by bringing the waters of the Rio to the mill of the
Juncal, it gives Fernando an official claim to them which
the millers of the upper valley do not have. This gives him
the right to complain of the abuses of the *hortelanos*. He has
clearly been thinking of this manœuvre for years, as his
attempts to obtain possession of the land above the stream
have shown. He paid a very high price indeed for one piece
of land.

His first move successfully split Juanito and Curro. They
do not support each other in resisting him until the very end,
when Juanito may have found difficulty in finding anyone to
stand as *hombre bueno* for him. Morally, Juanito's position is
weak from the start on account of the nature of his *huerto*,
founded upon stolen water. On the other hand, the fact
that he has had it long enough to grow fruit-trees, even
though they are still small, gives him a certain moral right on
a *de facto* basis. In the first incident he gained no sympathy,
for it was up to him to get his water without prejudice to the
community. Subsequently, Fernando paid him generously

for his interest. No one would have been sorry if he had lost his case.

Morally, Curro's case appears at first sight much stronger than Juanito's. It is the case of a powerful man attempting to override the rights of a neighbour. But Curro's action in refusing to consider an arrangement is unneighbourly, and his case is spoilt in the eyes of the pueblo by the vindictiveness which inspires him. His friendships are much more restricted for he is a poor man and commands little influence. His only strength is the support of his neighbours. While they felt themselves threatened, not knowing whether Fernando's scheme would turn out favourably to them or not, and felt that Curro was being victimised, they were prepared to support him. When Fernando reassured them that they would gain and not lose water, and when Curro refused to consider compensation, they were glad to reaffirm their solidarity with Fernando, even though they disapprove of the violation of the tradition upon which they depend for the security of their water. Not only is Fernando their spokesman, but they are all tied to him by obligations of friendship. "Fernando is a good friend, a good neighbour. He gives much. He has everybody in his debt." In view of his past kindness it would be shameless of them to go against him, moreover it would be impolitic. Curro's only allies are his cousin and *compadre*, Pepe, and a miller who is inspired chiefly by jealousy of Fernando and who soon withdraws when he sees the other millers are with Fernando—and "el Ranchero".

This man is *compadre* of Curro's uncle though Curro calls him *compadre*. He lives high up on the hill-side where he works at plaster burning. He is poor and without ambition, very proud and dependent on the favour of no man. He is the champion of equity, the enemy of corruption. He is quite uneducated, but he is feared for his outspokeness. It is his uncouthness and perhaps also his unwillingness to enter the system of reciprocal favours which has earned him the additional nickname of "the Bumpkin". He speaks much in moral sayings and laments the state of his country, but he is not a "Red". On the contrary, during the war he led a party of refugees from the Anarchist terror up into the mountains and hid them there, keeping them supplied with food. The story is told of how an official attempted to extort an illicit charge from him. He thumped the table and, in a voice that the whole pueblo could hear, he bellowed: "In this place there is neither mayor, nor manliness, nor shame!" The terrified official explained that he had made a mistake in his demand. He, it was, who took Curro's part in his first quarrel with Fernando over the sale of the mill. He remains with Curro throughout this quarrel, the disinterested friend.

It can be seen that "el Ranchero", the enemy of the system of patronage, retains his independence through remaining outside the system. His position as an independent craftsman with a virtual monopoly enables him to do this. He neither employs people nor is employed, he does not use water, he does not market his produce. People send a donkey for his plaster when they need it, and the demand is fairly steady. No doubt the independence of craftsmen generally accounts for the fact that the majority of the Anarchist leaders in the pueblos of the sierra came from that class.

The institution of friendship, based upon the moral notion of equality and the free exchange of favour, builds up, in situations of material inequality, a structure of patronage which links up the authority of the state through the economic power of certain individuals to the network of neighbourly relations. To make the point plainer: taking the incident described above, the powerful and wealthy Fernando Piñas is able to effect an improvement, to his own advantage, in the use of the waters of the valley at the expense of the rights of two persons of small importance, of whom, one, through a timely recourse to the law, manages to obtain ample compensation for the loss of his stolen water and the violation of his land, while the other, whose title to compensation for the loss of water was good, was defeated by a *chanchullo* (a dirty trick). In fact the corporal who placed the two in the same category was wrong. Curro did not seek, like Juanito, to exploit the violation of his rights, but to challenge the system of patronage. For this reason he was crushed. Fernando was able to defeat him owing to the support which he received from the authorities and also from the rest of the community, which remains loyal to him, thanks to the service which he renders in their relations with the source of authority and to his private generosity, a generosity which he is well able to afford in view of the advantages which he stands to gain.

In such a system the moralist may see a systematic abuse of principles; the social anthropologist, avoiding moral judgements, sees only the delegation of certain functions of representation through the medium of wealth and prestige. For reasons which will not be discussed here,[1] the law commands something which is highly prejudicial to the economy of the local community. The resulting conflict is resolved through a social personality who possesses an effective relationship with the pueblo, with the ruling group of the pueblo and with the representatives of the law outside the pueblo. Put in another way, the tension between the state and the community is balanced in the system of patronage. The element of balance in the situation becomes clearer when the relationship between the inspector and the pueblo is looked at through the inspector's eyes. If he pursued his duties with too much vigour he would, if he were successful, do the millers out of business altogether. They would stop milling, and he would get no more fines. He would deprive himself of a source of income which he needs, for he is poorly paid; he would ruin good men; and he would make enmities for himself, for those men have friends and *padrinos*. On the other hand, if he left the millers undisturbed he would not be taking full advantage of his position and he would not be thought by his superiors to be doing his job. Through the system of patronage the will of the state is adapted to the social structure of the pueblo. But patronage is only one aspect of the relationship between the two, and the incident which we have considered brought into sight only that part of the organisation of the state which is concerned with economic controls, the most recent and least essential of its organs, and one which at the present time is being greatly curtailed. In apposition to the structure of friendship built up from personal relations in the pueblo,

[1] The official reason given is that the primitive mills of the valley are uneconomical with the grain and cause additional waste in a time of shortage.

there can be seen to exist a structure of authority devolving
from the central state and defined explicitly by its laws.

To distinguish the two structures is to make an abstraction,
of course. The corporal has his friendships, however vulner-
able they may be to the demands of duty, and connives at the
activities of the millers. The humblest member of the
community depends upon the law. The two systems inter-
lock, not as juxtaposed groups of personalities but as juxtaposed systems of sanctions which operate with relative force
upon the individual in every situation, and define, through
the balance they strike, his social personality. We are dealing
not with rival groups but with rival, and not always rival
but often allied, systems of relationships.

Manners, friendship, the idiom of daily contact are based
upon a respect for others, a recognition of their right to
pride. This recognition is part of the egalitarianism of the
pueblo. But reciprocal service cannot assure concord in every
situation. Where two wills are in conflict one must overrule the
other. The other must be humiliated. They can be neighbours no longer. Fernando says, specifically, "I do not wish
to humiliate him" when envisaging his victory over Curro.
The lieutenant of the Civil Guard has not such concern in
his relations with members of the community. He speaks
another language. "It may be different in your country,"
he explains to the anthropologist, "the Spaniard requires
authority if he is to achieve anything." He illustrates what
he means with a gesture of the hand, that which is used in
threatening children with punishment. This opinion might
be taken to express nothing more than the contempt of a
person in authority for the people over whom he exercises
it. That he is feared and hated by the majority of the pueblo
there is no doubt, but the same belief is found among the
very people who resent his authority. Every family must have
a head who is obeyed, they say. A father who has no authority
over his family, a husband who has none over his wife, is
despised. Every property must have an owner. Every pueblo
must have an *alcalde*, a mayor, a person whose authority is
the guarantee of order, a person worthy of respect, whose
superiority makes it no humiliation to submit to him. Hence
"el Ranchero's" outcry that since there was corruption in

the pueblo, it had neither authority nor manliness nor shame. Authority is the guardian of the social virtues just as, within the family, it is the guardian of *vergüenza*; and it is a necessity, else the passionate egoism of men will carry the society into chaos. Therefore the dictator, the embodiment of authority, violates no value sacred to the social order[1] when he seizes power, but, rather, he reasserts one whose failure has brought society in danger of collapse. When General Primo de Rivera came to power it was to save the country from this danger, and the pueblo was well impressed by his first act which was to put all the *caciques* in jail. The old inn-keeper of the inn opposite the barracks of the Civil Guard smiles happily when he remembers the day when "there were forty-five guests across the road". All the prominent political personages of the *partido* were imprisoned in Alcalá for a few days. The pueblo, unlike the urban middle-classes, never reproached him with the destruction of constitutional government, which to them meant only *caciquismo*.

The idiom of command contrasts with that of friendship.[2] There comes the point when the pretences are dropped and the realities of power come into the open. An order is an order and not the request for a favour, and there can be no mistaking which is meant. The brusqueness of the former emphasises that it is based not upon any idea of reciprocity or sympathy but upon the unilateral force of coercion. Within the authoritarian situation the inferior is not entitled to feel pride. If he does, it is not legitimate self-esteem but *soberbia*. The second person singular is used here, not as a sign of *confianza* but, as in an army command, as a sign that no respect is accorded to the person addressed. But, on the other hand, he in whom authority is vested must possess the necessary manliness in order that he may be submitted to without humiliation. He who, for the sake of the principle of authority, viewed as socially good, submits to the person of "prestige through manliness" participates in his

[1] Cf. Guglielmo Ferrero, *The Principles of Power* (New York, 1942), for a somewhat fanciful view of the different values which attach to the exercise of political power in different European countries. Ferrero postulates "principles of legitimacy".

[2] This contrast is brought out in a dramatic passage in Zugasti's *El Bandolerismo* where the author describes his first interview with "el Niño"

commander's manliness and is not humiliated. Among the many popular songs sung in the valley is a *copla* upon a former dictator "el más valiente de España" ("the most valiant man of Spain"). But at the same time, within the value system of the pueblo, the mystique of authority is accompanied by exultation in the rebelliousness of the Spanish pueblo. Another *copla* of an earlier century was once quoted to me:

"Dice, cuando vino a España	"They said, when there came to Spain
el rey invicto Amadé	The unconquered king Amadeo,
A España no le gobierna	You are not able to govern the Spaniards,
Ni tampoco el Hucifé."	Nor is Lucifer either."

It is this rebelliousness which makes authority necessary it is thought—and the converse is equally true.

There exists, then, in the political structure of the pueblo two principles each attaching to a different aspect of social life. The principles of equality and authority. The former is associated with the relationship of neighbours, of people who live together in the pueblo. Equality has already been shown to be the essence of neighbourly relations and the sanctions of personal contact, jealousies, gossip and so forth prescribe it. A person's *vergüenza* is what makes him sensitive to these sanctions, and the matrilineal nature of *vergüenza* as well as the fact that neighbourly relations are largely conducted by women cause them to be particularly associated with the female sex. The principle of authority, on the other hand, is particularly associated with the male sex. And the quality of manliness is that which justifies its subjection of neighbourly values, for it is recognised as necessary to defend the social order and enforce the rule of right.

This is the ideal picture of the moral values of the pueblo,[1]

---

[1] It is interesting to observe that they are also those of Father Juan de Mariana, *De regis et rege institutione* (1599). [Spanish translation, *Obras del Padre Juan de Mariana* (Madrid, 1864)], both as regards the nature of authority and its relationship to equality, and also as regards the rights and duties associated with riches. Typically also, Mariana applauded the rebels of Fuenteovejuna in his history of Spain.

and if political authority enforced them all would be well. However, authority belongs to the state, and, so far from enforcing the rule of right, it frequently appears to the pueblo to enforce the opposite. Authority, in the eyes of many, does not enjoy the legitimacy which would make it the defender of *vergüenza*, and it is wielded for the most part by outsiders who do not belong to the pueblo. For this reason matters of government are regarded by many, in the tradition which comes down from the days of *caciquismo*, as the business of the state not of the pueblo, as something dangerous and immoral which sensible people have nothing to do with. Those who took part in anarchist politics under the republic are recalled as "those who had ideas".

"When they ask me to vote," an old farmer said, "I ask who for, and when they tell me who for, I vote. And if they don't ask me to vote I stay at home and mind my own business."

CHAPTER XI

Law and Morality

(i) Nicknames and the Vito

THE RELATIONSHIP between law and morality poses
problems which have preoccupied jurists and philosophers
for centuries, and which the anthropologist formerly side-
stepped by maintaining that in primitive society the distinction between the two cannot profitably be made. Neither
can be said to have emerged from the mother-concept of custom. The jural rules of simple autonomous peoples are carried by the memories of the elders of the community, but the
laws of a civilised country are codified by a central power
and must be applicable to a great variety of communities,
varied both as regards their local culture and also their social
status, and it is hardly surprising if they do not suffice in
themselves to give a complete picture of what the anthropologist, in contrast to the political philosopher, calls political
structure. The political philosopher sees only the framework
of legislation; the anthropologist must search for a system of
human relations. The data which he considers must include
not only the overt framework of law but also the discreet social relations through which it is interpreted. For this reason
it has been necessary in dealing with political structure to
devote some space to the institution of friendship. (Whether or
not it is properly named an institution is a point which need
not delay us.) It is in no way formalised, and the very ambiguities which enclose it have been shown to relate to its
role within the structure. It belongs not to the legislative
framework, but to another set of relations having their
origin not in the state but in the values of personal behaviour, and prescribing conduct, not through the sanctions of
organised force, but through those of community. The two
sets of sanctions are quite distinct and so, to the people of
the Sierra, are morality and law.

The next three chapters will be devoted to the examination of the role, within the total social structure, of the institutions deriving from the community[1] of the pueblo (*plebs*) and, standing in opposition to the powers external to the pueblo, the educated and the state. This aspect of the structure of the whole pueblo, I have been tempted to call the "infrastructure", but that the word has other uses already, because it lies behind the formal political structure and because its institutions are interrelated with one another.

Its nature is visible to begin with, in the system of naming people within the pueblo. How formal names are given has already been said. Everybody knows both his own surnames and usually, but not always, both those of his parents. Other people frequently do not know any but his Christian name, and they seldom know both his surnames unless they are closely related to him. When asked the name of the man who had been living opposite him, fifty yards away, for the last ten years (his only neighbour), the keeper of the tavern on the crossroads replied: "Francisco . . . Francisco . . . well, not to waste time over it, Francisco the Fishseller." His reluctance to use a nickname to someone as much an outsider as myself (with whom he was not well acquainted) came up against the obstacle of ignorance. He did not know his neighbour's name. After a further five minutes, spent largely thinking about the problem, he said: "His name is Sanchez. I know because I happen to know his son's name is Sanchez." To the pueblo he was Francisco the Fishseller.

Personal relations are conducted through Christian names as a general rule. The surname is not normally used as a form of address though there are instances of this. (There is no doubt that this has been encouraged by the influence of military service. Boys recently returned from it show a tendency to use surnames.) When referring to a person behind

1 Where the word "community" is used unspecifically, as in the contrast between the sanctions of community and those of organised force, it is not intended necessarily to have a strictly territorial basis. Sanctions of community are those which derive from inter-personal contacts wherever they effectively occur, and the "community of the middle class of the province" has been shown to exert sanctions upon its members. The community of the pueblo (*plebs*) on the other hand specifically excludes a number of people in so far as they do not participate in the life of the people who live there.

his back he is distinguished by a descriptive nickname.[1] This is never, or virtually never, used as a form of address. To do so would be bad manners, though exactly how bad would depend upon the nickname. Some are obscene and many are uncomplimentary.

A person possesses, then, a Christian name by which he is addressed; his surnames which are used in all his contacts with the legislative framework of society and the outside world but which may largely be ignored by the pueblo; and his nickname, which the pueblo knows him by, but which he is supposed not to know. In fact, of course, he always does know it. Whenever his name is written down it must be his surname. His nickname is never written, for there is no reason to write it in the daily life of the pueblo. A single exception to this occurred when the Town Hall sent round to the millers and *hortelanos* the forms which required them to state their water-rights. The properties were in some instances named, as in popular speech, by the nickname of the occupant. It appeared that the Town Hall did not know the official names of the mills and gardens in all cases and fell back upon the customary name. The name of the occupier entered on the form was always his proper name.

Writing is an activity which links a person with the world of formality. People who have to do with written matters tend to know many more surnames, and the staff of the Town Hall know who is who in the whole pueblo. (No one else knows the surnames of the whole pueblo.) But they also know the nicknames and, though they tend to use surnames more than other people, they will use nicknames when not in an official position. On one occasion I was sitting in the *casino* talking of Fernandito Piñas with the town clerk. We moved to the town hall, and when I referred there once more to Fernando Piñas the town clerk answered stiffly: "Don Fernando Castro Menacho." He felt that it would not be proper to mention a person by his nickname in such a place, particularly a person of Fernando's standing.

There is a feeling, not only among the officials but in the

[1] A similar system of nicknames is mentioned in Norman Douglas' *Old Calabria* (London, 1915). Douglas describes the difficulty of identifying a person knowing only his surname and without knowing his nickname (pp. 54–6).

pueblo, that nicknames are degrading and their use is a sign
of barbarity. People feel slightly ashamed that a foreigner
should wish to inquire into such matters, and fear that the
pueblo will be made to sound backward and uncivilised by
this feature. (A schoolmaster of my acquaintance even goes
so far as to maintain that the cultural standard of the population can make no advance while the nickname persists.)

The majority of surnames are common ones. The average
extension of a name within the population of the pueblo is
1·1 per cent. Some seven names claim more than 3·6 per
cent of the population each. That is to say that about one-
third of the population is called by one of those seven names.
The confusion is increased by the fact that a person's
matronym may be known but not his patronym. Yet, the
nickname, though it fulfils the function of identifying people
much better than does the surname, may also be hereditary,
and in a few instances nicknames build up genealogies which
rival surnames in their proliferation. Nearly a quarter of the
inhabitants of the valley are either "Conde" or "Gorrino".

First of all, the nicknames themselves. Perhaps the
commonest type refers to appearance in a purely descriptive
sense: "la Ciega" ("The Blind Woman"), "el Bisco" ("The
Squinting One"), "los Enanos" · ("The Dwarfs"), "el
Tartamudo" ("The Stammerer") are nicknames which are
given on the same principle as those of medieval monarchs.
There are also those, equally descriptive, which define the
person through his occupation: "el Panadero" ("the
Baker"), "el Pescadero" ("the Fishseller"), "el Herrador"
("the Blacksmith"), "el Electricista" ("the Electrician").
Such nicknames might be taken to be little more than descrip-
tions and barely to merit inclusion under this heading, but
that in many cases the description does not apply to them.
"The Baker" is not a baker but a farmer. "The Little Lame
One" walks sound. "The Toothless One" has all his teeth.
"The Bald One" all his hair. "The Ugly One" is considerably better looking than "the Pretty One". The nickname
was given not to the man but to his parent or grandparent or
great-grandparent. How far back they go cannot be said, for
men have no records of their families other than their own
memories provide and these people guard little from the past

Certain nicknames describe by analogy, using the names of animals. "el Piojo" ("the Louse"), "el Gorrino" ("the Piglet"), "el Rana" ("The Frog"),[1] or, by association, "el Peo" ("the Fart"), "el Papera" ("the Goitre"),[1] "el Jeta" ("the Snout").[1] These are already far from flattering, but a clearly mocking note is to be found in some: "el Rey" ("the King"), an illiterate small-farmer supposedly very unrefined, "el Monarca", "el Conde", "la Marquesa" for people who in all probability "gave themselves airs", "la Peseta Peligrosa" ("the dangerous peseta"), "la Santa" ("the saint"). "La Bonita de la Ribera" was given in irony to a lady who had goitre. Words of gypsy, known as slang, such as "el Choro" ("the Thief") or "el Pincho" ("The Handsome") refer to men who are not gypsies. Favourite terms of speech provide nicknames such as "Venga-venga" or "Justamente", which are plainly satirical in origin. Others inspired by some particular event are liable to be more damaging still: "el Cuerno de oro" ("the Horn of Gold", an idiomatic expression meaning a willing cuckold) was given to a man whose wife was the mistress of a rich man. "La Parrala" ("the Flirt") was the title of a song popular a few years ago and was given to a domineering matron of some fifty-five years. The more damaging and obscene names are very often supplementary ones, used only by persons of an unfriendly disposition, while friends continue to use some more harmless one. The niece of "el Peo" maintained that his nickname was "el Sacristán", though other people seemed to know him better by the former name. There are also those nicknames mentioned earlier which derive from an outsider's origin: "el Turco" ("the Man from Benamahoma"), "el Billongo" ("the Man of Villaluenga"), "el Malagueño", etc. Farms are commonly known by the name of the present or former occupier, but in certain instances the name of the farm has stuck to the children who were reared there. A man once explained at length that a certain farm was called "el rancho de Niebla" ("the cottage of Mist") because the mist hung there on winter mornings, and that the farmer was called Niebla from the name of his farm. In

---

[1] The gender of the article indicates the sex of the person bearing the nickname.

fact, however, Nieblas was his patronym. For patronyms and
also matronyms are adapted to serve as nicknames. Names
which have meaning lend themselves particularly to this,
such as "Calle", "Valle", "Pozo" ("Street", "Valley",
"Well"). The fact that they are "adapted to serve as nicknames" and are not merely being used as what they are, i.e.
surnames, can be seen from the way that the feminine is
formed: "Dianez" becomes "Diana"; "Jarillo" becomes
"Jarilla". In other cases again nicknames are adapted from
Christian names: "los Merchores" from Melchor, "los
Cristos" from Cristobal, "los Estebistas" or "el Estebano"
from Esteban, "el Amparucho" from Amparo or "la
Currichila" from Curro. Others become recognised by a
diminutive form of their own Christian name and are known
by nothing else. "Currillo", for example, once a prosperous
tenant farmer who ruined himself through drink and gaming
and became a beggar. Another beggar is called "Juanillón",
a name containing both the diminutive and also the augmentative termination which was once the nickname of a
famous bandit.

The circumstances which gave rise to many a nickname
have long been forgotten, though people will willingly
improvise a suitable story from their imagination. "Medio
Pan", "Peluquín" are names whose origin has been lost.
Others have been perverted by time; "Pataleón" from the
Saint's name "Pantaleon"; "el Montaburra" ("Get-on-the-
donkey") was originally "el Mataburra" ("Kill-the-
donkey"), a nickname earned by a man who, going home
late one night, got his donkey stuck in a stream and, being
drunk, left it there and went on alone. The donkey drowned.
Others have not even any known meaning, such as "Briole"
or "el Chamongo".

The nicknames, being transmissible, may be applied to
persons of either sex and may be used in the plural. The
grammatical anomalies are endless and apparently largely
fortuitous. The feminine tends to be formed by changing the
terminal letter to "a" or adding an "a" as in "la Zarzala",
"la Peluquina". "La Conda", not "la Condesa" ("the
Countess") is the feminine form of "el Conde" ("the
Count"). But masculine variants formed from feminine

nouns leave the terminal "a" unaltered. The article denotes the sex. In some cases no variant is formed, but a person is referred to as "she of So-and-so" or "those of So-and-so".

When we come to examine which nicknames are transmissible and according to what rules they are transmitted, we find them no more predictable than their grammar. Obscenities and those of strong personal criticism tend not to be transmitted though time takes the edge off them where they remain. Those of more than one word tend not to be transmitted for they are too cumbersome for general use. Some are invented for a person on some score or other and endure for a few years only, after which they give place to an earlier dynastic nickname. Others are supplanted by a newer and more libellous one. Any nickname is a potential heirloom. The nickname always passes with the blood, or more accurately perhaps (and more in keeping with the values of this society) through the household, for there is one case of a step-son receiving his step-father's nickname. In another it appears likely that the nickname originated with an elder brother. It is rare for a wife or husband to receive the nickname of his spouse though it may happen. Far more frequently each retains his own family nickname. A nickname may be inherited from either parent, and there are instances where some children inherit from one, some from the other. There is a tendency for the male children to inherit the father's, the female children the mother's, but this is by no means always the case. As a consequence of this, however, the nickname and the patronym become separated, and families bearing the same nickname have different patronyms. Even in one instance they no longer recognised their relationship as kin, though I succeeded finally in establishing that they were second cousins.

It might be expected that the nickname provided a principle of social structure, that those who shared a nickname were in some way bound together by it. This is not the case. To possess a common nickname is no bond. "The Condes" or "the Gorrinos" are never spoken of in the sense of all those who have one or other nickname. The transmission of the nickname is seen then to derive not from any dynastic principle but from the family situation. A child can never revert to a grandparent's nickname if his parent has not borne it (unless, as in one instance, he was brought up by the grandparent). He bears his grandfather's nickname only because he got it from his father or mother. Any further extension is only the work of time and nature. A nickname may be said, then, to define a person in the community either as himself or as the son of somebody else, as a member of a household. A certain difference between the two types of nickname exists, and there are people who have both personal nickname and also family nickname. José-Maria el Conde is also called "Tio Bigote" ("Uncle Whiskers") because he wears moustaches which is something rare among the farmers. As el Conde he is defined as the son of el Conde and the brother of Señ'Andrés el Conde, and others. As Tio Bigote, he is defined as himself. It is significant that those persons who stand out by virtue of their unconventional behaviour usually have a personal nickname. The more conventional characters tend to bear the nickname of their parent.

There is a family called "los Gorrinos" in Zahara, related to the Gorrinos of the valley. This is exceptional. As a rule a nickname is given by the pueblo to one of its members, and when he moves he will normally lose his nickname. To begin with, he is almost certain to be named according to the place of his origin, but later his new pueblo may find its own name for him. It may well not see him in the same light as the pueblo of his birth. It cannot, in any case, see him as the child of a particular household if he is a newcomer.

The nickname defines a person in his relationship to the community, defines him by his origin, his family, his place of upbringing, his office or his outstanding characteristic in the eyes of the pueblo. The professional people are not given nicknames, but are defined by their profession, "the vet", "the doctor", "the chemist". It is only in this way that they enter the community. For the same reason the *señoritos* are seldom given nicknames. Not only are they not expected to take such things in good part, they do not belong to the pueblo (*plebs*) and therefore to the community which the nickname defines. Only one, "el Señorito", is called by a nickname, and it might be possible to see in that the recognition of the fact that his relationship with the community is far more complete than that of any of the other landowners. In this as in other things he is old-fashioned. The relationship of the *señoritos* to the pueblo today is far more distant and impersonal than it was fifty years ago. In those times they were part of the pueblo. Today they are not. In those days they were given nicknames and the father-in-law of " el Señorito" was referred to as "Orejón" ("Big-ear"), even though he was the *cacique* of Alcalá.

The nickname is one way in which the sanctions of the community operate. An ugly nickname is very much resented, even though it may never be used in the owner's presence. It was only possible to discuss "la Rabona's" with her after years of friendship. Then, full of self-pity, she told the story of its origin, rounding it off with a grand tirade against her neighbours and human nature in general. "All is envy", she complained. "in this pueblo, all is envy". On the other hand, nicknames handed down from generations cause little offence. To be called "the Bald One" while you have your hair is no great hurt. The Condes and Gorrinos are prepared to speak of theirs in a situation of confidence with a friend. On the other hand, when a nickname is used by the young people in the street it is not usual to answer. However, Isabel la Marinita says: ". . . when I hear mine said to me in public I answer. That does not dishonour". Hers, derived from the patronym of a great-grandfather, can carry no malicious meaning, but others might not be too sure how, exactly, it was being said and prefer not to risk the humiliation of answering only to be laughed at. To hear one's nickname sung in the *Carnaval* by the anonymous mocking voices of the pueblo must indeed have meant humiliation.

The compactness of the pueblo no doubt lends force to its sanctions. They cannot be avoided save by going away. Therefore the code of manners ordains that respect be maintained for the pride of others. Aggressive or insulting behaviour is very "ugly" for it is liable to lead to a quarrel. And quarrels are ugly. People do not "tell so-and-so what I think of him" or give him "a piece of my mind". It is true that fights break out sometimes among the young men during fiestas when much wine is drunk, but they are stopped at once by those present who hold back the combatants. The assurance that the fight will not be permitted to take place enables the combatants to take up a very courageous stance. So goes the comment of older and more cynical folk. People do not go outside to fight, for all violence within the pueblo is bad. If they resort to it at all they do so secretly, aiming not to triumph over an opponent but to damage him for their own satisfaction, ambushing him at night and throwing rocks on him, without ever, if possible, revealing their identity. Where the enmity between two individuals reaches the point where they can no longer keep up the fiction of amicability then it is explained that "Fulano y Mengano no se hablan" ("X and Y do not speak with one another"). Convention allows them this mutual excommunication. Such people go to great lengths to avoid meeting and everyone respects this convention. A person cannot for any purpose join a group or go into a shop where there is someone to whom he does not speak. For the code of manners demands the participation in any gathering of those present, since the assumption that people are sensitive to the reaction of others is the corner-stone on which community is built. Where they wish to score off one another they do so with care and subtlety, either speaking evil of a person behind his back or putting him to shame through some innuendo which can always be declared unintentional, and therefore innocent, if offence is taken. Yet this prohibition applies only between private persons, and, cloaked by the anonymity of group action, the harshest insult may be delivered. Just as the sanctions of certain primitive societies are exerted not through a formally ordained institu-tion but through the violent action of the united community, whose members escape the guilt which such an action, indi-vidually performed, would involve, so the pueblo, through the imposition of a nickname, castigates the non-conformist in a way which permits the individual neighbour to remain guiltless of the offence of rudeness. It is not Fulano nor Mengano who has given the nickname, but *el pueblo*.

The same spirit of social satire, the same envy, inspires another institution which guards the moral standards of the pueblo, the *cencerrada* (literally, "the ringing of cow-bells").

This custom has been described at length by writers on European folklore, for it is not only general throughout Spain but it is also known in France and in other countries. It is similar in some respects to the public mocking which was formerly practised in English villages.[1]

The Andalusian *cencerrada* is generally described as a form of celebration of the remarriage of a widowed person, male or female. Upon the night of the wedding, the boys of the pueblo dance up and down the street outside the nuptial dwelling with cow-bells attached to their waist. They also blow upon cow-horns, drag strings of tins, and with the aid of such devices keep up a noise which ensures that there is no sleep all night for the newly wed couple. It was traditional in Alcalá to put on a *cencerrada* upon the eve of St. Peter, and various occasions are celebrated in this way in other places. The custom does not however find favour with the legislative powers, and it has long been the duty of the Civil Guard to suppress it. It is specifically mentioned in the Penal Code[2] as "an offence against public order".

It has nevertheless succeeded in enduring the displeasure of the forces of the law and is still practised in the pueblos of the sierra—in Alcalá under the name of *el vito*. In Jacinas it is known as *la pandorga* (the mobbing-up). The name *el vito* derives from a traditional dance of the same name associated, owing to the speed of its step, with St. Vitus. It is a popular dance no longer but was apparently a variety of *bulería*, a type of dance strongly infused with satire. Indeed, the words of the *vito* are clearly intended to mock.

The custom which this appellation covers is discovered, upon closer examination, to be somewhat different from that generally described as the *cencerrada*. The famous *vitos* of living memory did not take place in the pueblo of Alcalá, where the Civil Guard would presumably have suppressed them, but in the country, and particularly in the valley below the town. This was, no doubt, only due to the presence of the Civil Guard, for when, in 1951, the section of Civil Guard was withdrawn from Guadalmesí one took place

---

[1] Cf. the description of the "skimity-ride" in Thomas Hardy's *Mayor of Casterbridge*, or the "riding" in A. L. Rowse's *Cornish Childhood*.

[2] Art. 570. Cf. also E. Calatayud Sanjuan, *op. cit.*, p. 614.

within the pueblo. In addition, they were not provoked by the remarriage of widowed persons but in response to the flagrant immorality of persons who, being married, deserted their family and set up house with another. It would be difficult to do such a thing, save quite shamelessly, within the pueblo, on account of the presence of neighbours. It is also to be noted that the Civil Guard could, theoretically, take action in such a case since adultery is a criminal offence. (The law against adultery was abrogated during the period in which civil divorce was admitted, and this fact may have bearing upon the case to be discussed later.) Finally, the *vito* is a more enduring and violent ordeal than the common conception of the *cencerrada* supposes. An essential part of it is the composition and continual repetition of songs of remarkable obscenity about the victims.

The most famous *vito* of Alcalá took place about 1930. A man called Jacinto el Conde deserted his wife and children who remained in the pueblo, and set up house in an old mill in the valley with Mariquilla, the unmarried daughter of another farmer of the valley, "una que andaba con quién quería"—that is to say, she already had a bad reputation. Such a *vito* was put on as has never been seen before or since. Two hundred people came every night and not only boys but married men also. Jacinto called upon the Civil Guard for protection, which they sent, but, though they took prisoners, there were just as many next night. The Civil Guard came on a number of occasions and even confiscated the great "bell of the snow", a bell so heavy that it took two men to carry it, which had formerly been used by the snow-packers on the mountain and which the mockers had taken pains to bring on the scene. The Civil Guard soon gave up coming to protect Jacinto, and the pueblo, satisfied that it had gained a victory, redoubled the *vito*. In order to escape it the guilty couple moved house and took up their residence in a farm overlooking the lower valley in order to be farther from the pueblo, but people continued to come and those of Guadalmesí, which was now nearer, began to come as well.

Apart from the ringing of bells and the blowing of horns, they baked little mud figures with horns on them and placed them where he would find them the following day, and on more than one occasion they wired up the door of his farm-house so that he could not come out, and then eased the barrel of a shot-gun down through the thatch and sang their songs down it. It is said that the *vito* went on for three months and that then something inside Jacinto, near his heart, burst and it killed him.[1]

Jacinto appears to have been the chief victim of the songs but others were also sung to Mariquilla, nor were they any less severe on that account. The reproach contained in them does not refer to his deserted wife and children, though there is no doubt that this circumstance was responsible for the strength of feeling over the matter in the pueblo, they deride him, rather, as a cuckold, and indeed the reason given on one occasion of the *vito's* purpose was to warn him what manner of woman he was dealing with. This is clearly something of a rationalisation. A few of the more harmless rhymes may be given.

"El pobrecito del Conde   "Poor old Conde
   No se puede poner el   Can't put his hat on
    sombrero   For his horns go round and
   Tiene los cuernos revuel-   round
    tos   As if he were a ram."
   Como si fuera un carnero."

"Si la cabeza del Conde   "If the head of Conde
   Tuviera bombilla'   Had bulbs fitted on it
   Brillará tanto como   It would shine as bright
   La exposición de Sevilla."   As the Seville Exhibition."

(There was a world-famous exhibition in Seville in 1929)

A song was even sung to one of his brothers who came to visit him:

"Ten cuidado con tu her-   "Take care of your brother
   mano
   Que es un caballo   Who is a stud stallion
    sementa'
   Ten cuidado con la rubia   Take care of the blonde
   Que te le va a pesca'."   Who will fish him away from
    you."

[1] Death is frequently attributed to an emotional cause, shock or despair being the commonest. Thunderstorms are much feared for this reason. That the *vito* should have killed Jacinto is not therefore anything incredible but, on the contrary, just what might be expected.

Before considering the theoretical implications of the *vito* another example may be given. In 1946 (or thereabouts) el Cortadillo became engaged to marry a widow, a girl some eleven years his junior whose husband had died in the war. In the autumn she went to join the olive-pickers on the farm of el Cortadillo together with the other brothers- and sisters-in-law. They put on a *vito* which lasted three or four nights. The songs which they sang were personal and lewd, but they do not appear to have contained the implications of those addressed to Jacinto el Conde and Mariquilla. When it was seen that they were not going to desist, the brothers of el Cortadillo went out to reason with the jesters pointing out that the couple were neither married, which would have provided the conventional excuse for a *vito*, nor were they *juntos* (literally: "joined", i.e. living together), since he slept upstairs in the loft and she slept with her future sisters-in-law downstairs. The jokers retired for a short while, then returned to sing:

"El pobre del Cortadillo	"Poor old Cortadillo
Ni está junto ni está casa'o	Is neither joined nor married
Porque el duerme arriba	For he sleeps upstairs
Y ella duerme abajo."	And she sleeps downstairs."

At the second attempt, however, the brothers were successful and peace was concluded.

As a final example, the mock-*vito* of Señor José Puente ("Tio Puente") may be considered. An old farmer, famous for his jokes and good humour, he moved from his farm as he approached his eightieth birthday into a small house nearby, where a servant-girl of seventeen went to look after him. The neighbours decided to give him a *vito*, pretending that they believed he was the lover of his servant. The old man took full advantage to show that his wit had not deteriorated and he delighted everyone, answering in rhyme the rhymes they had composed for him. The jesters were invited into his house to drink wine. At no point was this *vito* in the least serious.

There are several points to be noted. The *vito*, viewed as a "jural sanction", applies, like certain articles in the Penal

Code, only to the flagrant breach of the moral code. The pueblo reacts not when its moral code is evaded but only when it is directly challenged. It has, though rarely, been put on in the case of an immoral relationship maintained through habitual visits, but only when the jesters were able to be certain of finding the habitual visitor in the expected place at the expected hour. Practical contingencies prevent it from operating otherwise.

A second point is that, clearly, it does not happen in every case. Within the pueblo it is no longer possible to do it, though there have been occasions on which it has been performed in a mild form, thanks to the fact that the commander of the Civil Guard and the other authorities shut their eyes to it. It must be remembered that it is not commanded by a judicial order, but by the desire which a sufficient number of young men feel to spend the night in that way rather than in any other. Consequently, in order to arouse these feelings a person must belong fully to the community, must be one in whom such behaviour is regarded as highly scandalous and the concern of the pueblo. There are certain persons, gypsies and recognised shameless ones, whose actions are not regarded as warranting the outburst of popular indignation. Nothing they could do would surprise the pueblo for they are regarded as already beyond the pale.

The *vito* is an outburst of aggressive ridicule on the part of the anonymous pueblo against one who transgresses, an outburst provoked, it might be said, by a manifestation of anti-social sex. There is no violence attached to it, and it is done under cover of the night. The mocking voices rise out of the darkness, but when the infuriated man rushes from his house to confront his assailants there is no one there; only the sound of scuffling, cow-bells, cat-calls and distant laughter. What can he do? If he invites the jesters in to wine or coffee, then there is an end of it, it is said. If not, then it goes on and gets worse. If one is wise, one smiles and takes it in good part, inviting one's insultors to be one's guests— "even though one may be black within". But even then it is up to them whether they decide to accept the offer of hospitality. If not, then the victim has humiliated himself for nothing, and his swallowed pride is rewarded with a blast on the cowhorn and a peal of laughter. Once they do accept then the anonymous pueblo disappears and those who advance into the light are individuals ready to resume personal relations. In the case of Jacinto el Conde there could be no solution. He reinforced his defiance of the pueblo by calling for the Civil Guard. Nor, after singing songs of such violence and crudity, would any of the jesters have been prepared to come forward and resume personal relations. In the case of el Cortadillo they ended by making peace, thanks to the good offices of his family, though not, as has been seen, at the first attempt.

It is the social personality not the person of the victim which is attained by this sanction. He is not harmed, but is humiliated and disgraced, and is, as it were, cast out of the moral community of the pueblo which has become anonymous and hostile to him. He must make atonement through the sacrifice of his pride before he is accepted back, or he must remain a moral outcast, a shameless one.

It can be seen that the custom of the *cencerrada* upon the remarriage of widowed persons is no more than a semi-serious application of the sanction. It cannot be an entirely serious manifestation of opprobrium since Church and State allow such remarriage. But it is, nevertheless, a manifestation of resentment in the face of that egoism which is the enemy of the social order. "What did she want to marry again for?" it is asked, "She had children already." Or "Now that we're alone," said an elderly farmer after his wife had left the room, "I'll tell you what women are—they're the devil, if they're not kept in subjection by a man." This was his conclusion to a conversation regarding a widow who had remarried. The value system of the pueblo is profoundly monogamous, and any return, after a person has been married, to pre-marital romanticism on the part of man or woman is regarded as a challenge to these values.[1]

There was formerly an occasion upon which the sanctions

[1] Where there are children of a previous marriage a second marriage cannot create a satisfactory family, for children must all be treated equally and parents cannot treat a child and a step-child as though they were equally attached to both. From this comes the belief that step-parents are always wicked, which is the usual reason given for disapproving of remarriage.

of the pueblo were institutionalised in yet another way. It is now fifteen years since it was practised and memories are not reliable. This was the festival of *Carnaval*, the traditional feast which heralds the opening of Lent.[1] As in other European countries, it had the character of a time of special licence and of the reversal of the social order. It took on an anti-clerical and political character during the years which preceded the Civil War, and the present government banned it on the grounds that if people were allowed to wear disguise they would take advantage of the occasion to pay off old scores. For an essential feature was that it was a time when people disguised themselves with masks. It also had the character of a time of authorised shamelessness, hence the saying "en carnaval todo vale" ("in carnival anything goes"). The reversal of values was illustrated in the relations of the sexes. A name for it was the "Festival of the Women" and it was supposed to be a propitious time for finding a *novio*. During *Carnaval* it was the girls who invited the boys to dance, who might ask them to marry and so forth.

"Ya viene el Carnavalito   "Here comes *Carnaval*
    El festival de mujere'   The festival of the women
    A la que no le caiga novio She who doesn't find a *novio*
    Qu'espere el año que   Will have to wait till next
        viene."   year."

Games were played in which *compadres de carnaval* found one another by a system of hazard and were then linked together for the rest of the festival. In this way persons who suffered from excessive shyness found their difficulty overcome. It is said that many *compadres de carnaval* became *novios* once the festival was over and consequently many happy marriages were owed to the custom. Other people, on the contrary, disapprove of *Carnaval*, for they say that it was a time when "ugly things" were done by those who had all too little shame in normal times and put the special licence which *Carnaval* offered to exaggerated use.

In relation to the moral sanctions of the pueblo, the songs of *Carnaval*, sung by the bands of masked people, possessed

[1] In many parts of Spain other festivals of the winter solstice are endowed with similar characteristics. Their relationship has been studied by J. Caro Baroja, *Análisis de la cultura* (Barcelona, 1949), pp. 183 *et seq.*

particular importance. A certain shamelessness must needs
be authorised for them to be sung, for they represented the
public exposition of the year's harvest of gossip. For weeks
before the arrival of *Carnaval* those who had talents of that
order spent their evenings composing these songs, and into
them put all the scurrilous events of the year. Things which
had been kept dark for many months came out in a couplet in
Carnaval sung hilariously by the masked figures as they
danced down the street. Shopkeepers who had used false
scales, municipal employees who abused their position found
themselves lampooned, but most of all the couplets were
intended to reveal illicit relationships between the sexes.
Through the masked voice of the pueblo the *novio* whose *novia*
had deceived him while he was away was warned of his
plight and exhorted to put off his horns. The songs of
Carnaval are recognised by some to have been the guardian of
marital and pre-marital fidelity. The supposed increase in
infidelity is often attributed to its suppression. "These days
nobody knows where he is. For who is to tell him of a thing
like that?"

CHAPTER XII

Law and Morality

(ii) Bandits and Gypsies

THE LEGAL and moral sanctions of this society each prescribe a code of behaviour, but the two codes are far from
being identical. An action is not wrong simply because it is
against the law, nor is a judgement necessarily just because
it follows the law. What has been referred to as "a distrust of
formal justice" is in fact no more than a reflection of this
distinction. Clearly, there is a large field of conduct which
both the law and moral values prohibit, delicts against
persons, property, and so on, but there is also a large part of
the Penal Code which to the pueblo is morally indifferent,
while inevitably much that is regarded as wrong is free of
legal injunction.

But there is a sphere, finally, where the two sets of sanctions,
instead of reinforcing one another, come into conflict. The
economic controls instituted by the government are regarded
as wrong, and those who attempt to enforce them are wicked.
To co-operate with the government by denouncing to the
inspector is an act of treason against the community. To go
to law against a neighbour over a minor matter is as un-
ethical as, among schoolboys, to sneak to the master. The
periodical instances of small theft which occur in the valley
are not brought before the law while the thief is thought to
be a resident in the valley. Private action is taken, counter-
theft or, if the thief can be caught in the act, violence. For a
poor man, when in need, to pilfer from the property of the
rich or to pasture his goats illegally on one of the large
properties is not considered immoral. It is a greater wrong
that some should go short when others have abundance.

On the other hand, legal sanctions may sometimes be invoked against the institutions which preserve the morality of

the pueblo, against the *vito* or against the activities of those persons to be discussed below who, in the terminology of the Penal Code, "abuse the credulity of the public". The law steps in to protect the adulterer against the sanctions of the pueblo, the thief against the *sabia* who would find him out.

Once more the intermediate position of the ruling group between state and community manifests itself. While they, or individuals among their number, have the duty of applying the sanctions of organised force, they are also members of the community. Though they have far more regard for the law than does the pueblo, they do not confuse it with morality. It is rather the instrument which provides them with the means of government. The incident described on page 129 illustrates how their use of that power is influenced by moral considerations.[1]

By distinguishing in this way between the sanctions of morality and those of organised force, tracing the former via the traditional customs and the value system of the pueblo to the structure of personal relations within the pueblo, and the latter via the formal political institutions and the code of law to the state, the nature of certain personalities, typical of Andalusia, becomes clear.

The bandit is a traditional and picturesque figure in Andalusia. He was already established there in the time of Cicero and has been there almost consistently ever since. In recent times he has been much romanticised, and has become the hero of a literary genre which might be compared with the American "Western". He is today one of the heroes of the cinema. This literary figure sprang from a folk tradition similar to that which surrounds the name of Robin Hood. Its essence is well expressed in a couplet referring originally to the name of Diego Corrientes, a famous eighteenth-century bandit, but frequently heard with another name in his place.

"Diego Corrientes, el ladrón de Andalucía,
    Que a los ricos robaba y a los pobres socorría."

"Diego Corrientes, the robber of Andalusia,
    Who used to rob the rich and help the poor."

[1] The values upon which such moral considerations are based, how far those of the educated are identical with those of the pueblo (*plebs*), will be discussed later.

According to Bernaldo de Quiros [1] there appears to be little justification for this assertion with regard to Diego Corrientes or any other bandit of the past, with the exception of José-Maria el Tempranillo whose style and gallantry did much to promote the legend in the early nineteenth century. This striking figure of whom Mérimée has left a portrait in his *Voyage en Espagne* is the subject of many stories told by those of Alcalá. One of the most popular tells how, riding one day through the campiña of Guadalmesí, he encountered a poor tenant farmer leading his aged and crotchety mule. José-Maria remarked that such a mule would be better off dead, and, drawing his pistol, he shot it. The poor man complained that it was the only beast he possessed but José-Maria told him to go to a *cortijo* nearby where they were selling a fine young animal and buy it. He threw the man a bag of money containing the required price. The man did as he was told and bought the mule, and no sooner had he ridden away on it than José-Maria galloped into the farm-yard and drawing his pistols demanded his money back. This story is one of the "chestnuts" of banditry for it is told everywhere of the local bandit hero. More reliable, historically, is that which records that he had a sweetheart from a pueblo of the sierra and that he attended the baptism of the child she bore him in the church of Alcalá. He obtained his pardon from the king while still quite young and passed into the royal service as a guard upon the mail coaches of Andalusia. He was killed defending a convoy against an assault led by his one-time lieutenant. In recent times the bandits have been mainly men who, either on account of a crime they had committed or to avoid military service, took to the hills rather than face capture by the Civil Guard and lead a precarious existence, robbing the isolated *cortijo* or capturing the member of a wealthy family for ransom. At different times the bandits have taken a distinct political colour, and those of the post-war period were led originally by former officers of the Republican forces and were supplied with arms from abroad. They were referred to as *los Rojos* ("the Reds") or *los de la sierra* ("those of the mountains") and were active in the country round Alcalá down to 1951.

[1] Bernaldo de Quiros and Ardila, *El Bandolerismo*.

The demographic background of the problem of banditry has been recognised for a long time. The colonisation of the wastes around Cordoba in the eighteenth century were undertaken with the avowed object of protecting the main road from the bandits who were endangering the communications between Madrid and that region.[1] Bernaldo de Quiros observes[2] that the principal characteristics of the social structure of the countryside are responsible for Andalusian banditry, and those he enumerates as:

(i) *El latifundismo*, the ownership and exploitation of agricultural property in large units.

(ii) The absence of a middle class.[3]

(iii) The great mass of agricultural proletariat, "almost entirely without roots, possessing no land, living . . . beside and in the view of the territorial aristocracy, witnessing their power, idleness and riches, while themselves enduring hunger and injustice. . . ."

He also notes, however, that in Extremadura where the same conditions obtain there is no tradition of banditry. He fails to note unfortunately that there is also a flourishing tradition of banditry in the mountainous parts of Andalusia where the conditions which he defines are not general, notably in the sierra of Ronda.

Ronda is like a provincial capital to the pueblos of the sierra. Like Jerez, it possesses a resident aristocracy. The pueblos to the south, in the valley of the Rio Genal, are small, less than one thousand inhabitants in number, and situated in wild country. The agricultural land of these pueblos and much of the low-lying forest is divided into small

---

[1] Cf. J. Caro Baroja, "Las 'nuevas poblaciones' de sierra morena y Andalucía" in *Clavileño*, 1952. No. 18. Also Bernaldo de Quiros, *Los Reyes*, etc.

[2] *El Bandolerismo*, p. 71.

[3] What Bernaldo de Quiros appears to mean by this statement, and it is one which is frequently made regarding Andalusia, is that the society is composed only of rich and of poor, that there is no middle class, in the sense of people of intermediary economic position. This is plainly untrue, even in the areas where *latifundismo* is most accentuated. What is missing is not the category of people of medium wealth but the ideal type of the *bourgeois*, distinguished by occupation and place of habitation and values from the landowners and the agricultural labourers. Where all live in towns the term "bourgeoisie" (taken in its literal sense) clearly becomes meaningless. Diaz del Moral uses the term *burguesía agricultora* in order to refer to this class. (See quotation on p. 61.)

properties. Large pastoral properties are owned by the state and by the aristocracy of Ronda who also own much of the better land round Ronda itself. An admirable article in *Estampa*, 1934, examines the condition of banditry in this region:

"Just as in some regions there are pueblos which strive to produce the most and the best bullfighters, so here they want to have bandits." It is a Civil Guard speaking to the journalist. "There are five or six from Parauta and you should see how proud the neighbours are of them." "All the folk of the sierra protect Flores" (a bandit). "In Igualeja the pueblo is on Flores' side. They are all spies who watch our every act. Only by a betrayal could we come to grips with him, and no one dares betray him for he would soon be avenged." The Civil Guard sees it as a permanent system: "When one dies, either a bandit or a Civil Guard, at once another steps forward to replace him and the show goes on. . . ."

The story is told of another bandit, Juan el Nene of Igualeja, described as *bandido de honor*, who attacked only the unjust, punished the peasants who got drunk and beat their wives, and gave alms to the needy. After twelve years he gave himself up and was pardoned.

The victims of these bandits are the *caciques* and the wealthy farmers.[1] The large landowners, on the contrary, enter into pacts with them for the sake of peace. A lady of the aristocracy explains the system: "The bandit respects our properties and the lives of our workers, in fact he protects them. On our part we never give him away." She goes on to explain how when she went once to visit a distant property Flores accompanied her, because as he explained, there were many petty robbers in the neighbourhood.

The different sections of the community ally themselves in different ways according to the locality. The only constants which can be established are the relationship between the bandit and the Civil Guard and the relationship of both

---

[1] The typical victim today is the farmer who has made much money from the black market. It is not only that people of higher social status are more difficult to catch. (When Don Antonio's family was in residence in the Pileta there used always to be a pair of Civil Guards on duty there.) The bandits also realise that the greater the importance of the person attacked the greater will be the outcry in the area and the demand for measures against them.

these to the pueblo. In communities such as the Andalusian pueblo it is not possible to hide, as it is in a large city. A person who is outside the law must either go far away to the city where his country ways will make him conspicuous, where his speech, vocabulary, dress, manners will betray him at once as belonging to the mountains and where unless he has a confidential contact he will soon be apprehended. Or he must take to the hills, retaining his confidential contacts in his own pueblo. His opposition to the Civil Guard assures him the sympathy of a large part of the pueblo. Theoretically, at any rate, a romantic and honourable figure, he is outside the law but he is not immoral. It is the fact that he remains a member of the moral community, at least in relation to certain sections of it, that he is able to subsist outside the law. Once the shepherds begin to inform upon him to the Civil Guard, once his friends in the pueblo fail him when he comes down for supplies, then he has reached the end of his tether. A clear understanding of this problem was responsible for the recent suppression of banditry in the sierra. The Civil Guard, unable to trap the elusive and well-armed "Reds", concentrated their efforts against their contacts in the pueblos. Finding their supplies endangered, the bandits took to plundering the shepherds and the latter reacted by betraying them to their pursuers.

Because he is not morally an outcast the bandit's reintegration into society was traditionally easier than that of other malefactors, and one is surprised at the number of bandits who, throughout the history of Andalusia, have obtained the royal pardon and settled down to a respectable old age. "Pasos Largos", a twentieth-century bandit of Ronda, is said to have become the guard on a property which he was sent to prison for robbing, and there are other examples of bandits who retired from law-breaking in order to defend the law. One is reminded of a similar pattern in another social sphere which is no less current in Andalusia, that recorded in the story of Don Miguel Mañara, the rebel against the sexual morality of his society who ended his days in extreme penitence and humility.

The *contrabandista* is another picturesque and traditional figure. The demand for foreign tobacco was perhaps responsible for his prominence in the nineteenth century, though he was established there long before the age of tobacco. A network of illicit commercial relations operated from Gibraltar over the whole of Andalusia. The smugglers appear to have used routes through the mountains which lie to the north in preference to risking the passage along the coast where they might be easily apprehended by the authorities. The main route appears to have led up the valley of the Rio Genal to Ronda past pueblos famous in the history of banditry: Gaucín, Cortes, La Sauceda, Parauta and Igualeja. Tío Puente can remember them in the days of his youth, coming with horse- and mule-trains of sixty beasts, a man to each animal and a cargo of tobacco on its back. They stopped at isolated farms for rest and supplies, and the farmer was glad to give them whatever they wanted for he knew that when they came to leave each man would pull a packet from his cargo and throw it down upon a pile in the *patio*. In those days there were few posts of Civil Guards in the mountains and fewer roads. Today the trains of contraband consist of no more than a few animals, and a host of individuals operate in different ways and on varying scales. But contraband tobacco can be bought anywhere and normally at steady and reasonable prices. Its distribution has at times contrasted favourably with the official systems of distribution.

The *contrabandistas* worked in similar areas if not in actual co-operation with the bandits, and the difference between the two was not great. Their position in the social structure was similar, and often enough a bandit turns out to have started his career as a smuggler and to have taken to the hills only after some unfortunate clash with the Civil Guards.

Shame as a sociological concept has been discussed in Chapter VIII, and what is meant by *sin vergüenza* has been explained. There are certain persons in this community who are recognised "shameless ones". Perhaps it would be better to call them self-confessed shameless ones, for they have no pretensions to shame, and do not respond at all to the sanctions which operate upon a person's shame. They cannot be threatened with loss of face, for they have morally nothing to lose. It is this which distinguishes them from those who

may be thought to be shameless and may even be said to be
shameless behind their back, but who keep up the pretence of
having shame. Such a shameless person is a kind of pariah,
and in contrast to the manners with which other people are
treated he is very often afforded scant courtesy. He is a person
who may be called shameless, to his face even, with impunity.
Structurally the opposite to the bandit, he is within the law
but beyond the pale, as far as the moral community goes.
Most commonly a beggar, though also a tinker or hawker, he
will never do "an honest job of work", nor indeed will
people employ such a person in any capacity which necessi-
tates a relationship of trust. Yet though such a person cannot
be made to respond to the sanctions of popular morality, that
does not prevent him or her from abusing them and playing
upon the sense of shame of others. Some of the old women
who come round the farms begging are feared rather than
pitied. They will accuse people of meanness at once if they
do not give, will make up lies about them and tell their
neighbours, will curse them and bewitch their dogs and so
on. Thanks to their own shamelessness they are able to apply
pressure to the shame of others, for shame is a self-regarding
sentiment, and the fact that the victim of such manœuvres
feels no moral compunction to give way does not prevent him
from reacting in order to save his pride. On the other hand, a
shameless one, having forfeited his moral membership of the
community, is no longer entitled to be treated like a neighbour and people show no hesitation in denouncing him to
the Civil Guard for an infringement of the law. When el
Tuerto came down to the valley with an accomplice and
robbed beehives, the victim went straight to the Civil Guard.
El Tuerto is used by the Civil Guard, on the other hand, as
an informer, a role in which his lack of shame is, to say the
least, convenient.

In the first instance the bandit is the ally of the pueblo as
long as he remains within the pale. In the second, the shameless one is free to molest honest people as long as he remains
within the law. When either puts himself outside the law and
also outside the moral community then the pueblo makes
common cause with the Civil Guard. At this point law and
morality join forces.

The Gypsies of Andalusia are partly sedentary and partly migratory. Before the war there were a number of families living in the pueblo of Alcalá of whom few remain now. Others come from other parts of Europe during the winter, but these camp away from the pueblos and have no lasting relationships there.

The gypsies are regarded as a race apart. The people of Alcalá referring to a non-gypsy say "a Castilian" or "a Christian" as though gypsies were neither, yet they are, for the most part, Spanish subjects and profess to adhere to the Church. They are distinguished by their appearance, and everybody is confident that he can tell a gypsy long before he opens his mouth. He can be told by his skin colour, by his hair, by his dress, by his gait or, in the women, by the style of doing the hair, by the ornaments they wear—all this before considering their language, the *caló*, and their customs. Such vast differences might imply the absence of miscegenation, but this is not in fact the case. There are mixed marriages in abundance, and whether the children of such marriages are gypsies or Castilians will depend very largely upon how they appear to the pueblo. There are in fact a number of dark skins among the Castilians and of fair ones among gypsies. They will appear one thing or the other to the pueblo according not only to their appearance but also according to their character and way of life. When I complained that some vagabonds, camped just outside the pueblo, lacked the physical characteristics of gypsies, I was told: "Even if they aren't, they're as good as gypsies." Upon another occasion, it was commented that there was a gypsy (he was in fact a half-caste), who worked in the fields "as if he were a Castilian". For gypsies do not undertake agricultural work. They are beggars, thieves, fortune-tellers, basket-makers, horse-dealers, and so forth, but a gypsy who does "an honest job of work" is simply not behaving like a gypsy. To define them sociologically, one might say that they are a caste of shameless ones, for even though there are gypsies who behave like Castillians it is recognised that gypsies are shameless. (It is said that a number have entered the ranks of their traditional enemies the Civil Guard and the pueblo comments humorously that

this is understandable, their lack of shame will not be noticed
there.) Borrow, whose insight into their nature was remarkable, observes[1]:

> "One great advantage which the gypsies possess over
> all other people is an utter absence of *mauvaise honte*; their
> speech is as fluent, their eyes as unabashed, in the presence
> of royalty, as before those from whom they have nothing
> to hope or fear."

He points out that they only feel shame before their own
people. How far it is true that they feel no shame cannot be
answered. Suffice that this is the general belief.[2] It is this
real or supposed absence of shame which defines their
position in society, makes them unemployable in any lasting
engagement, but at the same time fits them admirably for the
practice of the trade of horse-dealer in which they excel in
the fairs. No lie is so great, no deceit so ingenious that they
will not brazenly proceed with it.

Some explanation can now be offered both of the hero-
worship of the bandit in popular tradition and also of the
cult of the gypsy among the well-to-do. In the first, the
pueblo expresses its opposition to the state by romanticising
the figure who symbolises defiance to the state. The second is
of a different order. Throughout European history a tendency
may be noted for aristocracies to ally themselves with
dissident groups and castes, and the attraction which gypsies
have exerted upon them from the time of the famous Lady
Berners down to the modern Spanish grandee may have an
element of similarity with such alliances. Their skill in
dancing may also be adduced to make them symbolical of
gaiety, yet it is believed that they have not always occupied
the predominant position in Andalusian dancing which they
occupy today. Moreover, this would not suffice to explain the
quantity of pseudo-gypsy poetry which has been popular
since and even before Borrow's day. No, the gypsy has become the symbol of merry-making, not only because of the

---

[1] *The Gypsies of Spain*, p. 253.
[2] The general belief is frequently quite erroneous, as Borrow pointed out,
but I am not concerned here with the gypsies themselves so much as with their
significance in relation to "Castilian" society. In particular, regarding feminine
chastity among the gypsies, the Castilians are apt to be quite mistaken.

grace and wit of gypsy women but because of their accepted shamelessness. By donning the *traje de lunares*, the gypsy dress, for the fair, *romería*, or *flamenco party* the young girl or woman of good family can feel free of the excessive *vergüenza* which might make it impossible for her to enjoy herself. Through the pretence of disguising herself as a gypsy of whom shame is not expected, she can permit some of her habitual reserve to lapse, while at the same time she could never be taken seriously for a gypsy. Through their cult of the gypsies, people can participate in a realm of behaviour where they are not thwarted by the sanctions of a society which demands attitudes of shame and respect—the trammels of the social structure. Thanks to the privilege of their caste the gypsies are able to offer a world which appears free from such restraints because it is outside the moral community.

This explanation is valid not only in instances where the customs of the wealthy have assimilated items of Romany culture and use the symbol of the *gitano* in order to obtain the temporary release from those standards which the gypsies are thought not to obey. The recent history of Andalusia contains a number of examples of members of the aristocracy who have fled the society of their equals in order to live almost entirely surrounded by these people.

CHAPTER XIII

Law and Morality

(iii) The Supernatural[1]

THE POPULAR institutions which stand in opposition to those of the state are not only juridical in character. Within the pueblo are found others which aim to fulfil a variety of functions. It might be stated as a principle that wherever hostility is felt towards the formal structure the pueblo evolves its own supplementary institutions. A central figure in these is the *sabia* or wise woman.

There are two *sabias* in Alcalá; Juana de la Pileta and Redención. Juana is a woman of fifty-five who has been blind from childhood. She has nevertheless had two husbands (she was properly married in church to one of them) and several children. Redención is some ten years older but of a more retiring disposition and of more modest achievements as a *sabia*. She also has been married and has children.

A *sabia* is a woman who possesses powers of a supernatural order. These powers derive from the possession of *gracia* (grace). The word is used in a variety of contexts. It means a favour, a free gift. Also, in the sense of "well-favoured", it means grace in one's person, grace of movement, as, in English, grace in walking or dancing—the power to evoke admiration. It means humour—the power to evoke laughter. In the religious sense it means grace. In all its senses it means a divinely ordained privilege, a power which is a free gift, which demands no rational justification and no payment. (It is also the word used in saying thank you, for it is that which may be returned in acknowledgement of a favour.) Disgrace

---

1 The word is used in an admittedly subjective sense. "That which transcends the natural order", the natural order being that which the writer regards as natural. For many of the people of Alcalá, much that is here regarded as supernatural is part of the natural order.

consequently means a loss of this and *desgraciado* means both
"unfortunate" and, also, "in a shameful situation", as well
as out of favour. It may mean either out of God's favour or
out of one's neighbour's. Thus it comes to mean something
similar to a shameless one, though a less damaging term. A
desgraciado is an outcast through the will of God and not
through the fault of his mother.

It is her *gracia* which gives the *sabia* her powers. She must
have "grace in the hand" in order to cure by touch, but it
is a quality resident in her person. The signs of grace are
various. The five most generally recognised are:

(1) To be a twin.
(2) To be born on Good Friday.
(3) To cry out in one's mother's womb.
(4) To be visited by the Holy Virgin in dreams. This
normally occurs during childhood. Also "las Marías
tienen gracia" ("those called Maria have grace"), but
this is only in a purely minor way, such as having protection from such things as snakes.[1]
   (5) To have the two transverse lines of the hand joined
in one.

But possession of one of these signs does not bestow grace
automatically. They merely indicate that it is likely that the
person in question has it. Nor does possession of grace enable
a person to operate her power without knowledge and
training. Like shame, it is a matter both of endemic quality
and also of education.

The powers of the *sabia* vary in each individual case. But
the following are functions which, generally speaking, are
fulfilled by them.

(1) To find out the whereabouts of objects which are
lost, or animals which have strayed. (2) To discover the
name of the thief if they have been stolen, revealing the
circumstances of their disappearance. (3) To discover
whether an absent one is alright, in good health and so
on. To discover whether he or she is still *pensando* (thinking i.e. remains faithful). (4) To cause to fall in love, or

---

[1] It is significant that a particular taboo prohibits the mention of the words
for snake and lizard which are both referred to by some more general term. To
mention these words is thought to attract ill-fortune.

to fall in love again with a person for whom affection was waning. To operate upon the emotions in other ways, to end quarrels or pacify a violent husband. (5) To protect from acts of God or the fear aroused by them (which, as has been mentioned earlier, is liable to be physically detrimental, even dangerous). To ensure that a person who dies without receiving the last unction does not go to hell. (6) Curing, midwifery, etc., through medical, pseudomedical and supernatural methods.

The list is by no means complete. Juana can also assist in calming poltergeists and finding treasure and she gives advice to enable people to be successful in their choice of lottery tickets.

The powers to whom her invocations are addressed are mainly powers of the established religion. It is true that Astarte and Venus both make fleeting appearances, and that certain texts invoke directly the rosemary or the salt in an animistic manner as though they were possessed of magical power. But Juana is insistent upon her orthodoxy and devotion. "Nothing but the things of God" does she do, she assures. The belief in the miraculous powers of saints is general in Andalusia, and shrines, bedecked with the testimonies of those whose prayers have been answered, are common. The *sabia* is a person who by her grace and knowledge is able to manipulate these powers. Some of the signs of grace, it has been noted, imply a favoured relationship to religion. Moreover she takes a strict moral line with regard to the behaviour of girls. There is a passage in the oration of love in which she thanks God that her client has reached or is about to reach matrimony in a state of purity, and if this is not so then her grace enables her to be aware of the fact and her tongue cannot say the words. She confirms the general opinion regarding the decline in the standards of sexual morality. Formerly an occasional instance would occur when she could not finish the oration, but these days she is aghast at the number there are. While disapproving, she strives to see that matters go no further astray and to assure the fidelity of the *novio*. Her purpose throughout is highly moral. She uses her power to set right that which has gone wrong. But this is not on account of the power itself but simply because she is a good woman. The same power invoking "things which are not of God", may be used for evil.

Once more the intention, the state of the heart, is the important thing. A person possessed of such powers but of evil intent is not a *sabia* but a *bruja* (witch). She can cause people to lose not find things, can give the thief protection, can make a man blind to his wife's adulteries, can ensure that illicit passions are returned, can drive people mad, can afflict with illness or death.[1]

The forces of the supernatural operate, within the community, through immanent qualities such as grace and one which will be discussed later, *calio*, which are the specific attributes of women. A somewhat anomalous instance can be given to illustrate this. In the year 1950 there appeared in the valley a new phenomenon, a young man of markedly effeminate manner and dress named Rafael and referred to as "el Sabio de la Linea" (la Linea is the pueblo which acts as a contraband emporium opposite Gibraltar). Rafael had an original style in matters of curing. To begin with he was a townsman not a countryman, and he affected a certain education. He mixed an amount of medical jargon into his talk, though his essential ideas were closer to those of Juana than to those of the medical profession, and he impressed people as someone who "really knew" about these things. His pretensions in the supernatural world were certainly no less. "Others," he said, "may have their grace, but my grace is of the Holy Spirit itself. It was bestowed upon me at my birth." The report that he had cured the son of a miller who was thought to be incurable raised his prestige, and for a short time many people had faith in him. At the end of three months, however, he was discovered to be a confidence trickster, for he disappeared to Tangier with a large sum of money which had been entrusted to him by a patient. Yet before the time of this revelation he had seriously challenged the position of Juana and Redención. When they were

---

[1] Attribution of madness and illness to the power of witches is common enough. I have never come across a case in which death was suspected of being caused by a witch, but both death and also disappearance are thought to be possible achievements for them. I have known one instance of suicide resulting from madness attributed by some to witchcraft.

mentioned to him he said scornfully : "Those two old women do nothing, neither good nor harm. Or rather yes, they do, Redención is an *alcahueta*." He used the word in the sense of procureuse, for he went on: "She has a cupboard in the back of her house and in it she keeps a string with five sardines threaded on it through their eyes and various other charms." He explained that they had no grace but meddled immorally in sorcery and procured with the money of their clients favours which they attributed to their love-magic. He referred to them as witches.[1]

Rafael's words had considerable effect and for a time many people's confidence in the *sabias* of the pueblo was shaken. An ambivalence exists in the regard which people have for the *sabia*. Who knows? She may in reality be a witch. This is visible in the insistence which people who require her services praise her goodness. "Such a good woman, and how badly people speak of her, poor thing! Yet when they get ill they come running to her quickly enough."

People are shy of being seen going to visit the *sabia*, particularly if they are people of a certain standing, and very often they refrain from visiting the *sabia* in their own pueblo but visit one elsewhere. A number of people come from Ronda to visit Juana, and people of Alcalá go to visit others in the neighbourhood. How far this is due to a desire to avoid the suspicions of neighbours and how far to the belief in the superior powers of other *sabias* cannot be said. The people of the valley have not to face the curiosity of neighbours, for Juana comes round begging, and a message is easily slipped to her to call at this or that farm next time she is down that way.

Opposition towards the *sabia* has a structural background. Her practices are against the teachings of the Church, though she may well be regarded as harmless by the priest. At the same time the Civil Guard does not applaud her services in the repression of theft. A former sergeant warned

[1] The association between *alcahuetería*, in the sense of procuring, and *brujería* (from *bruja*) is an ancient and general one typified in the personage of *La Celestina*, a comedy of Fernando de Rojas, 1498. See also: J. Caro Baroja, *Algunos Mitos Españoles* (Madrid, 1944), p. 235: "los vocablos de bruja y hechicera de un lado, y de otro los de alcahueta y celestina estaban casi identificados . . ."

Juana not to dabble in accusations as it gave rise to violent quarrels. Educated people condemn such practices, on the grounds of "rationalism", as country nonsense and "superstition", the word by which they are officially condemned by the Church. In this sense, the ambivalence relating to her is the inverse of that which relates to the institutions of the formal structure. It is quite different from that which has been mentioned above which springs from the fear that she may be in reality a witch. In the first case she is condemned on the grounds that she effectively uses magic but uses it for evil ends; in the second case because she is a silly old woman who fools people. It is illustrative of Rafael's place in the social structure that he should have seen fit to attack her on both scores.

The *sabia* is not the only alternative to the doctor in matters of health. A whole range of practitioners presents itself to the person in need, ranging from simple quacks (male or female), who effect their cures through the application of a patent medicine without any pretensions to grace, down to the purely supernatural techniques of certain *sabias*. All these are grouped under the name *curandero(-a)*. The natural and the supernatural mingle together and it is not possible to draw any clear line as to where one ends and the other begins. One of the most practical and materialistic of the *curanderas* specialises in curing a painful and persistent boil, a common affliction in the area, with the aid of a powder the ingredients of which are a family secret. She pronounced herself on one occasion unable to cure a boil on account of its position on the patient's neck, and recommended that the patient make a vow in the shrine of our Lady of Remedies, the patron of her pueblo, asking that the position of the boil might be changed. The boil disappeared from the neck and reappeared upon the patient's nose whereupon the *curandera* cured it.

Another variety of *curandero* is the bone-setter. These men, for they are always men, have no particular grace and effect their cures through skill, a skill which at certain points comes near to being supernatural, for it is not a skill which anyone can acquire and it is most frequently hereditary, yet it involves the invocation of no supernatural powers and owes nothing other than to the knack and knowledge of the bone-setter himself. Neither their methods nor their achievements seem to differ very much from those of the medically recognised osteopath, though popular credence is sometimes given to stories of their exceptional ability. Men can never in fact have grace and consequently they are limited to methods which are purely manipulatory or herbalistic. El Sabio de La Linea is of course an exception—one which his effeminacy does something to palliate—but he is legitimately regarded as exceptional from every point of view. His influence, though great, endured only a few months and ended in a total eclipse. Following his disgrace all those whom he had helped suffered an immediate relapse. Rather than an institution of the life of the pueblo he was an exploiter of popular credulity, and his ability to combine the best of both worlds, his high-faluting language and his city suit, on the one hand, and his emotional appeal and his pretensions to exceptional grace on the other, were the keys to his success. His ambiguity in relation to sex merely reinforced his position as belonging at the same time to the male world of the formal structure and scientific medicine, and also to the female world of grace.

That supernatural power derived from grace belongs to women is made abundantly clear by an examination of the other forms of supernatural power. The distinction made by Professor Evans-Pritchard between witchcraft and sorcery,[1] while valid in this society as a method of analysis, does not in all cases find clear-cut exemplification. The *sabia* owes her powers both to her inherent grace and also to her knowledge of invocations and practical techniques. She is neither entirely one thing nor the other, neither witch nor sorceress.

There remain two varieties of supernatural power which fit Professor Evans-Pritchard's terms more exactly: sorcery and menstrual magic.

Sorcery is commonly associated with poltergeists in Alcalá, though its theoretical background is so uncertain that it is difficult to give a coherent account of it. It is admitted that the use of magical skills for malevolent purposes is possible

[1] E. E. Evans-Pritchard, *Witchcraft, Oracles and Magic among the Azande* (Oxford, 1937).

anywhere, but how, in fact, they produce their effect is, if not a mystery, at any rate a trade secret. From the few cases recorded the following facts emerge. Sorcery is recognised by the effect which it has on the victim, who suffers from sharp pains, whose needles are stuck into her, whose crockery is smashed and who, in one case, was locked into her own house and the key vanished. The victims were all women, as it happened. These phenomena were explained as the action of spirits who were sent by a person who had acquired control over them. Similar spirits appear in other beliefs and are particularly associated with Moorish treasure. These spirits are, according to some, the ghosts of the original owners of treasure who choose to reveal the whereabouts of their wealth to a particular person. Others believe that they are spirits sent by the ghosts. They manifest themselves through strange noises and voices which are very terrifying and are heard only at dead of night. They also throw things, crockery or stones, but are never seen save in the incarnation of a dog or cat or goat. In one instance a beautiful girl was seen in a tent lit up upon the mountain-side, but she was not thought to be the spirit but only an hallucination which the spirit had arranged. The person who has the courage to endure the ordeal of terror to the end is rewarded by finding the treasure. But treasure is also found by chance or simply by intuition, so people think.

The sorcerer who sends the spirits to afflict his victim obtains his power over them by reading a book of magic, and the expression used to explain this manœuvre is that he is "reading for so-and-so" ("está leyendo para Fulana"). To do this requires no grace and all that need be done is to follow the instructions in the book. Consequently, men can do it and in fact it is more often thought to be men who are responsible. It is done for motives of jealousy, a jilted *novio* in one case was thought to be responsible, a cousin's wife dissatisfied with the division of an inheritance in another. It is always done from far away, for it is explained that if it were done within the pueblo people would know about it. In one instance it was done by a small farmer of the valley to his sister-in-law who lived near-by. He did not do it seriously but only, having acquired the book during the war, to see if it worked. When it was proved effective he confessed and apologised. On one occasion an informant described it as "lo que hacen, estando ellos fuera" ("That which they do from outside").

The subject of menstrual magic is not easily discussed. During the time of their period women possess certain involuntary destructive powers. If they pick flowers they whither; they can kill bushes and trees with their touch and can wound the back of an animal upon which they ride. Their presence suffices to put out the fire in a lime-kiln or a plaster-kiln.[1] The vocabulary suggests an association between the emotion of jealousy and menstruation. *En celo* (literally, zeal or jealousy) is used to express the latter. Thus *la mujer celosa* (the jealous woman) is dangerous, for by association she possesses the powers which she would have while in that condition. Manifestation of the emotion of jealousy is no indication of their presence, however. There is little clarity in the minds or conformity in the opinions of the people of Alcalá upon this subject. People simply are not sure what the jealous woman is, nor how you can tell whether a woman is possessed of these powers or not. All that is certain is that any woman possesses them during that time while certain women are thought to be dangerous the whole time in this way as though they were permanently in such a condition, and this idea is expressed by saying that they have *calio*. No doubt there would be a great diversity of opinion if it were possible to know who was thought to possess it and who not, but such matters are only mentioned in strict confidence. The fear relating to *calio* is bound up with the fear of the potentially anti-social force of female sexuality which has been examined in Chapter VIII. Sexual passion is expressed through the idiom of heat—nicknames such as "el Calentito" and "la Tonta Caliente" were earned through a display of this quality—and the idea of heat is also associated with menstruation. The explanation of the wound inflicted upon the mule's back was that the rider was "burning". *Calio* is,

---

[1] Both these operations involve an element of hazard and their failure, unaccountable otherwise, is sometimes attributed to the power of women. The fire of the charcoal burner, equally subject to failure from inexplicable causes, is not affected by women on the other hand.

in sum, a secret and dangerous power possessed by a few women in the community and exercised independently of their will, and independently of their menstrual periods.

One final power, thought by the majority not to be connected with *calio*, is that of casting the evil eye.[1] The evil eye is a belief found in many parts of the world. It is the power to make a person, particularly a young child, sick and even to kill him, through bestowing a particularly bold and penetrating glance. Unlike other societies where the power may be possessed by members of either sex, it is the prerogative, here, of women. Gypsy women are particularly feared, perhaps, on account of the boldness with which they are accustomed to stare. Old gypsy women are often thought to be ill-intentioned and this may add to their power, but intention is not an essential factor. Stories are told of a Castilian woman who possessed it without any evil intent. She simply possessed that *desgracia*. *Calio* and the evil eye are seen, then, to be similar to grace but in a negative way.

There is no redress against sorcery.[2] Against the evil eye there are both defences and also remedies. Religious medallions and amulets, hung round a child's neck defend it against the evil eye and also against other mischances.[3] Juana de la Pileta is also believed to be able to prescribe or perform a cure for it, and other cures are commonly known by persons learned in such matters.

Within the community the powers of the supernatural are in the hands of women, and this fact accords with the view of the dichotomy of the sexes already given. Though the conceptions used to explain them are not associated with that of *vergüenza* except in so far as immorality signifies its

---

[1] Yet the glance of a menstruating woman is sufficient on occasions, to produce the same effect as her touch. It is her glance which puts out the fire in a kiln.

[2] The Church possesses the power to exorcise poltergeists.

[3] An evil wind is also a threat to the life of the young child. In C. J. Cela, *La familia de Pascual Duarte*, the story-teller relates laconically the death of his infant brother: "Un mal aire le entró y se murió" ("an evil wind entered him and he died"). A story recounted to me told of a child who was bringing a glass jug to his mother when an ill wind entered the jug and it broke in half. "What luck," the mother commented, "that it went into the jug and not into the child." The idea does not have the extended significance found by Redfield in Yucatan. (R. Redfield, *The Folk Culture of Yucatan* (Chicago, 1941).)

lack, both the danger to *vergüenza*, upon which the social
order of the community is founded, and the source of evil
magic within the community, derive from forms of female
sexuality, which are both sometimes expressed in the idiom of
heat.

It may well be asked at this point how among people who,
even though they possess but a low standard of book-learning,
belong nevertheless to a modern European culture, such
beliefs can persist and whether in fact they do believe in the
efficacy of the powers of the *sabia* and the practices which she
prescribes, or whether they do not observe such superstitions
in the same spirit as, say, superstitions regarding the salt or
the lighting of cigarettes are observed in an Oxford common-
room. Many people, and here again the difference between
the sexes is most noticeable, assert sternly that such matters
are nonsense, that the *sabia* can do no more than any other
person; that such beliefs are for old women and so on. The
young tend to be slightly more sceptical than the old, men
tend to be much more sceptical than women. It is thought
indeed to be credulous and unmanly to pay attention to all
this *alcahuetería*. Yet, members of the pueblo believe always
in some part of it. Though they may dismiss the *sabias* as
ineffectual, they do not doubt the possibility of supernatural
evil or the power of true grace. Curro, for example, an
avowed rationalist, dismisses the *sabias* in that way, yet can
give instances from his own experiences of the evil effects of
calio. The inn-keeper who thinks that Redención's cures are
for ignorant people who know no better, is himself convinced
that a local bone-setter can mend broken bones instantly
and far better than any doctor. He tells the story of an
apparently miraculous cure effected by this man. Their
beliefs show no logical consistency. Their consistency is to be
found in regard to their attitudes to the formal institutions
which oppose those of the "infra-structure". Doctors in
general, chemists, in general, are continually spoken badly of.
"Nothing grows in the chemist's shop" is the saying which
expresses their belief in the superiority of country cures to
the products of modern science. Yet this belief does not
prevent them from buying the latter. In the same way no

opportunity is lost to repeat stories in which *sabias* brought off spectacular cures after all the doctors had failed, and even stories of doctors admitting themselves defeated in their attempts to cure themselves or their children, and resorting to the practitioners whom they had always condemned. The humbled doctor is portrayed pleading with the *sabia* to cure him. For doctors have adequate reasons for condemning the practices of the *curanderos*, and even on occasions they have been known to take action against them.

What happens very frequently is that the patient goes to the doctor first and if he is not immediately cured he then resorts to the *sabia* or *curandera*. When he finally gets better, having followed the treatment of both, the credit is given to the latter. Neither are believed to be infallible and the *sabia* may well do you no good. But she is a good woman and does her curing out of goodness in return for what you choose to give her. She does not extort money like the doctor. The preference for her expresses a moral judgement more than anything else. As to their relative efficacity, the words of a man of Alcalá express the point of view of the pueblo: "When the hour of his death approaches no man can stay the clock. The same when the hour comes for his tooth to ache. But if he is given the right treatment it will ache less." The question of which is the right treatment, the doctor's or that of the *sabia*, is one each man must answer for himself.

The formally constituted institutions controlled by the ruling group or the state and the activities wherein the pueblo avoids them stand in opposition to one another. The latter spring from the network of interpersonal relations within the community and depend upon the memories and cultural traditions of the pueblo rather than on the written word. The former owe their existence to authority delegated by a central power. Pairing them together one can see, in place of the sanctions of law, the sanctions of the pueblo's mockery; in place of the food-control, the clandestine mills and the black market; in place of the matriculated shops, the *revendonas* and illicit traders; in place of the Civil Guard, the bandit and the smuggler. In place of the schools, the *maestros rurales*; in place of the doctor, vet and chemist, the

curanderos; in place of the *practicanta* (trained nurse), the
parteras (country midwives). And for the purpose of invoking
the powers of religion in such matters, in place of the priest,
the *sabia*.

In the attitude of the pueblo towards the ruling group a
certain ambivalence has been detected. Ambivalence is also
discernible in the pueblo's attitude not only towards the
witch but towards the whole "infra-structure". This might
almost be deduced logically from what has gone before.
When a man expresses respect for education he cannot but
deplore the humble achievements of the rural teacher. The
sabia's activities are condemned by the Church; the *curandero*
turns into a quack beside the wonders of modern medical
science. Where the values of authority reign, the bandit is a
criminal traitor, the *vito* is a breach of the peace inspired by
the envious nature of mankind, which, as la Rabona observed, is also responsible for the nickname. The food-control
admittedly can never be defended, but then it is equally the
enemy of the ruling group.

I have stressed earlier that the infra-structure is an aspect
of structure not a segment of the community. One personality
may stand closer to the sanctions of the law than those of
the community or vice versa, but every member of the
pueblo participates to a greater or lesser extent both in the
formal and also in the infra-structure. The ambivalences
reflect the individual's participation in two conflicting
systems of behaviour. It must be realised that neither could
subsist without the other. A man needs a surname whether
he has a nickname or not. When he has no nickname his
surname is used as one. He is at the same time a member of
the pueblo and a member of the state. The infra-structure
could not suffice to organise the relations of the community
without the law. Yet the law can only be applied through
personal contacts. The two systems are, at the same time,
interdependent and in opposition. They are both part of the
same structure. If a tension exists between the two, it is as
much a condition of the one as of the other. And what
requires to be explained is not only the source of this tension
but the ways through which it is resolved.

CHAPTER XIV

Conclusion

THE POSSESSION of *vergüenza* ensures the adherence of individuals to the moral standards of the pueblo, and thereby defines the limits of community. But possession of *vergüenza* is not enough in itself to determine conduct. It must be related to a common system of ethical values. The member of a polygamous society cannot be made to feel ashamed of committing bigamy. Common values are a necessity if the sanctions of the community are to be effective, and therefore it comes as no surprise to find that divergencies in values underlie the situations in which the elements of the pueblo oppose one another. Here we can summarise the main areas of these divergencies.

The attitude of the educated towards "village patriotism" has been noted. Even if they are sons of the pueblo and permanent residents there, their ties are wider than the horizons of the pueblo. They think of themselves as Andalusians, but above all as Spaniards. Their national patriotism is strong and highly emotional. They speak to the foreigner of themselves as "we Spaniards" and they are extremely sensitive to his opinion of Spain. Foreigners, they generally believe, make a derogatory and unjust evaluation of Spain. This belief owes much to Juan Valera's essay *La leyenda Negra* ("The Black Legend"), which records with great resentment all the untrue and unjust things which have been written with regard to Spain and Spanish history. The middle-classes of Andalusia are conscious of the Black Legend and believe it to inspire the attitudes of foreign governments towards their country. These feelings are sharpened by a political ideology (to which they subscribe at any rate superficially) which castigates even its compatriot critics with the epithet "anti-Spanish". Those who have no pretensions to education, however, often speak of themselves to the

foreigner as "nosotros de por aquí" ("we, of these parts") or
"nosotros Andaluces" ("we Andalusians"). They do not
take it upon themselves to speak for all their countrymen,
and when they speak of Spain they speak without emotional
bias. By nature they are Alcalareños and Andalusians. They
happen to be Spanish by nationality.

Certain differences in the values relating to sex have also
been observed. In general behaviour, women of the educated
class in Andalusia show a far greater reserve than their menfolk who possess an easy sociability. The uneducated, on the
other hand, are often shy compared to their womenfolk whose
self-confident ease in social intercourse with strangers has
often won the admiration of travellers.[1] In regard to religious
values the pueblo and the educated again diverge. Among
the former, faith is not found to be incompatible with grave
dogmatic errors and with a lack of respect for the temporal
order of the Church. Also, the women of the pueblo are much
more active in devotion than the men, whose attitude is more
often sceptical and indifferent, if not actually hostile.

The egalitarianism of the pueblo has been frequently
stressed. This inevitably comes into conflict with the feelings
of the well-to-do who, ever more responsive to the goals of a
social order not the pueblo's, tend to feel superior not on
account of their value as patrons within the community but
on account of belonging to a middle-class extraneous to the
pueblo, and who tend in social behaviour to claim an
exclusiveness which the values of the pueblo do not admit.
The present poverty of the pueblo is often blamed upon the
wealthy families who within the last few decades have moved
to Jerez. (The explanation was once given by a member of
the ruling group who added that the capitalists fled on
account of the activities of the Black Hand and took their
capital elsewhere, whereafter the industry of Alcalá declined.)
The resentment of economic inequality is not, as has been
noted, tantamount to a rejection of the idea of private
property. On the contrary, it is accompanied by the assertion that every man is master of his own property and has

[1] E.g. A. de Latour, *Voyage en Espagne* (Madrid, 1855): "Il résultait que
l'Andalouse n'existait qu'entre les filles du peuple." Byron made a similar
observation.

the right to dispose of it as he wishes. The resentment aims not so much at the existence of economic inequality as at the failure of the rich man to care for those who are less fortunate, at his lack of charity. It is not so much the system which is wrong, it is the rich who are evil. This accounts for the ambivalence which the pueblo feels towards the *señorito* and indeed explains how the system of patronage is morally possible. Patronage is good when the patron is good, but like friendship upon which it is based it has two faces. It can either confirm the superiority of the *señorito* or it can be exploited by the rich man in order to obtain a nefarious advantage over poor people. It covers a range of relationships from noble protection of dependents in accordance with the moral solidarity of the pueblo to the scurrilous coercions of the later period of *caciquismo*. The system is, clearly, only to be judged good in so far as it ensures that people do not go hungry, that injustice is not done. Where the majority of the community can look to a patron in time of need, such a system reinforces the integration of the pueblo as a whole. Where those who enjoy the advantages of patronage are a minority, then they and their patrons are likely to be resented by the remainder.

The values discussed so far have been deduced from observations of behaviour and commonly expressed judgements of behaviour. It is also possible to discern a reflection of these in the beliefs of the pueblo. The dangers to which children are exposed are not confined to evil winds and evil eyes. There is also a belief in a kind of "bluebeard" referred to commonly throughout Spain as the *sacamantecas*, though not so called in Alcalá, which refers to him only as a bad man, or baby-stealer. This personage comes always from outside, so that he is not known by anyone in the community. He may come disguised as a beggar or as a trader. He comes alone bearing either a sack or a pitcher and he comes for the blood of a healthy child. The disappearance of a child can only be accounted for in this way, and, though children do not normally disappear, most people can think of several stories which they have been told of children disappearing and the explanation is that they have been stolen. This belief might be derided by sophisticated people as something to which only the most gullible would grant credence. Yet I am told that cases have occurred during the present century of child murders which have been reported in the press under the title of "el sacamantecas de . . .". Given the existence of the myth it is only a matter of time before some deranged individual attempts to incarnate it. When asked why the baby-thief comes, the answer is that he is hired by a rich man whose child is ill and can only be saved by the blood of a healthy baby. Knowledge of the practice of blood transfusion in the hospitals of the large towns comes to underline the inherent probability of such a procedure. In the same way the nebulous character of the rich man comes to play a part in the contemporary myth-ology, and it is always the part of the villain characterised by the complete absence of morality. The belief that the land has in some way or other been spoilt by the rich men is common among the pueblos of the sierra. The explantion given in one instance was that the land was good cultivable land until the rich owner decided to pasture his flocks on it instead of cultivating it. This enabled him to go away and leave only a single employee to look after his affairs, and it had the effect of throwing the people into unemployment. (The man who held this belief was otherwise well aware that land which is turned over to pasture does not deteriorate but on the contrary improves.) This belief may be related to the land tenure of the pueblos of the sierra where the agri-cultural land is held in small-holdings in contrast to the large pastoral estates and which suffer chronically from over-population and unemployment. Opposition to the priests and the supporters of the Church is expressed in similar beliefs. "En la puerta del beato," the saying goes, "no cuelga el jato." ("In the doorways of the pious no beggar's blanket is to be seen.") In particular, beliefs regarding the sexual activities of those under vows of celibacy appear to relate not to known facts but to the desire to assert: "They're only men, just like us." Such beliefs may be held by individuals whose faith in other aspects of religion remains unassailed.

In the stories regarding treasure hidden by the Moors, the part of the villain is played by the state. Certain members of the pueblo are known to have discovered hidden treasure, but they can never admit to having done so because if the state knew, it would confiscate the treasure. Any neighbour who discovers the secret can demand half under threat of betrayal. Consequently it becomes impossible for the anthropologist to verify whether any treasure has ever been discovered or not. As with the practice of sorcery it is something which would never be admitted to. The fortunate individual to whom the Moor appears and gives instructions how to find the hoard will only be able to enjoy his good fortune on condition that he keeps the secret.

A symbolical meaning might be read into these stories. The hostile state wishes to get its hands upon the pristine wealth which lies buried in the pueblo. It can only be frustrated through secrecy. For information is a necessity to any system of government or, more precisely, to any system of sanctions—and the force of those of the pueblo have been shown to derive from the very closeness of the community. Secrecy, the witholding of information, permits conflicting social forces to co-exist and gives to this structure the resilience which enables it to persist. Thanks to secrecy the conflict between state and local community is resolved.

"The law" is an abstraction which it is useful to make for certain purposes of discussion. Yet when we consider individual situations it becomes a cloak for ambiguities. Instead, we must consider individual personalities and the way in which sanctions operate upon them. All laws are not of equal value even to the state. The inspector exerts one order of sanctions and himself is subject to another. Those which the corporal of the Civil Guard exerts are different again, and those to which he is subject also. The corporal knows that the millers mill, but he does not denounce them to the inspector. On the contrary, he connives in maintaining the fiction that they do not mill and closes them down only when they are in danger from the inspector, for he lives in Alcalá and must needs be on reasonable terms with the inhabitants if he is to fulfil his other duties in pursuing serious crime. The solidarity of the whole pueblo in face of the inspector permits clandestine milling, a secret shared by all, to go on. Anybody could denounce the millers, but nobody does. Secrecy operates, then, not merely in order to protect the community from the state, the inhabitants from the authorities, but also to protect the authorities, like the inhabitants, from each other. Within the pueblo, secrecy must be as complete as possible in order to be effective. To hide a secret from one person it is better to hide it from all, while the less you tell the less chance there is of the true story being put together. Hence the taboo upon gossiping (not merely upon old women's chatter but upon giving away information about your neighbour), and the continual spying which is its counterpart.

Things which are talked of openly in other societies become here matters of intrigue. *Calla'ito* (on the quiet), it is explained, is how things are done here.[1] Nobody, least of all the inspector, knows what the produce of the land is. Nobody can be quite sure whom a piece of land really belongs to. It may only be in a man's name and really belong to someone else. From this we can see the importance of the client in the relationship of patronage. He provides the information which enables a patron to appreciate the situation. When Curro spoke of selling his *huerto* the information went back to Fernando within a few hours, but Juanito kept his counsel and awaited his opportunity. To give away information about your affairs puts you in a weak position, for you can no longer keep the other man guessing. In relation to the same facts it is possible to understand the importance to these people of "confidence" and of its counterpart, deception; and the value which they attach to the state of the heart.

Yet the state of the heart is important not because society demands constancy but precisely because it does not. Where so many relationships are, in response to the fluidity of the structure, unstable, the heart provides a guarantee of fidelity in time. For it is characteristic of the "Andalusian temperament" (and we can here see a structural explanation for this fact) that only the present matters. Just as the secret and the conventional fictions of good behaviour permit the

---

[1] "Estas cosas son de mundo y no me pregunte su merced nada, porque mi oficio es callar" ("These are matters of the world and may Your Mercy not ask me about them, for my job is to keep my mouth shut"), says the smuggler in *El Ventero*. See Angel Saavedra, Duque de Rivas, *obras completas*, (Madrid); first published in *Los Españoles pintados por si mismos* (Madrid, 1843). Cf. also Simmel, *op. cit.*, p. 330.

adjustments of personal relationships in the present, so the "devaluation" of the past permits their readjustment. But the heart alone, outside the marriage bond and the *compadrazgo*, ensures a degree of permanency in human ties.

But if a margin of fiction exists between the ideal legal realm and the reality, it is no less true to say that another margin exists between the ideal community and the reality. As long as the law is "upheld" to all appearances, the power of the state is inviolate and the authorities are satisfied.[1] As long as the lack of shame of a person is not exposed, then manners demand that he be credited with the supposition of shame, for otherwise the principle of community breaks down. Both the law and the community can be seen, finally, as sets of sanctions which defend systems of values, both of them largely honoured in their absence.

What then is meant by values? I have assumed that they can be discovered by observing social behaviour, are a kind of short-hand term for the choice of conduct which a social system imposes. Yet they are not to be derived, in the last analysis, from the social reality of action, but rather from that other reality which exists only in the minds of the members of a society.

The chosen unit of analysis of this book was a community of about three thousand souls within which I have sought to find a system of social relations, yet if system it is, why should it stop there? The whole of Andalusia, of Spain or of Europe might equally claim to be a system. This is one of the hoariest problems of social anthropology and like most of its kind it turns out on closer examination to be a pseudo-problem. One delimits the area of one's data according to the techniques which one intends to use. In studying any society one must face two problems: What is the system of social relations within the community? and how is it affected by being part of the larger structure of the country, or of the continent?

The first chapter defined the limits of the community, the second how it was linked to the national structure, and, in

[1] Brenan rightly remarks upon the traditional lenience of Spanish justice (*The Spanish Labyrinth*, p. 85). No such tradition of lenience exists in Spain for the treatment of heresy.

effect, they contained the answer to these questions in embryo—an answer which subsequent chapters have done no more than unfold in different spheres. The structure is founded upon an evaluation of physical proximity which not only orders the grouping within it, through conceptions like the neighbour or the pueblo, but also runs through every aspect of its culture, from the conventions which govern its manners to its ethical principles or its evaluation of space and time. This value rests upon the assumption that there is no difference in the quality of men, that by nature all are equal.

Being part of a larger structure—in that the community is subject to the powers of provincial and central government and of persons allied to those powers, whose non-membership of the community enables them to escape the sanctions whereby its values are maintained—is shown to involve a violation of the principle of proximity, and the tension resulting between state and community is transfused through a ruling group thanks to the institution of patronage.

The nation is an agglomeration of interrelated communities, founded each upon a territorial basis and linked together by other communities of higher social status, greater economic means and a more comprehensive territorial scope. But it is also a state, a system of authority. Yet state and community are different not only in size but in nature. The community is essentially composed of identifiable individuals, while the state contains only anonymous categories, the products of abstraction and generalisation. The sanctions of the community apply inductively, for covert motives, while those of the state are deductive, devolving from some logical code. Law must possess a logical consistency since it is framed to apply not to particular individuals but to persons unspecified and, since it aims to antecede the situations which it will govern, unspecifiable. The goddess is blind, but the executive must keep its eyes open, for the law in application changes its nature and, no longer an abstraction, becomes materialised in the person of the town clerk or the tax-collector, a person who is a member of a community, who, to do his job must have particular information regarding individual personalities. The executive process can be expressed, if one wishes, as a syllogism : The law provides the major premiss, that which in general terms the legislative power commands. The minor premiss is filled in by the local executive who determines to whom it does in fact apply. The conclusion developing logically from these is the action to be taken.[1] But between the major premiss established by the legislature and the minor premiss which is supplied by knowledge of the community stands the hierarchy of the executive. The lower an administrator stands in the hierarchy the greater his knowledge of detail, and the less his concern with the logic of the policy, the greater his dependence upon the local community and the greater the number of administrative levels which separate him from the source of power. There are, then, a number of different levels at which the sanctions of law balance the sanctions of personal relations and permit the power of the state to adapt itself to the local community.

In this book I have been concerned only to show in detail how this adaptation is effected in the example of a distant mountain town. The facts are unique, but the principles which they illustrate are not. The tension between local community and central state is certainly not unique, if indeed it is not inherent in every structure of authority, but the mode of resolving it is particular to one culture and one environment, and to one time. Where similar conditions reign there will, I trust, be found similarities in the solution, and this study may then, as I would hope, be of some use.

[1] To illustrate this point I offer the following example which, needless to say, has nothing to do with Alcalá. Let us suppose that :
   (*Major premiss*) The legislature wishes to impose a tax upon taxi-drivers.
   (*Minor premiss*) The executive decides that X is a taxi-driver.
   (*Conclusion*) X must pay the tax.
But under certain social conditions the following variation is possible :
   (*Minor premiss*) It is said that X plies for hire with his motor-car, yet when the executive authorities ask him to drive them he does not charge anything.
   (*Conclusion*) X does not require a licence, he is a friend. He need pay nothing.

APPENDIX
The Present and the Past

I HAVE TRIED in this book to describe and explain the social structure of a pueblo of the Sierra de Cádiz as it exists in the present, and where I have referred to the more or less distant past I have done so haphazardly with no other object than to illuminate the point under discussion through an analogy or a contrast which the reader was left at liberty to take or leave. I have, in the main, resisted the temptation to account for anything observed today by a reference to its historical origin or to explain any historical facts through an analogy with the present. I have done this in recognition of the limitations of my theme and my material and not through any methodological stricture regarding the relevance of the diachronic view. On the contrary, the structure of a society at a given moment, whether its past has been recorded or not, appears to me to be very largely determined by its previous state. That this should be the case is not merely a matter of common-sense observation. The very perplexity which surrounds the use of the word "system"[1] in a sociological context relates to the fact that societies exist in the dimension of time (like a piece of music but unlike a drawing) in the sense that time is an element of their constitution and that their nature at any given moment is reducible to systematic terms only by extending that moment to include at any rate an hypothetical time-depth. What is done today makes sense only in conjunction with what was done yesterday, last year or in the last generation. Thus an analysis of the family system anywhere must consider the individual family over a period of several generations, while an even longer time-span may be necessary in order to evaluate the significance of the family within, say, the political structure. The term "social present" has been used in order to bring within a

[1] A problem touched on in the introduction

single conceptual scheme events which have in fact occurred at different times. But this mode of reasoning is open to the logical criticism that if they occurred at different times the whole system may have changed meanwhile. They may not be part of the same "social present" at all. Admitting this for what it is worth, social structure remains an abstraction of a moment in a temporal process which stands between a previous and a subsequent state and, thanks precisely to the disequilibrium in its component elements—what might be termed the functional maladjustments of the society—leads from one to the other.

This process is the study of the social historian, and the rules which govern it are the subject, ultimately, of the philosophy of history, though such historians as have attempted to schematise them have not seen their efforts greeted with universal approval, least of all among their colleagues. Entering the field of history, I certainly do not hope to improve upon the endeavours of its legitimate holders. But the formulation of sociological theory has been frustrated by the difficulty of agreeing whether any two societies are truly comparable, whether the rule formulated from the study of one can be expected to hold good in any other, or whether, on the contrary no rule can be formulated in terms which cover the contingencies as varied as are found in different cultures. Yet while it may with some justice be conceded that no two social facts drawn from different social contexts are comparable it cannot be denied that those of a given society are comparable with others of the same society at a different period. History offers, then, if the required historical data are available, the possibility of checking the formulations derived from the present by reference to the past. By looking backward in time the phenomena regarded as conditionally related together may be seen, or not, in coexistence with one another. The social anthropologist enters the field of history not to teach the historian but to seek to ratify his conclusions regarding the present. The purpose of this appendix is to take, briefly, such a backward glance.

The hypothesis which I have derived from this analysis of the way of life of the people of the sierra can be formulated for our purpose in the following terms:

A structural tension exists between the sanctions devolving from the local community and those devolving from the central government of the country. In this instance the tension is visible in every social sphere from the relations of the sexes to the medical techniques, and from the institution of friendship to that of the bandit. It corresponds to a conflict between the values of authority and those of equality. Indeed, a community such as this in which the principle of proximity is the foundation of social solidarity, in which the individual physical presence is evaluated above all abstract conceptions, cannot expect to find its needs respected five hundred miles away by masters whom it will never set eyes on. Yet these same conflicting values are both of them necessary to the structure of the community itself, as well as to the country as a whole. This tension is resolved through a hierarchy of patronage and through conventions of secrecy and fiction which have been shown to be essential to the system as it exists, even though they do not lack their native critics.

I have postulated that this tension stands in relation to the divergence in values and the degree of contact between the central government and the community, in the sense that the greater the difference in culture and values between state and community on the one hand, and on the other the shorter the effective spatial distance and the greater the political pressure exerted by the state, the more this tension increases. For conflict implies, by definition, first of all a basis of difference and secondly a ground of common contact, and applied to the situation in question these two factors can be seen to have changed considerably during the recent past. According to these changes, the postulated theory will, if it be true, apply as well in 1852 as in 1952, and as well in 1752 as in 1852. A review of the social history of the sierra during the past two hundred years should reflect changes in the social structure in terms of this contention.

The year 1752 happens to make a convenient chronological starting-point thanks to the survey carried out in that year by the agents of the Marqués de Campo Verde, Intendant-General of the Kingdom of Granada..

The government of Spain had made little effort to control

or inform itself of local affairs since the reign of Philip II, but in the middle of the eighteenth century a new spirit began to inspire the rulers of the state. Energetic measures were introduced with the object of simplifying and rationalising the process of government, and in order to achieve this end unification and centralisation became the order of the day. The eighteenth century saw the foundation of many of the state services. Communications, agriculture, industry, hygiene, even the dress of the populace became the objects of concern to the royal ministers, who for a hundred and fifty years had worried little about what went on outside Madrid. Systems of roads were built, schemes of agricultural credit and interior colonisation were put into effect. The royal enterprises extended all over the country. The Real Hacienda was entirely reformed. A great catastral survey was ordered in the middle of the century by the Marques de la Ensenada which should provide the information necessary to establish an economic and effective system of taxation to take the place of the myriad tithes, rights and participations which supported the different institutions of the central power. The Marques de Campo Verde's inquiry was initiated in this intention. A whole volume of statistics relating to the economy of each pueblo of the Kingdom of Granada—and Alcalá was still a part of that kingdom—was collected during the years 1752–54.[1] A total of forty questions lays bare the situation of the pueblo, its demography, its agricultural and industrial wealth, its wage—and price—levels, its municipal budget, the rights and taxes paid or enjoyed by its inhabitants and the economy of the ecclesiastical foundations within its confines. How far its figures are to be trusted need not concern us here for we shall not examine them in sufficient detail, but misgivings are inspired by a certain note of truculence which creeps into the text. Some of the answers, though they were sworn on oath before the parish priest as commissary of the Holy Office,[2] are regarded in Granada as unsatisfactory and in December the following year a further

1 Preserved in the Archives of the Casa de los Tiros, Granada, to whose director I am most grateful for the permission given to consult them.
2 The Church today does not regard the declaration required by the economic controls as morally binding. A false declaration is not a sin.

inquiry is initiated to supplement them. To the commissioner it is explained that the answers given in the first inquiry were not true anyway: "... they said that the declaration in question was made at the violent persuasion of Don Juan de Perez—the commissioner who conducted the first inquiry—who put down whatever he thought fit". Clearly, the ancestors of the modern Alcalareños knew as well as their descendants how to defend themselves from the authorities. Nevertheless, one is able to form some idea from this document of the structure of the pueblo.

In many ways it is remarkably similar. There are rather more inhabitants and rather more land under cultivation. The cloth industry is flourishing. Alcalá exports ice but no charcoal. The municipal organisation is much the same. A budget of 37,000 reales (roughly the same value as today, calculated in relation to individual wages) provides much the same services in regard to health, the protection of property, the organisation of religious festivals and commercial fairs. The significant differences may be summed up briefly.

To begin with, the position of the Church is very different both materially, and, as it would appear from subsequent events, morally. It is by far the largest land-owner. The income of the ecclesiastical foundations of Alcalá from their properties, tithes and chaplaincies is greater than the municipal budget. There are thirty-four ecclesiastics living there altogether—priests, chaplains and members of religious orders, and a convent of Discalced Carmelites as well. The parish priest bears a notably Alcalareño name as do most of the incumbents of chaplaincies, though there are probably outsiders among their number and there is also mention of "those that come and go". The services rendered to the community by the Church, other than its ritual functions, include education and the support of a hospital.

At court, rational ideas went hand-in-hand with anti-clericalism, and a struggle developed between Church and State which led to the expulsion of the Jesuits in 1768. Yet there is no reason to suppose that any such sentiments lurked in the pueblo of Alcalá, and when, much later, the troops of the French Revolution beseiged the town the inhabitants defended themselves stoutly in the same church which their descendants were to burn down in 1936. One of the more famous guerrilla leaders of the sierra during the French occupation was a priest of Ubrique.

Extensive common lands are owned by the inhabitants collectively, and the municipal budget is balanced by the rents which the Town Hall receives from its possessions. At this period the state takes no interest in local communications, and the municipality must pay for the work which it wishes to have done upon its roads and bridges. But on the other hand it is free of the charge of the services which the religious foundations perform. There is no indication of any absentee landlords drawing rent from the community and living elsewhere upon it. Nevertheless, the statistics claim no fewer than three hundred beggars "who go from door to door" against a mere two hundred and fifty journeymen. Such figures cannot be regarded without suspicion, for the object of the inquiry was to estimate the capacity of the pueblo to pay taxes and the poorer it could be made to appear the less it might reasonably expect to pay. Moreover, Antonio Ponz, passing through twenty years later, remarks on the prosperity of the place and the lack of beggars.

The status differences between the qualities of person no longer have any practical importance, but seigniorial rights are still of political and economic value. The Marqués de Cádiz, the ancestor of the Duke of Arcos, was given the seigniory of the town of Alcalá together with that of Jacinas, Benalurín and San Martín in exchange for that of Cádiz. (He had conquered them personally from the Moors, or more literally, he had sacked them and burned them to the ground.) These four towns are still, in the eighteenth century, administered integrally as the demesne (*estado*) of the Duke. He does not appear to have owned property there personally, but his seigniorial right entitles him to appoint the *corregidor*, the chief judicial officer of the demesne, and also certain other officials in the towns. As a result of this the political unity of the four towns appears closer than it does today. The Duke's agent lives in Alcalá and collects the tithes and taxes due to him. These comprise a third share of the grain and livestock tithes ("tercio diezmo grano y ganado"), a right of *veintena* worth 2,200 reales per annum, a tax which was farmed out to anyone who would rent it, and he also owns the monopoly of the seven ice-pits upon the mountain and a share in certain of the *censos*. Thanks to their belonging to the same demesne, the pastures of the four towns are common to the inhabitants of all and the services of certain municipal employees are shared. The Duke of Arcos is the magnate of the plains to the west where his great properties lie, yet Alcalá and the other towns of the demesne belong to the partido of Ronda and the Kingdom of Granada. The *rentas provinciales* and *alcabala* (excise) are paid to Ronda.

Other taxes are paid in various ways and to various recipients. The first fruits, *primicia*, are paid to the parish priest. The tithes (less the Duke of Arcos' third) to the Bishopric of Malaga, which also possesses a fiscal exemption for a business enterprise which it owns there. A *voto*, an endowment worth 150 fanegas of corn, is paid to the cathedral of Santiago de Galicia. The Royal Purse owns the salt-mines, a royal monopoly throughout the country. The only tax paid direct to the Treasury is the excise upon strong liquors, and that is farmed out to a neighbour of Alcalá. There are also two taxes, *utensilio* and *paja*, totalling the value of over 9,000 reales, paid to Seville for the support of the Army, and this tax is particularly resented. The poverty of the pueblo is explained as being due to it. This tax is distributed among the inhabitants by the Town Hall, which has the responsibility of paying it collectively for the whole community. The Mesta claims 60 reales per annum from the municipality.

The system is complicated, and its lack of unification is significant. Political power is not centralised in the hands of any one authority but is divided between institutions which have their seat in various places. Moreover, the people who occupy posts in the pueblo are not civil servants appointed from Madrid as members of a professional corps but employees of the pueblo. The majority have names which indicate that they are sons of the pueblo. Those whose names are qualified in the questionnaire with a mention of their origin are all from near-by pueblos.

This picture is far from adequate and gives no indication of the internal conflicts which may have divided Alcalá. The community is certainly not free from outside interference, though the authorities appear to allow the municipal government a high degree of autonomy. A host of powers external to the pueblo have the right to claim some tax or service there—even an agent of the Admiralty comes to demand wood from the forests. The high cost involved in collecting and forwarding in money or in kind these sometimes quite small sums is considerable without counting the legal expenses in which the Town Hall involves itself through challenging them in a quantity of lawsuits and pleas. Yet there are no signs at this time of the social unrest which characterises a later period, and the Church appears to be on good terms with the temporal authority. The Town Hall gives alms to the nuns and to the diocesan treasury, and rather unexpectedly one discovers the account of the sale of bulls inserted in its finances between the Treasury's tax upon strong liquor and the unpopular contribution to the support of the cavalry in Seville. (Almost as much money is raised by the bulls as is paid to the Army.) The Church still sanctions the authority of the state, and the state has not yet attacked the material position of the Church.

I shall perhaps be pardoned for recalling some of the changes in the Spanish social scene which separate this period from modern times.

The rationalisation of government in the second half of the eighteenth century took place within the traditional framework. Revolutionary ideas do not appear until the nineteenth century. Then, after a series of rebellions and counter-rebellions, of constitutions and absolutist decrees, the Liberal epoch opens. "Liberal", in Spanish politics, meant, first and foremost, anti-clerical. From the beginning of the century anti-clericalism, which had previously been confined to the court and the intellectuals, spread to the middle classes and the Army. It was not until the second half of the century that it became common in the pueblo. Under the influence of the Liberal government a social and economic revolution succeeded the political revolution. By 1852 the structure of the pueblo of Alcalá had changed fundamentally. The Kingdom of Granada and the seigniorial demesne have vanished. The province has come into existence. The church lands have been confiscated and placed on the market, and the great acorn forest which was common land has been sold into private hands also. A small part of it was cleared and distributed in small individual holdings among the pueblo. A new land-owning class has come into existence in Andalusia who owe their position to their skill in business, but whose landed possessions, acquired at the expense of the Church, soon convert them into good churchmen.

The Liberal government continued to extend its powers from the moment it acquired them and, faced with the rebellion in the north, found itself forced to build up a standing army, paid for at first by money raised from ex-propriations, which for political reasons no one could subse-quently afford to reduce. Shortly after the war, the creation of the Civil Guard relieved the local community of its responsi-bilities regarding the evil-doers and the highwaymen. The numbers of state servants multiply and re-multiply. Repre-sentatives of government-controlled institutions penetrate to the pueblo. So, when Garcia Oviedo [1] sees a tendency to-wards decentralisation from 1877–1935 this is true only in regard to the competence of the municipality in matters of law. The power which the state relinquishes is not given to the pueblo but to its servants in the pueblo. (It was precisely in 1877 that a law was first passed projecting schools for munici-pal functionaries.) We can see then that this development involves not only placing the affairs of the local community under the control of the state and accumulating information regarding the pueblo in the offices of the central administra-tion. It also means participation in the internal affairs of the pueblo by agents whose fundamental loyalty is to the state.

During the period in which all this occurs the schism in the values of the pueblo becomes visible. While the Church maintained its properties it appears to have held the loyalty of the whole pueblo, for, apart from the prestige which it enjoyed in the role of patron within the local community, its values were those of the pueblo. But the power of the people who replaced it in this respect was sanctioned by no

[1] Garcia Oviedo, *op. cit.* See footnote on page 14.

religious principle but only by their right of property or by
a state appointment. The impersonal, morally neutral
doctrines of liberal economy have replaced the theocratic
society. The place of the Church is taken by the *cacique*.
Authority comes no longer from God but from Madrid.

Even before the development of the Anarchist Movement
there are signs of a profound social discontent. The rising of
Perez del Alamo in 1861 raised an army of 10,000 men against
the established order, while the first Anarchist newspaper
was not founded until 1869. The popular rebellion thereafter acquires a political doctrine.

When, after the abortive federalism of 1873, the middle
classes of Andalusia made their peace with Madrid the extension of the Anarchist Movement was rapid. The pueblos of
the Serranía de Ronda were fertile ground for the new movement. Whether the scarcity of Civil Guards, which also
made the country favourable for bandits and smugglers,[1] encouraged Anarchism, whether the doctrine was propagated
through the network of the system of contraband, the mountains quickly became a stronghold. Of the sections which
sent either delegates or messages of sympathy to the Seville
Congress of the Federación de Trabajadores de la region
Española in 1882, those of the pueblos of the sierra represent
a far higher percentage of their total population than do
those of the larger towns of the plain. They appear to include
not merely the artisans who formed the main body of the
anarchists in the capitals and large towns but, in many cases,
the bulk of agricultural labourers. When the law forced the
movement underground it was here that the Black Hand
made its appearance.

Much has been written regarding the Anarchist Movement
which I shall not attempt to reiterate. What has not been
adequately stressed is the extent to which, in Andalusia, the
social background of the pueblo influenced the movement.
Its moralism, its naturalism, its millenarian belief, its insistence upon justice[2] and order in the organisation of social re-

---

[1] Bernaldo de Quiros and others have stressed the close association between
the anarchists and the bandits.

[2] The telegrams to the congress of 1882 which came from Catalonia and the
north ring with phrases like "ideas anarco-sindicalistas". Those from the sierra
talk only of justice and the just cause of the people.

lations, its refusal at the same time to tolerate any authority not vested in the community, to admit any basis of social organisation other than the pueblo, the natural unit of society, provide some justification for regarding it as the product of a tension within the structure of the local community. Yet this must not be taken as an excuse for overlooking the differences which can be seen to have existed in modern times between the values of the pueblo and those of the anarchists. Though the pueblo tends to show hostility to the temporal order of the Church the powers of religion play an all-important part in its institutions, and indeed its solidarity is expressed in its relation to the patron saint. Yet Anarchism went further than hostility to the temporal order, and even than church-burning. It prescribed a complete rejection of all religion, the substitution of salutations such as *Salud* (health or salvation) for the conventional *Vaya Vd. con Dios* or *Adios* and the elimination of the powers of religion from the vocabulary of everyday use. The anarchist sections from towns named after saints to the congress of 1882 frequently refer to their pueblo without the *San*, thus "José del Valle" for "San José del Valle". The avowed rationalism of the anarchists condemned the activities of the *sabias* as superstition and condemned the doctrines of religion on the same grounds. They attacked not only the idea of patronage and social inequality but also the festival of the bull-fight, alcohol and sexual promiscuity, all the flamboyant symbols of Andalusian culture. It would be quite wrong to conclude therefore that the anarchists represented the values of the pueblo as a whole. They represented, rather, a reaction against the imposition of new influences upon the traditional structure of the pueblo.

A further refinement is required at this point. In reality we can no more discuss "Anarchism" than we can discuss "witchcraft". We can only analyse the social significance of the latter by taking the witch and examining her relationship to the pueblo. Let us try therefore to see not Anarchism but the anarchist. Diaz del Moral has observed the importance of a small nucleus of convinced anarchists "los obreros concientes"[1] upon whom the whole movement depended. In

1 Diaz del Moral, *op. cit.*

the speech of those who today remember pre-war times "those who had ideas" (i.e. *ideas anarco-sindicalistas*) appear to indicate a similar category. The Anarchist Movement appears, then, as a certain number of convinced anarchists, a small percentage of the pueblo, who enjoy the support of the great majority of the pueblo upon certain occasions, but who are simply members of the pueblo for the remainder of the time like the *sabia* and who have no great influence upon events. The attitude towards them appears to have been ambivalent from the accounts of those who are prepared to discuss them. Moreover, such an explanation would account for the characteristics noted in the history of the movement, the lack of formal organisation and discipline, the suddenness with which the rebellions break out and the equal suddenness with which they subside. It would also account for the apparent indifference on the part of the rank and file towards the dogmas of the movement.

To what extent they accepted them as articles of faith is a thing which cannot be said, any more than it is possible to say whether the artisans of the capital cities attached the same significance to them as the peasants of the sierra. The evolution of the Anarchist Movement in Andalusia was away from the original millenairan Anarchism and towards a more urban conception of revolution.[1] The doctrine of the General Strike which dominated the movement from the beginning of the twentieth century implied collective action on a wider basis than the pueblo, however much this implication was resisted, and this tendency was carried still further with the organisation of the C.N.T. upon a national scale and the predominance within it of syndicalist ideas. Some evidence has been put forward to suggest that during the period of the Civil War certain tensions were visible between the anarchists of the large towns and those of the surrounding pueblos. The requirements of organisation in time of war made necessary a kind of authority which

---

[1] Millenarian Anarchism continued to exist in the country districts (e.g. the rising at Casas Viejas in 1934), and the mentality which goes with it remained the basis of the faith upon which the political association was founded. The resistance to becoming a national organisation was very strong, for it was recognised that it involved the sacrifice of an essential value, the sovereignty of the local community.

inevitably ran counter to the conceptions of the anarchists of the pueblo. It is said that since the war the underground political opposition in Andalusia has been entirely communist, this in spite of the fact that Communism had no previous importance there.

Seen in the dimension of time, the Anarchist Movement in the pueblos of the sierra does indeed appear as a development in the relationship of the pueblo to the state, in the conflict between the values of the community and those of the central power and its allies. It is born after the power of the Church has been destroyed by the growing state and its place in the structure of the pueblo has been taken by a class of no longer anti-clerical property-owners. It ends when the state, having destroyed the anarcho-syndicalist syndicate, imposes the reign of syndicalism. During that time the spirit of the Anarchist Movement has changed and its centre of balance has moved from the pueblo to the big city.

In this process the state is seen encroaching upon the functions which were formerly vested in the community, increasing its influence there and imposing decisions made in Cádiz or Madrid upon the internal affairs of the pueblo. Yet today the divergence between the national rulers and the pueblo grows less. State education, the radio, the cinema, easy communications and the experience of military service all in their different ways carry the culture of urban society to Alcalá. The pueblo adapts itself to new political and technological influences. Meanwhile, the fundamental values of Andalusian society persist, for they are common to the whole culture, the whole population of the South. Thanks to them the different elements of the structure hold together. They give to Andalusia its historical continuity, the stamp of its character.

Glossary of Spanish Words

These words are defined as they are used in Alcalá; certain variations of meaning will be seen to exist between that given in this Glossary and that given in a dictionary.

agua robada. Literally, stolen water, i.e. water diverted clandestinely from the communal stream.

alcahueta. A gossip; hence **alcahuetería**, scandalmongering.

aparcería. An arrangement whereby land is exploited in partnership between two or more people; hence **aparcero**, a person with whom such an arrangement is made.

bruja. A witch; one who employs magic for evil ends; an uncomplimentary way of referring to a *sabia*.

cabrón. Literally, he-goat (not used in this sense); a cuckold; **cabrito**, a kid or he-goat.

cacique. A local political boss; usually, in Andalusia, a landowner; hence **caciquismo**, the system whereby, during the epoch of constitutional government, political elections were arranged by the *cacique*.

calio. An evil and involuntary power associated with menstruation.

camelar. To compliment; to deceive with flattery; hence **camelo**, a tall story or nonsense.

campiña. The agricultural plain.

cara dura. Literally, hard-faced; shameless.

casino. The recreational club to which leading personalities of the pueblo belong.

celos. Jealousy or zeal; **en celo**, on heat (used of animals); **celosa**, jealous or zealous; a person possessing *calio*.

cojones. Literally, testicles; hence courage, masculinity.

compadrazgo. The relationship between the parent and the god-parent; hence **compadre**, the person in such a relationship to another.

confianza. Confidence; willingness to enter into friendship with a person.

consuegro. The parent of a person's child's spouse (from **suegro**, a parent-in-law).

corredor. A professional broker; a person who assists in arranging deals.

curandero. A person empowered either by knowledge or grace or a combination of the two to heal human beings or domestic animals, other than a person officially qualified to do so.

desgracia. The loss of grace; hence **desgraciado,** unfortunate; disgraced; ill-blessed.

encargado. Charged with a duty; hence a person placed in charge, a bailiff.

feria. A fair.

la fiscalía. The food control organisation or the members of it.

flamenco. Popular music of Andalusia.

forastero. A person from outside the pueblo, translated in the text as "outsider".

ganado. Livestock; hence **ganadero,** one who has to do with livestock; herdsman or herd owner.

gracia. Grace; a favour or free gift; grace in movement; the power to evoke admiration or laughter; supernatural power; grace in the religious sense; **gracias,** thanks.

hombre bueno. One who intervenes in a law suit on behalf of one of the parties engaged.

hombría. Manliness.

huerta. An irrigated farm; an irrigated valley; hence **hortelano,** one who cultivates irrigated land; **huerto,** small plot of irrigated land.

jopo. The tail of an animal; penis; augmentative, **jopón,** person living in the upper quarter of the town; **jopiche,** diminutive of *jopo,* a person living in the lower quarter of the town.

maestro. A schoolmaster; **maestro nacional,** a schoolmaster qualified by the State who teaches in State schools; **maestro rural,** a man who gives lessons to children on the farms.

matador. A killer, either of bulls or pigs.

matón. A bully or thug; a person employed to intimidate others.

matriculación. The municipal tax upon industrial and commercial enterprises.

a medias. Half-shares; hence **medianería,** an arrangement whereby an enterprise is shared between the owner and the exploiter; **medianero,** one who exploits an undertaking on such a basis.

naturaleza. Nature; essence; the place of a person's birth; hence **natural,** native of a place.

novio, novia. Fiancée; boy-friend, girl-friend; hence **noviazgo,** the institution of courtship.

padrino. God-parent; sponsor; a powerful person who protects and favours.

partido judicial. A number of municipalities grouped together for certain administrative purposes.

patrono. A patron; an employer.

población. Population; an inhabited place.

primo. Cousin; foolish person; mug; **primo hermano,** first cousin.

pueblo. Town or village; those who live in the place; plebs; people.

rancho. A cottage outside the town; hence **ranchero,** a country-dweller, particularly a small farmer.

reja. The iron bars upon a window; the place where courting is sometimes done.

remanentes. The waters of a mill-stream or irrigation channel which continue to flow after the main stream has been cut off. Also mispronounced, **romanientes.**

sabia. A wise woman; one empowered by grace and knowledge to perform magical acts. See *bruja.*

sacamantecas. A "bluebeard"; a baby-stealer.

sin vergüenza. One who has no shame; a social outcast.

término. The territory of a municipality.

tertulia. A group of friends, united in an habitual meeting-place.

los terrazgos or **terrajos.** An area of very small cultivable land holdings.

vecino, vecina. A neighbour; the status of an emancipated person inscribed in the Parish Register; formerly the head of a family.

vergüenza. Shame.

INDEX